MW01480307

THE TWELVE TRIBES OF ISRAEL
Around 1200-1050 B.C.
(according to the Book of Joshua)
0 (km) 100
0 (mi) 60
Mediterranean Sea
Sidon
Ijon
Dan
Tyre
ARAMEANS
ASHER
NAPHTALI
Kedesh
Hazor
Chinnereth
Ashteroth
Achshaph
Hamath
BASAN
Helkath
ZEBULUN
Mount Tabor
Jokneam
ISSACHAR
Edrei
Dor
Japhia
Camon
Megiddo
Jezreel
Taanach
Bethshean
Ramoth-Gilead
MANASSEH
Tirzah
Shamir
Zaphon
Shechem
Mahanaim
River Jordan
Pirathon
Gathrimmon
Aphek
Joppa
Shiloh
DAN
EPHRAIM
GAD
AMMON
Bethel
Jazer
Bethoron
Ai
Gilgal
Rabbath Ammon
Eltekeh
Gezer
Gibeon
Gibbethon
BENJAMIN
Jericho
Heshbon
Mephaath
Ashdod
Ekron
Jerusalem
Bezer
Mount Nebo
Ashkelon
Gath
Bethlehem
Jarmuth
REUBEN
PHILISTIA
Lachish
JUDAH
Jahaza
Gaza
Hebron
Dead Sea
Debir
Eshtemoa
Gerar
Arad
Beersheba
MOAB
SIMEON
Kirhareseth
AMALEK
Zoar
Wilderness of Zin
EDOM
Tamar
Zalmona
Bozrah
Kadesh
Punon

ISRAEL

THE CHOOSING PEOPLE

עם הבוחר

By:
Avraham Russak

The History & Foundation of Jewish Tradition

Dedicated to my grandchildren -

When you learn your history, where you come from and where you are going, only then will you know who you truly are!

Remember Hellen Keller's lesson that a well-educated mind will always have more questions than answers!

INTRODUCTION
By Rabbi Eytan Feiner

It is a fundamental principle of Judaism – indeed, intertwined with the core of any honest existential perspective, that we are all endowed by the Almighty with *bechira chafshis*, absolute free will. Each and every one of us possesses the power to choose freely, an idea so basic, explains Rav Yitzchak Hutner in his <u>*Pachad Yitzchak*</u>, that the Rambam (Maimonides) felt no need to incorporate it into his Thirteen Principles of Faith. After all, free will is something we grasp instinctively – we naturally sense to be axiomatic, that we are not prodded to have to work on "believing" it to be true. Our innate feelings clearly vouch for its veracity, while those who espouse determinism are compelled to try and prove otherwise.

When G-d's heavenly angels questioned the inexplicable suffering of the saintly Rabbi Akiva at the hands of the ruthless Romans, G-d responded by instructing them to remain silent. Otherwise, He continued, "I will return the world to its original state of utter desolation." G-d was not threatening his celestial court, explains Rav Berel Povarsky, the current Dean of the Ponovezh Yeshiva. Rather, He was highlighting for all the generations one of the key purposes of mankind's creation.

From the beginning of time, man was put into this mundane and material world to tap into the latent power of his free will to choose truth over falsehood and good over evil. If we were to comprehend the ways of the Almighty, to resolve, for example, the age-old dilemma of why the righteous suffer and the wicked often prosper, there is no longer any reason for man's placement in the physical realm. For our souls to truly enjoy basking in proximity to the Divine Presence, we must earn our material reward by first journeying on the figurative roller coaster of life's vicissitudes, enduring life's struggles and surmounting the myriad obstacles in our path to self-perfection.

If the omniscient Creator provided us with all the answers, explained world history in a more lucid fashion, unraveled His intricately woven tapestry of all life's events before our eyes, then we will have lost a paramount purpose to our very creation. We will have been stripped of our precious free will, our priceless commodity that G-d wishes for us to incessantly tap – to choose freely how we live our lives and which perspectives and attitudes we opt to adopt to deal with our many queries and daily challenges. If all is explained in clear fashion before us, the world may as well return to its initial emptiness, for man's noble task of *choosing on his own* to follow G-d and His Torah under all circumstances will be no more.

With the aforementioned in mind, we now turn to the wonderful work before us. The author explains his book's intriguing title at the very outset: "We are," he writes, "The People that Chose, or The Choosing People. What did we choose? To follow G-d and the Torah. That is who we are!"

And how right he is. That poignant concept strikes at the very core of our existence, through thick and thin, persevering through pogroms, crusades, rampant anti-Semitism, and the indescribable atrocities of the Holocaust. We remain – as we have been from time immemorial – a unique People that never ceases to choose. To choose freely, with our absolute free-will forever intact, to follow G-d and to follow His hallowed Torah. Even when plagued by predicaments, inundated with endless questions and the ever-present paradox of Jewish suffering permeating their thoughts, there always remained a formidable nucleus of righteous Jews who continued to choose to follow the ways of the One above, no matter what life threw their way.

A chief ingredient in maintaining our lofty status as both the "Chosen" and the "Choosing" People, is learning about and appreciating our roots, our illustrious lineage, and sacred heritage. And Reb Avraham Russak's well-researched and informative presentation on the pages before you is perfectly suited for such a task.

Believe me, I know. Yes, I read through it and enjoyed the journey. But also, I take pride in being his nephew. I have known the author all my life and have witnessed his wondrous achievements, especially in the domain of conveying the principles, history, and foundation of Jewish tradition that every Jew needs to know to people of all ages, educational and cultural backgrounds, and levels of observance.

Over many decades, Reb Avraham (my "Uncle Larry") has taught these crucial ideas to so many in Seattle, Washington – and indeed, way beyond – and has done so with a gusto, a dynamism, and a passion for exploring Jewish history and the fundamentals of our faith. All while displaying an unquenchable thirst for Torah truths – and of course, always accompanied by his well-know wit, humor, and broad-based secular knowledge. You will find a delightful taste of all the above in the pages that await you.

Imbued with an unbridled love of Torah that he inherited from his dear father, my beloved Saba Joe Russak A"H, the author has carefully studied through *Tanach*, delved deeply into many diverse sources, and has provided us with an excellent resource and guide that we can share with families and students for years to come.

Keep it nearby and put this valuable resource to great use. It is replete with information that every Jew needs to know, and the author has sprinkled it with interesting and exciting tidbits along the way. Reb Avraham Russak has surely succeeded in making this brief journey through our fascinating history a most enjoyable one indeed.

Rabbi Eytan Feiner

Congregation Knesseth Israel ("The White Shul")

Chanukah, 5781

REFLECTING ON TANACH

A few years ago, I was walking through the Old City of Jerusalem with my niece, Rabbanit Shani Taragin. She was showing me some of the hidden neighborhoods and historical sites that most tourists do not visit.

She took me to a square in the Jewish Quarter up the hill from Yeshivat Ha'Kotel and just below the Armenian Quarter. It is a unique neighborhood with a circular public park just outside an elementary school.

She asked me to take particular note of the many senior citizens sitting in the square with their canes or walkers, watching the children playing. She then showed me an inscription on the back of one of the seating areas, where a prophecy of Zechariah has been carved in relief into a wall.

It comes from the Book of Trei Asar, Zechariah, perek 8, pessukim 4-5 and reads as follows:

כה אמר ה' צבאות, עד ישבו זקנים וזקנות ברחובות ירושלים, ואיש משענתו בידו מרב ימים. ורחובות העיר ימלאו ילדים וילדות משחקים ברחבתיה

Translation: "So said the Lord of Hosts. Old men and women will sit in the streets of Jerusalem, each with their staff in hand because of old age. And the streets of the city will be filled with boys and girls playing."

This prophecy of Zechariah has been fulfilled. We see the words of our prophets coming-to-life every day and we need to listen to them. We must study our history, learn Torah, Neviim, and Kesuvim, and educate ourselves so we can pass along our Mesorah to our children.

Let our generation read, hear, and heed the words of our prophets.

TABLE OF CONTENTS

INTRODUCTION	3
REFLECTING ON TANACH	7
WHAT IS THE PURPOSE OF THIS BOOK?	10
JEWISH HISTORY	12
HISTORY Part 1 – From Creation to the Forefathers	12
HISTORY Part 2 – From Moshe to the Conquest of Israel	15
HISTORY Part 3 – Joshua, Judges, and the Early Prophets	17
HISTORY Part 4 – Kings and the First Temple	18
HISTORY Part 5 – From Babylon to Purim	20
HISTORY Part 6 – The 2nd Temple Period	21
HISTORY Part 7 – Greeks, Romans, Destruction and Exile	24
HISTORY Part 8 – Jewish Rebellion and the Time of the Mishna	27
HISTORY Part 9 – The Talmud	28
HISTORY Part 10 – Centuries of Commentary, Persecution and Survival in Exile	29
HISTORY Part 11 – The Crusades, the Rishonim & the Spanish Inquisition	31
HISTORY Part 12 – The Achronim	33
HISTORY Part 13 – Return to Eretz Yisrael	36
HISTORY Part 14 – Jewish Life Grows in the USA	38
HISTORY Part 15 – The Holocaust	39
HISTORY Part 16 – Independent Israel	43
HISTORY Part 17 – Reflections on Israel	50
CHRONOLOGICAL ORDER OF THE KINGS OF ISRAEL	54
THE KINGS OF YEHUDA - the SOUTHERN KINGDOM	54
THE KINGS OF YISRAEL – THE NORTHERN KINGDOM	59
THE PROPHETS OF THE JEWISH PEOPLE	61
THE EBB AND FLOW OF NACH – An Outline	64
TRANSMISSION FROM GENERATION TO GENERATION	81

FUNDAMENTAL JEWISH CONCEPTS	96
THE TEN LOST TRIBES	102
THE JEWISH CALENDAR	105
WHERE DID OUR STRUCTURED PRAYERS COME FROM?	110
TRADITIONAL JEWISH DRESS	117
KEEPING KOSHER	122
ORTHODOX, CONSERVATIVE & REFORM JUDAISM	126
FUNDAMENTAL MISHNAIC & TALMUDIC CONCEPTS, ADAGES, & PRINCIPLES	130
THE WHAT & WHY of ANTISEMITISM	141
THE TRADITIONAL ROLES OF MEN & WOMEN	147
JUDAISM vs. OTHER RELIGIONS	154
BIBLICAL NAMES WE ALL NEED TO KNOW	167
QUOTES TO LIVE BY	188
THE 613 MITZVOS	242
A PERSONAL LIBRARY and a LIFETIME OF STUDY	331
BIG QUESTIONS	335
TAKING PRIDE IN BEING A JEW	346
ADDITIONAL TERMS – A SHORT GLOSSARY	349
FINAL MUSINGS	360
AFTERWORD	363
Acknowledgements	370

WHAT IS THE PURPOSE OF THIS BOOK?

The foundation of the Jewish People is the Torah, our history, and our shared experiences. For thousands of years we have cherished our connection to a singular G-d who is the Creator of our world.

The purpose of this book is to provide the reader or student with enough knowledge to heighten their understanding of Tanach, Jewish practice, and our progression through history. Too few Jews have ever taken the time to properly learn what is in this book and I urge educators to use this as a curriculum to teach these fundamental concepts and facts to their students and as a springboard for deeper discussion and exploration.

The first principle that guides our existence is to know who we are and where we came from. For too long we have been called "The Chosen People." That is a misnomer. We are, instead, "The People that Chose" or, "The Choosing People." What did we choose? To follow G-d and the Torah. That is who we are! With that in mind, let us first review the basics of our history so we can better understand where we came from.

In learning history, it is important to always keep the timeline of events in perspective. I will often follow two sets of dates and calendars. The first is the Jewish timeline which counts the years since creation. For instance, the exodus from Egypt was in the Jewish year 2448 from creation. That same year in today's secular calendar (originally called the Gregorian Calendar) is minus 1313 (1313 years **B**efore the **C**hristian or **C**ommon Era, "**BCE**"). As I finish writing this book, we are in the Jewish year 5781 which correlates to the secular year 2021.

The two main sources I have used for dates are the <u>Codex Judaica Chronological Index of Jewish History</u> and the <u>Jewish Timeline</u>

Encyclopedia, both by Mattis Kantor. You will notice that many of these dates are different than those taught in school or written in history books. For instance, most sources list the date of the destruction of the 1st Temple in Jerusalem as 586 BCE. My listing here is 423 BCE.

The commonly accepted dates (until the time of the early Roman presence in Israel) are off by over 160 years. There is an opinion that during the Greek period the timeline was thrown-off due to poor time keeping. There is an additional theory that the calendar was disrupted during the period of the Persian kings. Tanach speaks of four kings, but there are an additional ten recorded elsewhere.

The timeline followed in this book is based on the teachings of Rabbi Yosi ben Charlaftah in his *Seder Olam Rabbah* (The Great Order of the World) written in the 2nd century CE.

It is important for students to understand the chronological order of our history, but it is not critical that dates be committed to memory. I am trying to help the reader develop perspective on the progression of Jewish history.

I suggest that when you study this material you set certain historical dates and events and landmarks to help you establish the correct order of events and have some knowledge of the time-period in which they happened.

JEWISH HISTORY

HISTORY Part 1 – From Creation to the Forefathers

Following the Creation account in the Torah, there were ten generations from Adam to Noah. There were an additional ten generations separating Noah from Avraham.

The Great Flood during the time of Noah was in the year 1656 from Creation (2105 BCE). It is important to remember that Noah was not a Jew. Nevertheless, we (and our Arab cousins, the children of Ishmael) are descendants of Shem, the eldest son of Noah, and are "Semites."

The first Jew was Avram, (later, **Avraham** – Abraham), who was born in the year 1948 from Creation, over 3800 years ago (interestingly, the creation of the State of Israel was in the secular year 1948). The lives of Noah and Avraham overlapped by 58 years. Technically, the term "Jew" for Avraham is not accurate since that term was not used until much later when we became known as descendants of Yehuda (Judah – son of Yaakov). Avraham was often called *Avraham Ha'Ivri – Abraham (who came from) across the river.*

The Tower of Babel story and the subsequent dispersion of mankind was in the year 1996 from Creation (1765 BCE). The Covenant between G-d and Avraham which we call the "**Bris Bein Habesarim**" was established 22 years later (Avraham settled in Canaan five years after that). Our sages are divided on the subject of how old Avraham was when he discovered G-d and rejected the pagan ways of those around him. Some say that he was only three. Others say that he was either 40 or 48.

Avraham introduced monotheism into the world and was able to influence a large group of followers. Although they became monotheists, they were not Jews. Later, when Yaakov and his family went to Egypt, the only Jews were the 70 members of his extended family. It is important to note that in the beginning, our roots were in *avodah zarah* (idol worship) since Avraham was born into that environment. Later, he discovered G-d and rejected the pagan environment around him.

Avraham was tested by G-d ten times. There are two popular listings of the tests, one by Maimonides (the Rambam) and the other in Avos D'Rebbi Nassan.

Rambam:

1. Avraham was told by G-d to leave his homeland
2. Famine in the Promised Land – descent to Egypt
3. Pharaoh seizes Sarah, Avraham's wife
4. The battle between Avraham and the 4 kings to save Lot
5. Taking Hagar as a wife since Sarah could not have children
6. G-d orders Avraham to circumcise himself
7. Avimelech, king of Gerar, seizes Sarah
8. G-d tells Avraham to send Hagar and Yishmael away
9. Estrangement from Yishmael

The final test, #10 – Akedas Yitzchak – the offering on Mt. Moriah

Avos D'Rebbi Nassan:

1. Avraham thrown into furnace by Nimrod
2. Being told to leave his land
3. Famine in Promised Land
4. Pharaoh taking Sarah
5. Avimelech taking Sarah
6. War against kings to save Lot
7. Taking Hagar as a wife to have children in Sarah's stead
8. Circumcision

9. Expulsion of Hagar and Yishmael

The final test, #10 – Akedas Yitzchak

Avraham's first child, borne to him by his maidservant Hagar, was Ishmael. The Torah then tells us of the circumcision of both Avraham and Ishmael and follows with the story of the destruction of the city of S'dom.

The birth of Yitzchak was in the year 2048 and the "offering" by Avraham of his son (which is called "Akedas Yitzchak") was 37 years later, followed by the death of Sarah, Yitzchak's mother.

Yitzchak married Rivka, who gave birth to **Eisav and Yaakov**. Avraham died when these two grandsons were fifteen which is important to note so that one can understand the overlap of the generations. Yitzchak never left the land of Canaan his entire life.

Yaakov, in his exile to Charan (when he ran away from his brother Eisav after "stealing" the birthright) married sisters, Leah and Rachel, and returned to Canaan in 2205. He had twelve sons (with his wives Leah and Rachel and two maidservants, Bilhah and Zilpah), the Twelve Tribes of Israel. It is important to commit these names to memory as they will appear in our study of history repeatedly. They were Reuven, Shimon, Levi, Yehuda, Yissachar, Zevulun (sons of Leah), Dan, Naftali (sons of Bilhah), Gad, Asher (sons of Zilpah), Yosef, Binyamin (sons of Rachel) and Dena (daughter of Leah).

Yosef was sold by his brothers and brought as a slave to Egypt in the year 2216 (1545 BCE) at the age of 17 and his grandfather Yitzchak died twelve years later. Yosef became the viceroy of Egypt at the age of 30 and the story of his brothers coming to Egypt during a famine and finally reconciling with him was in 2238. That year, the descent of Yaakov's family to Egypt marked the beginning of 210 years of exile. Yosef had been separated from his father and his family for 22 years (the same number of years his father Yaakov had been separated from Yitzchak when he fled to Charan - he was away for 20 years plus 2 years of travel).

Yaakov remained in Egypt with his twelve sons for seventeen more years and died in 2255. Yosef died 54 years later. Following the death of the last of the 12 brothers in 2332 (Levi), the actual physical enslavement and servitude in Egypt began. It was the year 1429 BCE.

We have briefly covered the basic timeline and progression of Jewish history leading up to the period of slavery in Egypt. The next 156 years would see 116 years of harsh servitude, the birth of Moshe, the deliverance from Egypt, and the journey through the desert to the Land of Israel.

HISTORY PART 2 – FROM MOSHE TO THE CONQUEST OF ISRAEL

Moshe was born on the 7th of Adar of the year 2368 (1393 BCE) (and died 120 years later on his birthday in 1273 BCE).

On the 15th of Nissan, 79 years later, Moshe spoke with G-d at the burning bush. From that point, it was exactly one year until the exodus from Egypt. Following Moshe's return to Egypt, the plagues began on the 1st of Av. The Exodus was exactly 430 years from the Bris Bein Habesarim, the covenant G-d made with Avraham. The exodus from Egypt was in the year 2448 from Creation, 1313 BCE, and followed the ten plagues, which took place over the course of one year.

The Ten Plagues

1. דם – the Nile River and all the waters of Egypt turned to blood
2. צפרדע – frogs emerged from the water and filled the land
3. כינים – the desert dust turned to lice, affecting man and animals

4. ערוב – wild animals attacked the Egyptian people
5. דבר – livestock died of an epidemic of pestilence
6. שחין – people and animals inflicted with boils on their skin
7. ברד – a downpour of hail (ice and fire) destroyed Egypt's grain
8. ארבה – a plague of locusts ate any remaining plants
9. חשך – day turned to night with thick darkness over Egypt.
10. מכת בכורות – final plague, death of the firstborn

Seven days following the Exodus, B'nei Yisrael crossed the Reed Sea (the name of the Sea in the Torah is *Yam Suf* – literally, the "Sea of Reeds," not the "Red Sea").

Following the crossing, on the 15th of Iyar (30 days after departure) G-d began to provide food in the desert – the Mana.

On the 1st of Sivan, 45 days after leaving Egypt, they arrived in the wilderness of Sinai. Friday night, the 6th of Sivan, marked the revelation on Sinai of the Ten Commandments (literally, "The Ten Statements") and the next day, Moshe ascended Mount Sinai. While on the mountain for 40 days, Moshe received both the Written and Oral law.

Moshe came down the mountain on the 17th of Tammuz, saw the people worshiping the golden calf, and broke the tablets. On the 18th he went back up the mountain and spent another 40 days praying for the Jewish People.

Following his return to the camp he was told by G-d to carve two tablets like the original ones and return to the mountain. He went up for a final 40 days and returned on the 10th of Tishrei, the day that would be marked forever as Yom Kippur.

The very next day, B'nei Yisrael began bringing gifts for the construction of the Tabernacle, the Mishkan, which was completed on the 25th day of Kislev. It is interesting to note that Chanukah, a holiday celebrating the re-dedication of the Temple in 138 BCE falls on the 25th of Kislev as well.

The next year, Moshe sent the spies to scout the Promised Land and they returned with their report. That night, the 9th of Av (Tish'a b'Av) the Jews bemoaned their plight, openly proclaiming their fear of fighting to conquer the Land of Israel. That resulted in G-d cursing that generation and Moshe telling them that they would aimlessly wander the desert for the next 38+ years. Soon after that was the incident of the rebellion of Korach and his followers.

The entire book of Devarim is filled with the speeches made by Moshe to the Jewish People in the last few weeks of his life, and ends with a description of his death and burial. He died on the 7th of Adar at the age, to-the-day, of 120, which corresponds to the total number of days he spent on Mount Sinai.

HISTORY Part 3 – Joshua, Judges, and the Early Prophets

B'nei Yisrael crossed the Jordan River on the 10th of Nissan and entered the Land of Israel in the year 2488 (1273 BCE) under the command of Yehoshua – Joshua, where they observed the first Pesach since the exodus from Egypt.

It took fourteen years to complete the initial conquest of the Land and the apportioning of its territories among the twelve tribes. Joshua died thirteen years later, beginning a difficult period during which there was a vacuum of leadership. For the next 350 years, until the period of

Shmuel the Prophet and the kingship of Shaul, the Jewish People were led by a series of judges, military leaders, prophets, and priests.

This was a time marked by such leaders as Devorah the prophetess, Gideon, Shimshon (Samson), Eli the Kohen and Shmuel the Prophet. King David was born during this period and began ruling as king at the age of 30.

HISTORY Part 4 – Kings and the First Temple

The first King of Israel was Shaul (Saul) who was anointed by Shmuel the Prophet. He was the first of 43 kings who would serve in Yehuda (the southern portion of the land) and in Yisrael, (the northern portion) until the destruction of the 1st Temple.

The full description of the early history of both Shaul and his successor, King David, is covered in the third book of Neviim, the book of Shmuel.

David became king following the death of Shaul but only ruled over his own tribe – Yehuda. Later, he became king over the entire nation and remained as king until his death at the age of 70. He was succeeded by his son, Shlomo Hamelech (King Solomon) who built the first Temple in Jerusalem.

Prior to the building of the Temple, the Mishkan (Tabernacle) had stood in multiple locations including Shilo, Nov, and Givon. The Talmud says that the components of the Mishkan were buried under Solomon's Temple during construction. In the year 827 BCE the Temple was completed and the holy Ark was welcomed into its new home. 30 years later, Shlomo died and was succeeded by his son Rechavam.

Shlomo is credited with authorship of Mishlei (Proverbs), Koheles (Ecclesiastes), and Shir Hashirim (Song of Songs).

Following the death of Shlomo and the beginning of the rule of Rechavam, the entire country of Israel split into two pieces. The Southern Kingdom which became known as "Yehuda" was made-up of the tribe of Yehuda, the southern portion of the tribe Binyamin and those Kohanim and Leviim who lived in close proximity to the Temple in Jerusalem. If you look at popular maps of the territories of the 12 tribes, you will notice that they place the tribe of Shimon in the south-west of Israel. Their tribe was mostly absorbed by the tribe of Yehuda as described in the first perek of the book of Shoftim when they joined Yehuda to battle against the Canaanites. Any remnants of Shimon were exiled by the Assyrians prior to the destruction of the 1st Temple.

The Northern Kingdom was ruled by Yeravam who was popular with the majority of the populace. It encompassed the territories of the other ten tribes and became known as "Yisrael." Today, the two territories of Yehuda and Yisrael are associated with Yehuda and Shomron.

This split of the nation continued for more than 240 years. The beginning of the end of this period was marked by the exile of the tribes who lived across the Jordan River; Reuven, Gad and half the tribe of Menasheh. They were conquered by Tiglat Pil'esser of Assyria. Later, the remaining northern tribes were also conquered by the Assyrians. The final conquest of the Northern Kingdom, Yisrael, took place in 556 BCE.

The Southern Kingdom, Yehuda, remained mostly intact through multiple attempts by Assyria to destroy Jerusalem. King Chizkiyahu (Hezekiah) was instrumental in repelling the Assyrian army. His son Menasheh and subsequent kings reigned during a period of downfall.

The Babylonians (under the leadership of King Nebuchadnezzar) destroyed Jerusalem and Yehuda and sacked the Temple in 423 BCE, 410 years from the beginning of its construction.

The siege of Jerusalem as described in the megillah of Eicha led to mass starvation and a plague that decimated the city. After the Babylonian conquest, those Jews who were not exiled became known as *Yehudim* (those who remained from the southern kingdom, *Yehuda*).

The Babylonians exiled the majority of Jews and many others ran away to Egypt and parts of southern Europe, sowing the seeds of new communities. Over 500 years later, following the Roman conquest of the 2nd Temple, large numbers of Jews would be taken as slaves to Europe, further exacerbating our "dispersion."

HISTORY Part 5 – From Babylon to Purim

Many Jews had been exiled from Yehuda to Babylon prior to the final destruction of Jerusalem. Included in their numbers was Yechezkel (Ezekiel the Prophet) who had prophesied the exile.

For the next 50 years Babylon was a great world power under the leadership of Nebuchadnezzar. Yirmiyahu (Jeremiah the prophet) wrote the book of Melachim (Kings I and II) and the megillah of Eicha. Daniel became an advisor to the king. Many of the stories of this time period are chronicled in the Book of Daniel which is written partially in Aramaic and partially in Hebrew.

The Persian Empire began its ascent at this time and conquered Babylon. Their leader, Cyrus, encouraged the Jews to return to Israel and rebuild the Temple. Over 40,000 returned with a member of the royal family, Zerubavel, but the vast majority remained in Babylon. The effort to rebuild the Temple was not successful after an internal conflict erupted between the returnees from Babylon and the Samaritans, otherwise known as the Kuthim.

The Purim story took place at this time, with Achashverosh II succeeding Cyrus. The story of Esther being taken to the palace to become his wife took place in 362 BCE. The decree by Haman as signed by the King, which called for genocide against the Jews of Persia and Media, happened five years later. The holiday of Purim was proclaimed in 355 BCE as Mordechai wrote and distributed the Book of Esther. Two years later, the rebuilding of the Temple in Jerusalem resumed (as encouraged by Darius II, the son of Esther and Achashverosh).

Zechariah prophesied in 351 BCE that there was no reason to mourn the First Temple any longer. This ushered-in a new era and marked the first year of the 2nd Temple, which stood until year 69 of the modern era, a total of 420 years.

HISTORY Part 6 – The 2nd Temple Period

Ezra, the head of the Sanhedrin in Babylon, led a return of refugees to Israel. The majority of Jews still chose to remain in Babylon. A few years later, Nechemia led another return to Israel. Together with Ezra and the 120 leaders of the Great Assembly – the Anshei Knesses Hagedolah, new laws and customs were instituted including daily prayer services, the Shmona Esrei, Kiddush, Havdalah, and many other blessings and prayers were formalized. This period also marked the beginning of the establishment of Rabbinic *s'yagim* (fences) around the Torah to prohibit or pre-empt sinning.

Under the leadership of Ezra, the books of Neviim and Kesuvim were written-down and published in classic holy script. Ezra thus became known as Ezra Ha'Sofer – Ezra the Scribe. He is also credited with designing many of our daily prayers and instituting the public reading of Torah on Mondays and Thursdays.

These books became known as "Nach" (נך) an acronym for the Hebrew words נביאים כתובים - The Prophets and the Writings. The first five books of the Torah as well as these books are known collectively as "Tanach" or: **תורה-נביאים-כתובים**

The following is an outline of the books and writings that contain divinely inspired texts. Although each was originally written-down on parchment by a human author from Moshe to Nechemiah, our tradition is that they were transmitted as follows:

Torah – from G-d, directly to Moshe

Neviim – the words of prophets based on messages received from G-d

Kesuvim – words of human authors based on divine inspiration

תורה – The Torah

The 5 books of the Torah:

B'reishis – Genesis

Sh'mos – Exodus

Vayikra - Leviticus

Bamidbar - Numbers

Devarim – Deuteronomy

נביאים – Nevi'im - Prophets

Yehoshua – Joshua

Shoftim – Judges

Shmuel I and II – Samuel 1 and 2

Melachim I and II – Kings 1 and 2

Yeshayah – Isaiah

Yirmiyah – Jeremiah

Yechezkel – Ezekiel

Trei Asar – The Twelve (Prophets)

כתובים – Kesuvim – The Writings

Tehillim – Psalms

Mishlei – Proverbs

Iyov – Job

Shir Hashirim – Song of Songs

Rus – Ruth

Eichah – Lamentations

Koheles – Ecclesiastes

Esther

Daniel

Ezra and Nechemiah

Divrei Hayamim I and II – Chronicles I and II

I completed my first cycle of studying all of Tanach including Rashi and Radak on July 30th, 2020 just after Tish'a B'Av 5780, two days before my 65th birthday.

HISTORY Part 7 – Greeks, Romans, Destruction and Exile

Alexander the Great conquered Persia and began to expand the Macedonian (of Greek origin) Empire. He was mentored by the great Greek philosopher, Aristotle.

Upon arriving in Israel to conquer the land in 313 BCE, Alexander was convinced by Shimon Ha'Tzaddik, the last of the leaders of the Great Assembly, to allow the Temple to stand. Although Alexander's armies physically took control of Israel, they allowed Jewish spiritual practice to continue.

Alexander died very shortly after his conquest and his generals divided the conquered lands into four provinces. Israel was caught between two of those areas, controlled by the Egyptian Ptolemies and the Seleucids of Syria. During this time the Ptolemy administration ordered 72 Jewish scholars to translate the Torah into Greek. Each scholar was sequestered in a separate location and ordered to translate the Torah. When completed, all 72 copies proved to be the same and the resulting final document was called "Septuagint." The Greek version of this story tells of 70 scholars, thus the Latin/Greek name: "Septuagint" – "Seventy." It is also known as: *Targum Ha'Shivim – The Translation of the Seventy*.

Life in Israel began to change under Greek occupation as some Jews became Hellenists and promoted Greek culture. The Samaritans gained strength as did the Tzedukim – the Sadducees, who only followed the

Written Torah and did not accept the orally transmitted Torah laws. They were literalists.

By the year 161 BCE, Israel was dominated by the Syrian Greeks. The office of High Priest in the Temple was held by a Hellenist named Yeshua who called himself "Jason." Antiochus, as king, enforced new rules against traditional Jewish practice. Keep in mind that at this time, the Jews in Babylon were thriving (and continued to do so for many centuries), but in Israel, Jews were ordered not to keep Shabbos, circumcision, and the laws of family purity.

In 140 BCE, Matisyahu and his five sons led a rebellion against the Greeks. They were called "Hashmonaim" after the area adjacent to Modiin from which they came. Following the death of Matisyahu, his son Yehuda became the leader and was given the name *Ha'Maccabee* (The Hammer). The rebels gained control of the Temple, cleaned out its desecrated areas, destroyed the Greek idols that had been installed there, and re-dedicated the Temple. The story of finding a cruse of oil for the Menorah of the Temple is central to the Chanukah story and its declaration as a holiday in the year 138 BCE (some say 165 BCE).

The word "Chanukah" is composed of the word "chanu" – (חנו)ך ("dedicated") and the letters "chaf" and "heh" (כה) which stand for "25" since the Temple was re-dedicated on the 25th of the month of Kislev of that year.

Many battles with the Syrian Greeks followed, leading to the death of Yehuda's brother Elazar (crushed by an elephant in the first major battle). Yehuda was killed in the battle of Elasa. Their brother Yonasan became ruler of Yehuda and another brother, Yochanan, became the High Priest. Their family established a dynasty and ruled over the land of Israel until the Romans under Pompey were invited into the land to help settle a civil war in 66 BCE.

The Romans quickly took control of the land and called it "Judea."

Herod, a Jew who had been educated in Rome and courted favor with Emperor Augustus, was installed as ruler in 36 BCE. He proceeded to kill-off the Hashmonaim and rebuilt much of the infrastructure of the country. He built palaces in Masada, Herodian and Caesarea. By the year 11 BCE he completed his renovation of the Temple in Jerusalem, and others continued improving the Temple site through the year 4 CE.

During this time, Hillel, a direct descendant of King David, returned to Israel from Babylon, became the Nassi of the Sanhedrin, and established a beis midrash. This began a new era which is called the period of the Tannaim.

The Tannaim were the scholars of the period prior to the destruction of the 2nd Temple (by the Romans) through the 2nd century CE. They include such scholars as Hillel, Shammai, Rabban Gamliel, Rav Yochanan ben Zakkai, Rabbi Akiva, etc. These scholars are also called: "the Rabbis of the Mishna."

Multiple Jewish rebellions against Roman occupation resulted in Rome sending Vespasian and his legions to Judea. Rav Yochanan ben Zakkai escaped the city of Jerusalem that was controlled by warring Jewish militias and was able to meet with Vespasian. He predicted Vespasian's imminent declaration as Emperor following the death of Nero in Rome. He asked the Roman general to set aside the city of Yavneh where Jewish scholars could continue teaching their traditions and pleaded with him not to kill-off the remnants of the Davidic Dynasty.

Vespasian granted his wish and protected Yavneh and its scholars including Rabban Gamliel and Rav Tzadok. He then returned to Rome and Titus, his son, initiated the siege of Jerusalem.

The second Temple was destroyed by the Romans in 69 of the Common Era on the 9th of Av – Tish'a B'Av.

Approximately 100,000 Jews were taken to Rome as slaves, while some scholars continued to teach in Yavneh under Roman protection as promised by Vespasian.

HISTORY Part 8 – Jewish Rebellion and the Time of the Mishna

The Romans fought a war against Jewish rebels, but a small outpost of less than one thousand Jews survived in the former palace of Herod at Masada, by the Dead Sea. In the year 74, after a long siege, the rebels committed suicide rather than allow general Flavius Silva to capture them and take them into slavery.

The next fifty years saw the land of Israel ruled by a series of harsh Roman leaders. Emperor Hadrian issued decrees against religious Jewish observance and built a temple to Jupiter on the site of the 2nd Temple. He also changed the name of Jerusalem to Aelia Capitolina (Hadrian was the head of the Aelius clan and wished the city of Jerusalem to be named after his family). This led to a Jewish revolt led by Shimon Bar Koziba (Bar Kochba). He was able to recapture Jerusalem and was so successful that Rabbi Akiva declared that Bar Kochba was the Mashiach.

Over the next few years, the Romans continued to wage war against an army of rebels who were driven back to the city of Betar which fell on the 9th of Av. Bar Kochba was killed along with over 580,000 Jews. Judaism was banned and Rabbi Akiva and other leaders were tortured and murdered. They became known as the Ten Martyrs. On Yom Kippur and Tish'a B'Av we tell their story as part of our liturgy.

Hadrian, as Roman emperor, also directed a war at this time against the Philistines who had rebelled against Roman rule. He ordered the total destruction of the Philistine people. He changed the name of Judea to Philistia (later, Syria Palaestina) which changed the name of the land of Israel (Judea) to a name honoring two enemies, Syria and the Philistines.

The massacres and retaliation by the Romans continued until they decimated the Holy Land. In many areas they literally salted the earth so nothing would grow. By this time, many of the Tannaim of Yavneh had died or been murdered and most of the others fled the land.

One scholar (some time between 160 and 180 CE), Rav Yehuda ben Rav Shimon ben Gamliel, appealed to the new emperor, Marcus Aurelius Antoninus, who granted the rebuilding of one academy. Rav Yehuda became known as Reb Yehuda Ha'Nassi, otherwise known as "Rebbi." He took upon himself the task of writing-down and clarifying the Oral Law, fearing that our tradition of passing this information from generation-to-generation by word-of-mouth was at risk of being lost. His voluminous work was organized into the six books of the Mishna. The Mishna was completed sometime between the years 189 and 229 of our modern calendar.

HISTORY Part 9 – The Talmud

Following the death of Reb Yehuda Ha'Nassi, the Roman persecution in Israel continued. A disciple of his, Rav (Abba Aricha), moved to Babylonia (Bavel), establishing an academy there. Those scholars who discussed and taught the Mishna (in the cities of Nehardea, Sura, Pumpedisa, etc.) became known as Amoraim. Following the death of Rav, Shmuel became the leading authority in the schools of Bavel.

The next few hundred years were a period marked by increased study and analysis of the Mishna. The subsequent teachings, discussions, arguments, stories, and clarification of laws, were collected by the competing academies in Bavel (as well as in Israel) into a major work called "Talmud." Rav Yochanan in Tiberias, Israel, expounded on the Mishna based on what he had been taught by Reb Yehuda Ha'Nassi. This became the basis of the Talmud Yerushalmi. The teachings in Bavel became the basis of the Talmud Bavli. The Bavli closed after the Yerushalmi and is therefore considered the final word.

The Mishna is the original written version of the oral law as codified by Rav Yehuda Ha'Nassi around the year 200. It includes six major categories of law: Zeraim, Moed, Nashim, Nezikin, Kadshim and Taharos.

The Gemara is the written record of rabbinic discussions of the Mishna (as organized and edited by Ravina and Ravi Ashi around the year 400).

The Talmud is the name of the overall comprehensive written version of the Oral Law and subsequent commentaries in 38 volumes. It was completed around the year 427 (year 4187 from creation). The version that is most common today is the Vilna Shas. The word "Shas" is an acronym for (משנה) סדרי ששה – the six books (of the Mishna), and includes the Mishna and the Gemara (as well as the commentaries of Rashi, Tosafos, etc.).

HISTORY Part 10 – Centuries of Commentary, Persecution and Survival in Exile

The academies of Bavel continued to thrive and Jewish study and practice survived in cities like Baghdad. The growing influence of the

Church in Rome led to conflict with the Eastern Roman (Byzantine) Empire.

The greatest of the Jewish scholars of the time congregated in the city of Pumpedisa in Bavel and were given the title "Gaon." The next four centuries (apx. 600 to 1000 of the modern era) are known as the period of the Gaonim.

Many of the descendants of the Jewish slaves who had been taken to Rome were further dispersed by the Barbarians (Goths, Huns, Franks, Vandals, Saxons) who conquered Rome, leading to a further expansion of the Jewish population to other parts of Europe, from Germany to Spain.

This period of time also marked the beginning of Islam, founded by Muhammad in Arabia. It was a time of perpetual war, with the Persian Empire conquering Eretz Yisrael and the Byzantines taking it back a few years later. Caught in the crossfire were the Jews, living among the destruction and chaos in horrible conditions. The Muslims under Muhammad's successor conquered Jerusalem and built a wooden mosque on the site of the Beis Hamikdash.

As Islam spread, the North African Muslims (Moors), invaded Spain and were welcomed by the Jews. Under Moorish rule, Judaism flourished in Spain and North Africa leading to a golden age in Spain of writing of Torah commentary, music, song, and liturgical poetry.

Most of Europe at this time was embroiled in a state of internal war between the remnants of the Roman empire, the Byzantines, the Franks, the English, the Moors, and others. The average person lived in terrible poverty and a feudal system controlled most of society. There was a terrible chasm between the rich and poor. The Church in Rome and Constantinople (the Eastern Catholic Church) wielded tremendous power, hoarding its wealth. As always, the Jews were caught in the middle, making life in most of Europe extremely difficult.

The time period in Europe from 500 to the early 1000's is commonly referred-to by historians as "The Dark Ages." Nevertheless, out of this emerged a period of unparalleled Jewish writing and commentary that would change Torah study forever. Jewish scholarship began to grow around the year 1000 under such leaders as Rabbeinu Gershom, the Rif, Rashi, the Rambam, Ramban, and others, and became part of a golden age of written Torah commentary.

HISTORY Part 11 – The Crusades, the Rishonim & the Spanish Inquisition

Between the years 1095 and 1270 there were eight officially sanctioned Crusades. The first was ordered by Pope Urban who called-to-arms knights and soldiers to retake Jerusalem from the Muslims. Over 90,000 volunteered to serve. Many Jewish communities were destroyed by marauding soldiers as they traveled through Europe, making their way to seaports along the Mediterranean on their way to the Holy Land.

The First Crusade decimated Jerusalem as Christian knights conquered it in 1099. Jerusalem and the Holy Land were fought-over for the next 170 years and were repeatedly passed between Christian and Muslim control. As usual, Jews were caught in the crossfire and often massacred.

Rashi lived in Troyes, France during the period of the 1st Crusade. Although he was a wine merchant, he spent his life writing a definitive commentary on Tanach and the Talmud. Rashi and the Rif (Rabbi Yitzchak Alfasi from Algeria and Spain) are commonly identified as the early "Rishonim" ("first" or "early" commentators and codifiers).

Rashi died in 1105 and was succeeded by his grandson, Yaakov Ben Meier (known as Rabbeinu Tam) and his descendants, who we call the Ba'alei Ha'Tosafos. They were contemporaries of other commentators and codifiers of Jewish law including the Rambam, Radak, Ramban, etc.

In the 1200's, the intensity of antisemitism in Europe increased. The Catholic Church was at the center of this, promoting Jew-hatred as a way of deflecting other problems in society and diverting attention from the growing wealth and control of the Roman Catholic Church.

What we call the Spanish Inquisition actually had its roots in the Church in Rome. It spread to Paris, where, in 1242, there was a massive public burning of the Talmud. In 1290 the Jews were expelled from England. In the 1300's, Germany saw an explosion of antisemitism. The Black Plague (Bubonic Plague) hit Europe in 1349, killing millions and stoking the fires of antisemitism. Jews were expelled from France in 1394.

Because the Jews had defied all odds and continued to flourish in Europe as merchants, traders, and money-lenders, antisemitism intensified. Since the Catholic Church did not allow Christians to charge interest on loans (a law from the Torah), many Jews were used as intermediaries and became bankers, pawn-shop owners and direct lenders. This led to a projection in the public media of Jews like "Shylock," Shakespeare's notorious Jewish character from his play, The Merchant of Venice.

Following the re-conquest of Spain and the defeat of the Moors, Christian control of Spain was re-established by Ferdinand II and his queen, Isabella. They proclaimed an Inquisition in 1478 as a way of further consolidating Spanish power and as a way of forcing the Jewish population of Spain to convert to Christianity.

In previous centuries, Spanish and Portuguese Jews had thrived under Moorish control and built affluent communities. Jews were influential in medicine, government, banking, import-export businesses, and many trades. All of the remaining 800,000 Spanish and Portuguese Jews who had not yet converted to Christianity were ordered by the Office of the Inquisition to convert by August 2, 1492 (which was Tisha B'Av). Any remaining Jews were to be officially expelled from Spain as of that day. Columbus departed the next day on his voyage to discover the "new world." He was accompanied by a Jewish "converso" interpreter, Luis de Torres.

Those Jews who converted to Christianity included a large number who pretended to follow the Christian faith, while secretly maintaining their Jewish identify. Today, we call them "conversos." Later, many of these Jews were able to emigrate to other countries including Italy, where they were given the name "marrano" (swine) as a way of categorizing them as Jews who had previously converted.

Those who left Spain and Portugal earlier and had not converted, went to Amsterdam, Italy, Greece and throughout the Middle-East as they fled from the Inquisition. Formally, the Inquisition continued to 1834 and stretched as far as South America, with many of its Jews living as conversos in cities such as Recife, Brazil. The descendants of those who came originally from Spain and Portugal became known as "Sephardim" (Spanish Jews).

HISTORY Part 12 – The Achronim

The period of the Achronim, the "later" Jewish commentators, covers the period from the early 15th century to just after World War I, from the writing of the Shulchan Aruch to the Mishna B'rurah.

Due to the expulsion of Jews from such countries as Spain, Portugal, England and France, Jewish life in Europe consolidated in Eastern Europe; Poland, Germany, Czechoslovakia, Romania, Hungary, Ukraine, Lithuania, and Belarus. The Jews of this region became known as "Ashkenazim." There was also a resurgence of scholarly life in Israel in places like Tzfat (Safed) following the last of the Crusades and the conquest of Israel by the Ottoman Empire (Turkey). Surprisingly, Jewish life in Italy thrived even though it was the home country of the Catholic Church.

The printing press was invented by Guttenberg in the 1440's, making it easier to publish scholarly works and to make them widely available.

Rav Yosef Karo wrote the Shulchan Aruch, a definitive codification of Jewish law (based on the halachic codes and commentaries of the Rif, the Rambam, and the Rosh) in 1563. Rabbi Yitzchak Luria, the Ari'zal, taught and wrote in Tzfat about "Kabbalah" and its mystical ways, based on the Zohar, the Book of Radiance. Our Mesorah teaches that the Zohar was revealed to Moshe on Mt. Sinai and was passed orally until it was written-down by Rav Shimon Bar Yochai during the Roman occupation of Judea.

In Eastern Europe, Moreinu ha'Rav Loew (the Maharal of Prague) and Rav Shmuel Eidels (the Maharsha in Lublin) as well as the Rav Moshe Isserles (the Ramoh) and Rav Shlomo Luria (the Maharshal) became prominent commentators in the late 1500's.

By the mid 1600's the Jewish population in Poland and Western Russia was growing rapidly and a new series of persecutions and massacres began. The Cossacks under the leadership of Bogdan Chmielnitzki rebelled against Polish rule in the Ukraine and tortured and forcibly converted Jews to Eastern Christianity. Up to 300,000 Jews were killed in the Chmielnitzki pogroms (localized massacres) of 1648 due to the fact that they were caught in the crosshairs of someone else's rebellion and became scapegoats.

By 1654, Jews had begun settling in New Amsterdam (New York) opening the door to increasing Jewish immigration to the United States from places in Europe where they had been victims of increased violence.

Through both the 1600's and 1700's Jewish writing of Torah commentary and written codification of law became more common, partially due to the ease at which the written word could be copied by the printing press.

The Bal Shem Tov, Rabbi Yisrael ben Eliezer, rose to prominence in Europe. During the Chmielnitzki period many Jews had put their hopes in a rising Jewish leader, Shabtai Zvi, who they believed could be the Mashiach. They despaired when he converted to Islam and died in 1676. Against this backdrop, the Bal Shem Tov brought hope to many communities with his innovated teachings that became the foundation of Chassidic Judaism. He brought Jewish mysticism to the masses, de-emphasizing intensive Torah study in favor of fervent prayer (including the adoption of much Sephardic liturgy), song, and a culture of stories, magic, and miracles. This was also the background through which Chabad Lubavitch under the Bal Hatanya (Rabbi Schneuer Zalman of Liadi) was established.

The Vilna Gaon and others took exception to the teachings of the Chassidim and the late 1700's was a time of conflict in Eastern Europe between Chassidim and Misnagdim (the "Opponents").

This was also the time of the French Revolution, Napoleon's conquests, and the formation of an independent United States of America. The Constitution of the United States gave Jews full citizenship and freedom and this concept spread to other countries. Jews re-settled in England, France, and many other Western European countries. Israel was beginning to see a return of Jews who had fled European pogroms, and Jewish life in the Americas was growing rapidly.

HISTORY Part 13 – Return to Eretz Yisrael

It is important to note that from the 1820's to the 1870's, the Jews of Israel survived with the assistance of numerous benefactors and subsidies from the "Chalukah," a fund that collected charity money overseas. The biggest benefactor was Sir Moses Montefiore, who not only contributed funds, but helped build the first suburb of Jerusalem outside the Old City walls, Mishkenot Sha'ananim.

Prior to any formal movement of immigration of Jews into the Holy Land, a group of observant Jews from Jerusalem and a few new immigrants from Hungary established Petach Tikva (Opening of Hope), the first new settlement in Israel in over 2000 years. Today, it is a suburb of Tel Aviv, and is known as "Aym Hamoshavot" ("The Mother of Settlements"). At that time, the Jewish population of the Holy Land was estimated at no more than 25,000.

Zionism as a political movement was begun in 1897 by Theodore Herzl. It was designed to re-establish a Jewish homeland in Israel (called "Palestine" even under Ottoman-Turkish control as it continued to be labeled by its late-Roman name).

Prior to the establishment of a political movement called "Zionism," there was an earlier return of 25,000 to 35,000 Jews (mostly from Eastern Europe) who traveled to their traditional homeland in Ottoman-controlled Palestine. This took place from 1881 to 1903 as is called "The First Aliyah." It is also called "The Agricultural Aliyah." The word "Aliyah" means "rising," "coming up," or "returning." Early immigrants fled pogroms in Eastern Europe and established agricultural settlements such as Rishon Le'Zion, Rosh Pina, and Zichron Yaakov. They received assistance from Baron Edmond Rothschild who helped finance their land purchases. These early agricultural settlements were called "moshavot."

1904 to 1914 marked the period of the Second Aliyah and the establishment of new agricultural collective communities called "kibbutzim." Following the Russian Revolution of 1905 (as opposed to the Communist Revolution of 1917), over two million Jews left Russia. Most made their way to the United States, South Africa, Australia, Mexico, and South America. About 35,000 Jews took part in the 2nd Aliyah. They were fleeing the aftermath of the 1905 Russian revolution and its accompanying pogroms. The first kibbutz, Degania, was built in 1909 near Tiberias.

The Third Aliyah followed World War I, from 1919 to 1923, during which time almost 40,000 Jews fled Russia, Lithuania, and Poland for Palestine. The Russian "October" Revolution of 1917 had brought the Communists into power and it is estimated that over 500,000 Jews were murdered in pogroms. In 1917, during World War I, the British Empire conquered Palestine, taking it back from the Turkish (Ottoman) Empire, that had held it for over 400 years. That year, The Balfour Declaration was proclaimed. It was a public statement by the British government calling for the establishment of a national homeland for the Jewish people in Palestine.

The Fourth Aliyah was from 1924 to 1928. It followed an economic crisis in Poland that had inflamed anti-Jewish sentiment. Many Jews tried to come to the United States, but strict immigration quotas kept them out. Over 80,000 Jews came to Palestine, which was now under British control (the British having taken Palestine during World War I). Due to the rapidly growing Jewish population, the local Arabs became increasingly hostile. Over 23,000 Jews left Palestine during this time period (including my mother's family) due to Arab riots and attacks.

The Fifth Aliyah started when the Nazi Party rose to power in Germany in 1933. It continued until 1939 and the beginning of World War II. Estimates of the number of new immigrants during that period run from 250,000 to 300,000.

The British, under constant pressure from the Arabs (and needing oil from the Middle East), increasingly cut Jewish immigration into Palestine and made it difficult to continue the mass exodus of European Jews.

HISTORY Part 14 – Jewish Life Grows in the USA

In 1881, the United States had a Jewish population of around 280,000. It is estimated that there were about 200 synagogues, only twelve of which were not reform. The majority of Jews who had come to America following its independence gave up their religious observance, especially Shabbos, since they were required to work on Saturdays.

The pogroms in Russia and growing anti-Semitism in Eastern Europe in the late 1800's were the key factors that fueled Jewish immigration into the United States, with over two million Ashkenazi Jews (mostly Yiddish speaking) immigrating between 1881 and 1914.

In France, in 1895, a Jewish officer in the French army, Alfred Dreyfus, was accused of being a spy. This began a period of anti-Jewish sentiment throughout France. He was tried, found guilty, and sent to the worst prison in the French colonies; Devil's Island in French Guiana.

A Jewish newspaper reporter from Austria, Theodore Herzl, was moved by the story of the Dreyfus trial and its injustices. He subsequently developed the idea of a Jewish State with self-rule. He was successful at winning-over statesmen and idealists and established the Zionist movement. Emile Zola, a French writer, took-up the cause of Dreyfus and proved him innocent. He wrote a famous newspaper article in which he accused the French army leadership of anti-Semitism, entitled: J'Accuse. The French army leadership never apologized for their accusations, but did release Dreyfus from prison in 1900.

The anti-Semitism of the French as well as attacks on Jews in North Africa and many other communities, also spurred many Sephardic Jews to emigrate. Jews from Algeria, Morocco, Greece, Turkey and France began moving to the Americas.

An influx of traditional Jews into the United States contributed to the growth of orthodox synagogues and observance, yet the period from World War I through World War II (1914-1945) also saw tremendous assimilation and the relaxing of standards of Jewish observance. There was no system of formal Jewish education, especially for girls. Most communities had after-school Jewish classes at their local synagogue, but the large-scale Jewish schools and yeshivas we have today were very limited at that time.

The growth in traditional Jewish education began following World War II and the immigration of survivors of the war including many great yeshiva leaders from Europe and the remnants of their institutions.

HISTORY Part 15 – The Holocaust

The aftermath of World War I had a devastating effect on Germany and caused instability, inflation, and a rising resentment of Jews. The Nazis, an extreme right-wing party led by Adolf Hitler, came to power in

Germany in 1933. The German Jewish population of over 500,000 suffered economic sanctions, violence, torture, murder, and imprisonment. Life for Jews in Germany became intolerable, but it was difficult to enter the United States due to strict immigration quotas. Some Jews went to Central and South America and others to British Palestine, but it became increasingly difficult to get out of Germany.

In 1938, a Nazi-incited large-scale pogrom swept through both Germany and Austria. Over 300 synagogues were destroyed, Jewish businesses attacked, 30,000 Jews arrested, and cemeteries desecrated. So much glass was shattered in the violence against Jewish homes and businesses that November 9th, 1938 became known as "Kristallnacht" (The Night of Broken Glass).

In May of 1939, the British government announced further restrictions on Jewish immigration in Palestine (the White Paper) allowing only 10,000 Jews per year to enter the country. By that time, there were over 400,000 Jews in Palestine and the British were feeling tremendous pressure to appease the Arabs. With war looming, the British wanted to ensure their oil supply would not be interrupted.

On September 1, 1939, Hitler attacked Poland. His armies used a new technique utilizing speed and overwhelming power called "Blitzkrieg." His tanks, artillery, and air force destroyed the Polish army (elements of which were still fighting on horseback) and took control of the entire country in eighteen days. The Germans immediately began organized systematic attacks on Jews. They destroyed the Jewish section of Czestochowa, Poland, eight days after the start of the war and killed several hundred Jews. This was the beginning of their campaign to kill the Jews of Europe.

No Jew was safe from the Nazis. Immediately upon the conquering of any town, a special killing unit of merciless German soldiers, elite members of the SS (Schutzstaffel Protection Squadron) called "Einsatzgruppen" (Deployment Groups), would round-up all the Jews in "aktions" such as Aktion T-4 that specifically targeted mental patients and those with physical disabilities, and murder them. Often, they enlisted local villagers (as in the Ukraine) to do the killing.

Early in the war, most of the killing was done by shooting the victims. The Germans deemed this to be too slow, and searched for ways to kill mass numbers of Jews in a more efficient and cost-effective way. From 1939 through 1942, especially after the invasion of Western Russia, hundreds of thousands of Jews were murdered by SS soldiers. 34,000 Jews from Kiev were rounded-up in two days (erev Yom Kippur of 1942) and were shot in a ravine called Babi Yar. All 30,000 Jews of the Berditchev ghetto were killed. Throughout Poland and Russia, the Germans established ghettos where Jews could be concentrated and segregated from the general population.

The word "ghetto" was first used (in Italy, 1516) when the Jews of Venice were restricted to living in one neighborhood on land previously used by a cannon foundry, a "ghetto." Later, that word came to designate any neighborhood where minorities concentrated. During World War II, the Germans established over one thousand ghettos in Europe. The most infamous was the Warsaw Ghetto in Poland, which housed at its peak over 460,000 Jews.

Following the initial conquest of Poland, the Germans took a small, poor neighborhood of Warsaw and herded thirty percent of the city's population into it. They built a brick wall around the ghetto and were successful in concentrating the city's Jewish population by the end of November, 1940. Starvation and disease decimated the population.

in January of 1942, the Germans conducted a meeting (known as The Wansee Conference) at which fifteen leaders in specialized areas of dealing with the "Jewish problem" gathered to find a way to enact a "final solution" to killing Jews in the most efficient way possible. Included in the attendees were the head of the Gestapo (secret police) Heinrich Muller, the head of the SS – Heinrich Himmler, and Adolph Eichmann, chief of the Department of Jewish Affairs. Eichmann became known as the architect of the Holocaust, helping to design and implement the large-scale killing centers in Poland and Germany. These included Auschwitz-Birkenau, Belzec, Bergen Belsen, Buchenwald, Dachau, Gross Rosen, Majdanek, Mauthausen, Sobibor, Treblinka, and many others.

By the summer of 1942, 254,000 Jews had been sent from the Warsaw Ghetto to Treblinka, a newly designed concentration camp that used gas chambers for mass killing. On April 19th, 1943 (during Passover), an uprising by the desperate ghetto population (now down to 35,000) began, led by Mordechai Anielewicz. On May 16th, the German army began liquidating what remained of the ghetto.

The primary method of killing, as designed at this conference, was to provide a constant flow of Jews (transported by railroad in cattle cars) to large-scale killing facilities (concentration camps). There, some prisoners were chosen as temporary factory workers and laborers while the majority were taken directly to the gas chambers. The Nazis utilized a blue crystalline chemical formula called Zyklon B (previously used to kill gophers) that turns into poisonous gas when exposed to air. Following the gassing, the bodies were burned in crematoriums or huge pyres.

Over 1.1 million Jews were gassed in Auschwitz-Birkenau, 925,000 in Treblinka, 435,000 in Belzec, 167,000 in Sobibor and the list goes on. The total killed by the earlier shootings and other methods (by the SS in Poland and Western Russia) is estimated at almost 1.5 million.

The number of Jews murdered in the Holocaust is generally estimated at six million but most likely was higher due to poor standards of documentation early in the war.

In 1945, the Russian army advancing from the east liberated numerous camps including Majdanek and Auschwitz-Birkenau. Forces of the United States army advancing from the west liberated many of the camps in Germany including Bergen Belsen and Dachau.

Jews who had survived the Holocaust were placed in displaced person camps (known as "DP" camps) and began searching for surviving friends and relatives. Later, many of them made their way to the United States while others tried to find their way to British Palestine.

HISTORY Part 16 – Independent Israel

Following the Holocaust, Jewish leaders in British Palestine increased pressure on the government in London to allow more Jews to find a safe haven. Jewish resistance against the British immigration blockade began to grow. At the same time, Palestine's Jews had to deal with an increasingly agitated and violent Arab population. During World War II, one of the Arab leaders (the Grand Mufti of Jerusalem) had been hosted and protected by Adolf Hitler in Berlin. After the war, he fled, and continued to call for the murder of the Jews, this time in Palestine.

Jewish underground resistance movements began to grow. The most famous were the Haganah, Irgun, Palmach, Lechi, and the Stern Gang. Some took-up the cause of smuggling European Jews into Palestine (often, the boats they used for smuggling were turned-back by the British navy and sent to Greece, France, Italy, or Germany, like the ship *Exodus*).

Others primarily attacked British military installations to pressure them to leave Palestine.

In 1946, Jewish resistance fighters of the Irgun blew-up the south wing of the King David Hotel (British army headquarters in Jerusalem). This was a landmark event that discouraged the British government (due to the loss of 91 lives) and was one of the keys to their decision to end their mandate in Palestine.

The United Nations recognized the problem of the Jewish survivors in Europe and voted, in 1947, to withdraw the mandate of the British that had given them control of Palestine at the end of World War I. The date for independence from the British was set as May 15th, 1948. The British evacuated Palestine and the Jewish governmental authority headed by David Ben Gurion, called for the establishment of a new country called Israel. Ben Gurion became its first prime minister.

The Arab armies of Egypt, Jordan, Syria, Lebanon, and Iraq attacked Israel immediately, with the intention of throwing the Jews into the Mediterranean Sea.

The armed forces of Israel – the separate groups of the Haganah, Irgun, Palmach, Lechi, and the Stern Gang, were organized into one cohesive fighting force by an American Jewish colonel who had served under general Patton during World War II. David "Mickey" Marcus became the first general (*aluf*) of the Israeli army in thousands of years, but was killed during the attempt to break the Arab blockade of Jerusalem. Marcus combined all of the previous paramilitary organizations into one army called "Tzahal" which is an acronym for Tzva Haganah le-Yisrael ("the Army of Defense of Israel").

The fighting against the Arab armies continued into 1949. The British released over 25,000 Jews who had tried to enter Palestine and had been held in internment camps on the Island of Cyprus. Many of them were conscripted into the new Israeli army immediately upon arrival in Haifa harbor. Jews from around the world came to Israel to assist and swelled its Jewish population to over one million.

Military equipment was purchased from Czechoslovakia and a few other countries as Israel fought for its survival. Over four thousand Jewish soldiers and two thousand civilians died in the fighting. An armistice agreement ending official hostilities was signed in May of 1949.

The War of Independence against the Arab armies had substantially changed the boundaries of the land originally designated for Israel in the United Nations Mandate and the resulting partition plan, with Jerusalem split. Israel was stuck with borders that were difficult to defend. In one area to the east of Tel Aviv and stretching north to Haifa, the country was anywhere from nine to eleven miles wide. This boundary, as designed in the armistice agreement, became known as the Green Line and remained that way until the 6-Day-War of 1967.

The Arabs had been offered a large swath of Palestine in the initial partition plan of the United Nations. That plan had called for the creation of two countries, one for Jews and one for Arabs. That plan was rejected by the leaders of the Arab League and had triggered the War of Independence.

Arab leaders in Jordan and Egypt openly called upon the Arabs living in Palestine in cities such as Acre, Jaffa, Haifa, and Jerusalem, to leave their homes until the Arab armies could massacre the Jews. These citizens were told that they could come home and reclaim their property after an Arab victory. Unfortunately for them, the Arabs were not victorious, which led to many of these Palestinians (those who had lived in the land when it was called "Palestine" under Turkish or British rule) being displaced and unable to return to the new country, "Israel."

There was another war in 1956 prompted by the Egyptian closing of the Suez Canal to Israeli ships. Israel invaded the Sinai Peninsula and conquered most of it in a brilliant armored campaign.

Arab infiltrators conducted constant incursions into Israel over the next ten years. In 1967, the Egyptians, Jordanians, and Syrians amassed their armies on the border of Israel and blockaded the Straits of Tiran to Israeli shipping.

On June 5th, 1967, Israel launched its entire air force in a bold pre-emptive strike to attack Egyptian, Jordanian, and Syrian airfields. It was successful in destroying the enemies' air forces in the first few hours of the war. Over the next six days Israeli forces captured the entire Sinai Peninsula from Egypt, the Golan Heights from Syria, and East-Jerusalem all the way to the Jordan River from Jordan. This became known as The Six-Day-War.

In the aftermath of Israel's Six-Day-War victory there was an awakening of religious fervor and pro-Israel sentiment in the Western World. It began a wave of immigration to Israel (its population reached almost 2,400,000 Jews by 1969), a return to religious observance and Torah study (the Bal Teshuva Movement), as well as Zionist fervor among many secular Jews in the United States.

The Arabs still refused to recognize Israel as a legitimate country and a group calling itself the Palestine Liberation Organization, the PLO, began attacking Israeli citizens, hijacking airplanes, and committing acts of terror in Israel. Egypt continued its harassment of Israel by firing artillery shells on an almost daily basis into southern Israel.

By 1973, the Arabs had re-armed with the assistance of Russia. Under the leadership of Egypt, Arab armies attacked Israel on Yom Kippur day, 1973. This began The Yom Kippur War. Over 70,000 Egyptian soldiers flooded across the Suez Canal into the Sinai Peninsula and the Syrians attacked from the northeast. Jordan, for the most part, stayed out of this fight.

It took over a week for Israeli forces to stage an effective counter-attack and they did so with re-arming from the United States as Phantom and Skyhawk fighter planes and other weaponry were airlifted to Israel as directed by US President Richard Nixon, cooperating with Israeli Prime Minister Golda Meir.

The Israeli army was successful at pushing the Egyptians back across the Suez Canal and Israeli tanks and paratroopers pursued them into North Africa. In Syria, Israeli forces advanced to within a few miles of Damascus. The Russian government intervened and pressured the United Nations to call for a cease-fire. The war lasted 29 days and over 2,500 Israeli soldiers were killed. The Arabs lost almost 20,000 soldiers.

Young Jewish nationalists began to build settlements in the Golan Heights, Gaza Strip, Judea, and Samaria, as a way of populating conquered land and preventing future attacks. They called themselves "Gush Emunim" (Bloc of the Faithful).

Around this time, the Soviet Jewry movement in the United States and Western Europe began working to exert political pressure on the Soviet Union to relax their emigration standards (this began a wave of Russian Jewish immigration that has seen almost 1,300,000 Russians move to Israel). Israel began consolidating its hold on previously conquered land, and in an effort to created more housing and increase internal security, the construction of new suburbs, settlements, and towns exploded.

On June 27th, 1976, a group of PLO and German terrorists hijacked an Air France flight and took it to Entebbe, Uganda. They sought and found the protection of its leader, Idi Amin, and negotiated with the Israelis for the release of 40 PLO terrorists held in jail. The terrorists eventually released about half of the 248 passengers (the non-Jewish ones), and kept the Jews in the airport as hostages. The French air-crew chose to remain with the Jewish hostages. On July 3rd, armed commandos of the Israeli special forces conducted a successful night raid on the Entebbe airport and freed the hostages, flying them back to Israel. This became known as Operation Thunderbolt.

In 1979, President Anwar Sadat of Egypt visited Israel at the invitation of Prime Minister Menachem Begin. A peace treaty was signed that returned the Sinai Peninsula to Egypt.

In 1981, Israel bombed and destroyed the Osirak nuclear reactor near Baghdad, Iraq, following threats from the Iraqi government.

Subsequent years have seen Israel's invasions of Lebanon to stop Iranian-backed militias as in the 1982 Lebanon War. There have been two "intifada" insurrections (Arabic for "shake off" – to shake off Israeli control), with the first from 1987 to 1993 and the second in the early 2000's. There have been constant rocket attacks from the Gaza Strip (which was given back to the Palestinians in 2005, along with its 21 settlements) and terror attacks continue. Israel armed itself with anti-rocket "Patriot" missiles (The Iron Dome) and is engaged in an ongoing war of attrition with Hamas and Hezbollah terrorists.

Israel has built over 350 miles of walls to separate it from Arab towns and Palestinian-controlled area as a way of trying to stop suicide bombers from infiltrating its borders. It has been a successful campaign but has damaged Israel's image around the world.

Today, Israel had gone from being the "underdog" who was like David fighting Goliath, to being viewed as a "Goliath" attacking David. Its strong army and air force as well as its position as an economic and scientific power have raised the ire of many.

Nevertheless, Israel has grown into a nation with a stable economy, energy independence (following the discovery of two natural gas fields, Leviathan and Tamar in the Mediterranean) and the largest single population of Jews – almost 7,000,000 (as well as 1,916,000 Islamic Arabs, 441,000 Christians - both Arab and "western", and Druze).

Israel has grown through an unparalleled influx of immigrants from all corners of the earth. We are beginning to see the fulfillment of what is written in the book of Devarim chapter 30, *pessukim* 1-5. There, G-d promised that there would be a future return to the Land of Israel (which we refer-to as קיבוץ גליות – The Ingathering of Exiles.

The government of Israel has conducted numerous operations assisting large numbers of Jews to "return" and make Aliyah. This movement began in 1949 with Operation Magic Carpet that airlifted 49,000 Yemenite Jews to Israel as well as some from Shanghai and Calcutta. The air operations were conducted by Alaska Airlines, which was the only airline to offer assistance. Many airlines turned-down the request from Israel and the Jewish Agency for charter services and none of them remain today (including Pan American, TWA, and others).

In 1984, during a civil war in East Africa, over 8,000 black Jews from Ethiopia (who were called either Beta Yisrael or Falasha) who traced their heritage back to the union of King Solomon and the Queen of Sheba, were airlifted from the Sudan to Israel in Operation Moses. Operation Yachin brought almost 97,000 Jews from Morocco and North Africa from 1961 to 1964 and Operation Solomon in 1991 evacuated about 49,000 more Ethiopians to Israel.

HISTORY Part 17 – Reflections on Israel

Discussion Point: Is Israel racist? Who is a Palestinian? Who is an Israeli?

Many Jewish students are subjected today to challenges on college campuses by well-funded protestors who call for the abolishment of Israel and call it a "racist" or "apartheid" country. There has also been a strong effort to push for the defunding of Israel through a boycott, divestment, and sanction movement called: "BDS."

It is critical that all Jewish students study the modern history of Israel and the conflict with the Palestinians, and prepare for confrontations with students and professors. Israel cannot logically be defined as racist. It is made-up of people of every religion and every race. Jews are not a race, but a religion. There are Jewish whites, blacks, Indians, Asians, and Africans. I encourage the reader to study the history of apartheid and its enforcement by the South African government and come to your own conclusion as to whether Israel endorses or enforces apartheid policies.

As noted earlier in my overview of history, the first mention of Israel in the Torah was a reference (in the days of Abraham) to the Land of Canaan. Israel's first name was "Canaan." Later, when Joshua led the Jews into the land, the Torah refers to it as "Yisrael," the same name He had given to Jacob (Yaakov) following his struggle with the angel.

The next name was the one given by the Romans when they called the land "Judea." Following the Temple's destruction and subsequent rebellions by the Jews, the Romans renamed the land "Palaestina" using the name of a Jewish enemy (the Philistines) to punish the Jews. This name remained in one form or another throughout the Turkish and British occupations until May of 1948.

My mother was born in 1924 in Jaffa, Palestine, under British rule. I still have her passport and it lists her country of origin as Palestine. She was a "Palestinian." Today, there are still Jewish, Arab, Christian, Druze, and other Palestinians, having been born before May of 1948 in pre-Israel British Palestine. Now, the name of the country has changed. If you are born in Haifa, Tel Aviv, Acre, Jerusalem, Beersheba, etc. you are Israeli, no matter what your religious affiliation or racial identity.

If an Arab currently lives in an Israeli city they are Israeli. If they live in a territory that is under Palestinian administration, they are Palestinian.

To be clear, there is no such thing as a Palestinian nation and there never has been. Never has any single ethnic or religious group in the Middle East existed under the name "Palestinian." That name has been used to identify the government administration under which one was born but is not the name of a specific people or nation. Only the Philistines could make a claim of peoplehood and they are long-gone following the Roman genocide against them almost two thousand years ago!

I encourage the reader to do their own research and to clarify for themselves the claims of peoplehood that others make and to reach your own educated decision.

We, as Jews, are an enigma. What is the secret to our survival? How do you explain our continuity, our perseverance, and our dedication to a singular God? Perhaps it is precisely this mystery that keeps us going.

In 1898, the great American writer, Mark Twain (Samuel Clemens) was visiting Austria. He witnessed the use of Jews as scapegoats by leaders of the Hapsburg Empire and wrote an article titled: "Stirring Times in Austria."

An American reader wrote to Twain and asked if there would ever be a time when a Jew could live honestly, decently, and peaceably like the rest of mankind. In response, in 1899, Twain penned: <u>Concerning the Jews</u> and this is an excerpt from his essay:

"The Egyptian, the Babylonian, and the Persian rose, filled the planet with sound and splendor then faded to dream-stuff and passed away. The Greek and the Roman followed, and made a vast noise, and they are gone. Other peoples have sprung up and held their torch high for a time, but it burned out, and they sit in twilight now, or have vanished.

The Jew saw them all, beat them all, and now is what he always was, exhibiting no decadence, no infirmities of age, no weakening of his parts, no slowing of his energies, no dulling of his alert and aggressive mind.

All things are mortal but the Jew. All other forces pass but he remains.

What is the secret of his immortality?"

For centuries, both our friends and enemies have marveled at our ability to survive times of persecution and times of plenty.

We defy understanding. We should all take pride in our history, our peoplehood, and our resourcefulness.

As George Santayana, the famous Spanish writer and poet said:

"Those who cannot remember the past are condemned to repeat it!"

Over a thousand years ago, Rashi predicted that the time would come when our enemies would claim that the Jewish nation stole the Land of Israel from the indigenous tribes that occupied the land.

Rabbi Morris Besdin at Yeshiva University used to make all of his incoming freshmen students in Chumash class memorize this Rashi in the first week of school. I still know it by heart and suggest that other educators teach this Rashi to their students.

The first Rashi in the Torah beginning with the words אמר רבי יצחק states that the nations of the world will perpetually fight our claim that the land of Israel is ours. They will say: "You conquered (and stole) the land of the seven nations."

Our response is supposed to be: "Yes. G-d is the creator of the land. He originally gave it to them and later, gave it to us!"

This is our best defense against the claims of others who are against the "occupation" of Eretz Yisrael. G-d created the world. As such, He can do with it as He sees fit!

The Torah is the fulfillment of G-d's promise to our Forefathers (which is reiterated every year at the Passover Seder) that Israel will be ours at a time of G-d's choosing. This is our inheritance, it is the will of G-d. Does that sound simplistic? Does it sound too "fundamentalist?" Perhaps, but it's the truth and that's what matters. Rashi warned us in the 1100's and nothing has changed.

We must study our history and commit it to memory. Only then will we have the tools to help us avoid many of the pitfalls of the past.

CHRONOLOGICAL ORDER OF THE KINGS OF ISRAEL

King Saul, Shaul. The first king following the period of the judges. Became king in the Jewish year 2882, 879 BCE.

Ish Boshes, son of Shaul. Following the death of Shaul in battle with the Philistines at Mt. Gilboa, Ish Boshes became king, reigned for two years. At the same time, David was declared king but only reigned over the area of Yehuda in Hevron. Ish Boshes was assassinated by two of his officers, opening the way for David to become king over the entire nation.

King David reigned for 40 years. He moved the capital to Jerusalem and prepared the site for the future First Temple.

King Solomon (son of King David) also reigned for 40 years and built the First Temple in 833 BCE. It stood for 410 years and was destroyed by the Babylonians in 423 BCE (Jewish year 3339). Following his death, the kingdom was divided by competing factions – the tribes of Yehuda and Binyamin comprised the Southern Kingdom of Yehuda and the other ten tribes formed the Northern Kingdom – Yisrael.

THE KINGS OF YEHUDA - the SOUTHERN KINGDOM
(all were descendants of the House of David)

Rechavam, son of Solomon, was the first king of Yehuda after the death of his father. He was king for 17 years, mostly spent fighting with Jeroboam (Yeravam), the first king of Yisrael.

Aviyah, son of Rechavam, reigned for 3 years.

Asa, son of Aviyah, reigned for 41 years.

Yehoshafat, son of Asa, reigned 21 years.

Yehoram, son of Yehoshafat, reigned 8 years.

Achazyahu, son of Yehoram, reigned one year. He was assassinated by Yehu, one of the kings of Yisrael.

Athalya, the daughter of king Achav of Yisrael was the mother of Achazyahu. She took over as "king" and reigned for 6 years. She was killed by order of Yehoyadah the priest, so that her grandson, Yehoash, the son of Achazyahu, could become king.

Yehoash reigned for 40 years.

Uzziah (or Uziyahu), the son of Yehoash reigned for 52 years.

Yotham, son of Uzziah, reigned for 16 years.

Achaz, son of Yotam, reigned for 16 years.

At this point there is a disagreement as to whether Hoshea or Chizkiyahu, son of Achaz, became king. Nevertheless, in the Jewish year 3199, Chizkiyahu (Hezekiah) began his reign.

Chizkiyahu, son of Achaz, reigned 29 years. During his reign the northern 10 tribes of Yisrael were exiled to Assyria by Shalmanessar (in 3205). The southern kingdom of Yehuda was besieged by Sannecheriv from Assyria eight years later, but king Chizkiyahu was prepared. He had re-directed the water source for Jerusalem and the city survived (in the book of Melachim II, the miraculous defeat and retreat of Sannecheriv is documented).

Menasheh, son of Chizkiyahu, became king and reigned for 55 years. He was evil, allowed idol worship, and erected a statue in the Temple.

Amon, son of Menasheh, reigned for 2 years but was killed by rebellious servants.

Yoshiyahu, son of Amon, took over as king at the age of eight. He reigned for 31 years. He renovated the Temple and found a hidden Torah that was ascribed to Moshe. The Torah was opened to the section describing the fate of Israel and Yoshiyahu consulted with the prophetess Chulda to see what this meant. He buried the Ark in an underground chamber that had been prepared by King Solomon and prepared for the eventual fall of Jerusalem. He was killed in battle by the king of Egypt who was traveling through Israel on his way to do battle with Assyria.

Yehoachaz, son of Yoshiyahu, reigned for only 3 months. He was replaced with his brother, Eliakim (also, a son of Yoshiyahu) whose name was changed to Yehoyakim.

Yehoyakim, son of Yoshiyahu, reigned 11 years. He was captured by the Babylonians and exiled. He died on the way to Babylon.

Yehoyachin, son of Yehoyakim, reigned for three months. He was exiled to Babylonia. He was succeeded by his uncle, Mataniah, whose name was changed to Zedekiah – Tzidkiyahu.

Tzidkiyahu (Zedekiah) son of Yoshiyahu, ruled for 11 years. Eventually, at the end of the Jewish year 3338, he was captured by the Babylonians, blinded and taken in chains to Bavel. Nebuzardan, a general of the king of Babylonia (Nebuchadnezzar), burned the Temple and exiled the Jews, leaving Jerusalem desolate. In 3410 the prophet Zecharyah declared there was no longer a need to mourn the Temple and that the rebuilding should begin. The Temple was rebuilt and completed in 3412, with the encouragement of Darius II, the son of Queen Esther.

2nd Temple Period:

Initially, both Ezra and Nechemiah led the people, followed by Shimon HaTzadik, but they did not adopt the official title of "King."

Following the revolt by the Maccabees against the Greeks, the family of the Hashmonaim became rulers over Israel from 139 BCE to 36 BCE and established a dynasty. They were followed by King Herod and his descendants.

Here is the order of their rule:

Yehuda (Ha'Maccabee – son of Matisyahu)

Yonasan (son of Mattisyahu)

Shimon (son of Mattisyahu)

Yochanan Hyrkanus (son of Shimon)

Yehuda Aristoblus (son of Yochanan)

Alexander Yannai (son of Yochanan)

Queen Shalomis (Salome – wife of Alexander Yannai)

Aristoblus II (son of Alexander Yannai)

Hyrkanus II (son of Aristoblus II)

The Romans were invited into Israel to help quell an internal civil insurrection, which resulted in their taking control of the country. From this point forward, all rulers were selected and approved by the Roman leadership.

Herod became ruler in 36 BCE (and killed-off the remainder of the Hashmonaim, ending their dynasty. He rebuilt the Temple, completing his renovations in 11 BCE, and built magnificent palaces at Masada, Herodian, etc.)

Archelaus, son of Herod, ruled in year 1 of the common era, but was deposed by the Roman leadership who selected Agrippa to rule.

Agrippa I, grandson of Herod, ruled 23 years.

Agrippa II, son of Agrippa I, ruled. He was the final Jewish ruler of the land and continued in office until Vespasian came to Judea in the year 66 of the common era.

THE KINGS OF YISRAEL – THE NORTHERN KINGDOM

Yeravam ben Nevat was the first ruler of Yisrael, the Northern Kingdom of 10 tribes and ruled for 22 years.

Nadav, son of Yeravam, ruled for 2 years. He was killed by Ba'asha who rebelled and became the new king.

Ba'asha, from the tribe of Yissachar, reigned for 24 years.

Elah, son of Ba'asha, ruled for 2 years. He was killed by Zimri, one of his military captains, who became king.

Zimri ruled for only one week. He was killed by Omri, a general in the army of Elah. Omri became king.

Omri ruled for 12 years.

Ach'av, son of Omri, ruled for 22 years. He, and his wicked wife Jezebel (Izevel) expanded the northern kingdom's rejection of the Torah, and killed-off almost all of the prophets, but did not succeed in killing Eliyahu (Elijah).

Achazyahu, son of Ach'av ruled 2 years.

Yehoram, son of Ach'av, ruled for 12 years.

Yehu, from the tribe of Mesasheh, ruled for 28 years.

Yeho'achaz, son of Yehu, ruled for 17 years.

Yeho'ash, son of Yeho'achaz, ruled for 16 years.

Yeravam II, son of Yeho'ash, ruled for 41 years.

Zecharyahu, son of Yeravam II, reigned for 6 months and was assassinated by Shalom ben Yavesh, who became the next ruler.

Shalom ben Yavesh ruled for one month and was assassinated by Menachem ben Gadi who took over as king.

Menachem ben Gadi ruled for 10 years.

Pekachya ben Menachem, ruled 2 years. He was killed by an assistant, Pekach ben Remaliah, who became king.

Pekach ben Remaliah ruled for 22 years. During this period the king of Assyria attacked Yisrael and exiled the two tribes of Naphtali and Zevulun. He was assassinated by Hoshea ben Elah who became the last ruler of Yisrael, the Northern Kingdom.

Hoshea ben Elah, from the tribe of Reuven, ruled for 19 years. During his reign, the king of Assyria exiled the remainder of the ten tribes, completing his war against Yisrael in the Jewish year 3205, 556 BCE.

This marked the end of the Northern Kingdom and the rulers of the territory known as Yisrael.

THE PROPHETS OF THE JEWISH PEOPLE

The Talmud in Megillah (14a) says that there were 48 prophets. Rashi lists 46 and says that he does not know who the other two prophets were. In addition, there were 7 female prophetesses. Our sages say that prophecy was not limited to only these men and women, but the listing below covers those whose prophecies are written in Neviim and Kesuvim.

Here is a listing of all of the known 53 (of 55), including men and women, in chronological order:

1. Avraham
2. Sarah
3. Yitzchak
4. Yaakov
5. Aharon
6. Miriam
7. Moshe
8. Yehoshua (conquest of Israel)
9. Pinchas (period of judges and early prophets begins)
10. Devorah
11. Elkana
12. Chanah
13. Eli Ha'Kohen
14. Shmuel (period of the kings begins)
15. Avigail
16. Gad
17. Nathan
18. David
19. Shlomo (building of the 1st Temple)

20. Shemaya
21. Ido
22. Michayahu
23. Ovadia
24. Achiyah Ha'Shiloni
25. Yehuda ben Chonani
26. Azariya ben Oded
27. Chaziel Ha'Levi
28. Eliezer ben Dodo
29. Hoshea
30. Amos
31. Micha
32. Amotz
33. Eliyahu (Elijah)
34. Elisha
35. Yona ben Amitai (Jonah)
36. Yishayahu (Isaiah)
37. Yoel
38. Nachum
39. Habakuk
40. Tzefania
41. Chulda
42. Uriah
43. ==Yirmiyahu (Jeremiah) (destruction of the 1st Temple)==
44. Yechezkel (Ezekiel)
45. Baruch ben Neria
46. Neria
47. Saria
48. Machsiyahu
49. Chaggai

50. Zechariah (Zachariah)
51. Mordechai "Bilshan" ben Yair
52. Esther
53. Malachi

THE EBB AND FLOW OF NACH – AN OUTLINE

It is easy to lose track of time. In school we learn a few chapters of the Torah and try to build proficiency in reading and translating so we can hone our skills and begin to learn on our own. Unfortunately, the majority of students do not make it very far into Tanach before giving up.

The purpose of this chapter is to travel through Tanach, highlighting its major events and themes. I will effort to give some perspective as well on where these events fall on the timeline of our history.

The five books of the Torah span Jewish history through the death of Moshe in the Jewish year 2488 which equates to 1273 BCE.

The Book of Joshua – Yehoshua:

The first book of Nach was authored by Joshua himself and the books of Neviim begin with Joshua assuming command of the Jewish People and making preparations to cross the Jordan River.

We are told of the mission of the spies in Jericho, the crossing of the Jordan, establishment of a camp in Gilgal, and the destruction of the city of Jericho.

This is followed by a description of numerous campaigns to conquer the land and the defeat of 31 kings. Next, the land is divided among the tribes and each is apportioned their land. Cities of refuge are established and assigned to the Leviim. Reuven, Gad, and part of Menashe, return to the east side of the Jordan to settle the land they had asked Moshe for.

The end of the book of Joshua has his farewell address and warnings to the Jewish nation. It also describes the burial of Joshua, Joseph, and Elazar (son of Aharon), as well as the sarcophagus of Yosef.

The Book of Shoftim – Judges:

Shoftim begins with continued conquest of the Land of Israel. It was authored by the prophet, Samuel. The first judge, Osniel ben Kenaz from the tribe of Yehuda, ruled for 42 years. He was followed by Ehud ben Gera.

We are told of Devorah, prophetess and judge, the oppression of Jabin, (a king of Canaan), and the defeat of Canaan and its general Sisera.

The Song of Devorah is the fifth chapter. It is followed by stories of oppression, war against Midian, internal strife, rebellions, and ongoing trouble with the Philistines. The Jews never fully completed the conquest of the land and did not fully exile its indigenous population. Therefore, conflict continued.

The stories of Shimshon (Samson) and his battles against the Philistines, are in the 13th through 16th chapters.

The 19th chapter is the famous story of the *pilegesh* (concubine) of Giveah. The Book of Shoftim ends with internal civil war against the tribe of Binyamin and eventual reconciliation.

One recurring theme is that the periods of peace and relative tranquility in Israel lasted for forty years each. They were usually followed by a return to sin and war with our enemies.

The period of the judges was a time of instability, lack of centralized leadership, and ongoing battles due to alien nations being allowed to remain in Israel. The land was ruled by the judges and early prophets, but there was public desire for the rule of a king.

The Books of Samuel (Shmuel) I and II:

This book opens with the leadership of Eli the High Priest, the prayer of Chana for a child, and the birth of Shmuel.

Shmuel grew to be a prophet during a period when the country was conducting continuous wars with the Philistines. In a shocking defeat, the army of Israel was routed and the golden Ark of the Tabernacle was captured.

The Ark was eventually sent back to the Tabernacle following a plague against the Philistines, yet not long after that, a new war with the Philistines broke out.

Shmuel became a judge over Israel, the people asked for a king, and the stories of Shaul (Saul) and his anointing by Shmuel are described. Under King Shaul there were wars against the Philistines and Amalek. Following the defeat of Amalek, Shaul allowed their king, Agag, to live. Shmuel was enraged and executed Agag himself.

Shmuel searched for a new king, and, through prophecy, was led to David, the youngest son of Yishai. This is followed by the story of David and Goliath on the battlefield during a stand-off between the Philistines and the army of King Shaul. David defeated Goliath and the Jewish army routed the Philistines.

David was accepted into the court of the king and became the friend of one of Shaul's sons, Jonathan (Yonasan). David was popular among the people. Shaul became jealous and tried to kill David, who fled. The first book of Shmuel ends with King Shaul dying on the battlefield along with three of his four sons in another battle with the Philistines at Mt. Gilboa.

The second book of Shmuel opens with David being informed of the death of king Shaul, his mourning, and his being anointed as king. Shaul's remaining son, Ish Boshes, was anointed by Avner ben Ner, resulting in a power-struggle and a period of conflict between the forces of David and those of Ish Boshes. David's personal guard, Yoav, killed Avner. Two captains in the army assassinated Ish Boshes.

David became the king over all of Israel, captured Jerusalem from the indigenous Yevushim (Jebusites). He arranged for the holy Ark to be brought to Jerusalem. During this move, the wagon carrying the Ark began to tip over and Uzzah, while trying to steady the wagon, touched the Ark and died.

David's numerous wars are described. During one of these, David sent Uriah to the front lines of battle (certain death) and took Bathsheba, his wife (numerous commentaries say that King David saw, through prophecy, that he was destined to marry her and establish a dynasty). David married her, but was rebuked by the prophet Nathan. Bathsheba eventually gave birth to Solomon.

A large portion of this book is dedicated to the conflict between David and his son, Avshalom. Multiple conflicts arose, David embarked on more campaigns in battle, and put-down a rebellion between tribes led by Sheba ben Bichri.

The book ends with David's census of the nation and his subsequent punishment for having conducted an unwarranted counting of the people. His speech to the prophet Gad following the resulting plague (and the death of 70,000 men) is the basis of our daily prayer of *tachanun*. David purchased the site of the eventual Temple from Aravnah the Jebusite and the plague ended.

The Book of Melachim (Kings) I and II:

The Gemara in Bava Basra 14b says that the prophet Jeremiah wrote the Book of Kings. It begins with the reign of King Solomon and his construction of the First Temple and ends with the destruction of the Temple and the exile of the tribes of Yehuda to Babylon. Melachim covers a time period of 421 years.

The construction of Solomon's Temple, its inauguration, the later years of the king and the split in his kingdom (into Yehuda and Yisrael) make up the first 12 chapters of Book 1. Following this, the rule of multiple kings is described. Special attention should be paid to the stories of the prophet Elijah (Eliyahu Ha'navi), especially the challenge of Eliyahu to the prophets of Baal on Mount Carmel and his troubles with King Ach'av (Ahab). In the beginning of Book 2, Eliyahu ascended to heaven after blessing his protégé, Elisha, who became the moral leader and chief prophet of Israel.

The balance of the Book of Kings covers the chain of kingship in Israel, internal battles between the north and the south, the Assyrian conquest of the north, and the defense of the south by King Chizkiyahu (Hezekiah). The persistence of idolatry led to the eventual destruction of the Temple by the Babylonians.

Melachim ends with the looting of the Temple, the exile of much of the Jewish populace, and the fleeing of many Jews to Egypt to escape Nebuchadnezzar.

Thematically, the Book of Kings is filled with many highs and lows. Kings would sin, a prophet (e.g., Eliyahu, Elisha, Isaiah, Chuldah) would warn of impending doom, the king would repent, and the people would be saved. Occasionally a righteous king arose, but his son did not follow in his path. At least in the Southern Kingdom, the kingship remained limited to those who descended from the House of David, maintaining a dynasty.

The pervasiveness of this cycle, the attraction of idol worship, immorality, and sin, are difficult to understand in light of the fact that the Temple in Jerusalem was standing the entire time and the Temple service and its miracles were ongoing. It is a mystery for the ages how Jewish kings and queens could commit such acts of evil, often murdering their own families.

The Books of Isaiah (Yeshayah), Jeremiah (Yirmiyah), and Yechezkel (Ezekiel):

The first of these books is credited to multiple authors. Isaiah the prophet wrote the first 39 chapters and the remainder was completed during the Babylonian exile. It overlaps the Book of Kings and is considered, by many, to be a branch of that book.

Thematically, the book of Isaiah and the books of Jeremiah and Ezekiel (Yirmiyah and Yechezkel) are filled with prophecies and warnings of impending doom for Israel as well as hope for the future. Nevertheless, these same prophecies hold eternal messages for our people and are relevant to this day. The multiple prophecies of the eventual return to Jerusalem after the Babylonian exile and the rebuilding of the Second Temple, contain hidden messages about the days of the Mashiach, the World-To-Come, and the End-of-Days. It is as if the prophets were speaking to multiple generations at the same time with the same words.

All three of these prophets (Isaiah, Jeremiah, Ezekiel) overlapped the time of the Kings of Israel and in the case of Ezekiel (Yechezkel) extended into the period of the Babylonian exile, where his prophecies were recorded by the Men of the Great Assembly (*Anshei K'nesses Ha'gedolah*).

The visions of the prophets and their warnings to the Jewish People are vivid and fill the reader with fear. Nevertheless, they give hope for the future. That is why the book of Yechezkel concludes with a lengthy description of the future Temple and the eventual boundaries of Israel and its tribal lands.

One of the common themes that runs through these prophecies is the fact that our enemies, despite being allowed to conquer and exile us, will have to pay the price for what they have done. The fact that they gloated over our destruction and took joy in our sorrow will lead to their downfall. We are also told that the day will come when the remaining nations in the world will realize that we are right, that G-d is the only One, and will recognize Judaism as the one true religion.

The Book of T'rei Asar (the Twelve Prophets):

Following the return from exile in Babylon, the Men of the Great Assembly wrote-down the prophecies of these twelve men. There is an opinion that Chaggai, Zechariah, and Malachi wrote-down their words because they saw that the time of prophecy was coming to an end.

The twelve prophets of this book are Hoshea, Yoel, Amos, Ovadiah, Yonah, Micha, Nachum, Chabakuk, Tzefaniah, Chaggai, Zechariah, and Malachi.

The most famous of these writings are the story of Yonah (Jonah) that we read on the afternoon of Yom Kippur (during Mincha) and the prophecies of Zechariah. He prophesied during the period of Darius II, the son of Esther, who had given permission for the Jews to rebuild the Temple.

These prophesies are filled with visions and riddles and are very difficult to comprehend. Zechariah's final prophecy is of the eventual war between Gog and Magog and our return to the Land of Israel.

Psalms – Tehillim:

King David is commonly given credit for authoring the Book of Psalms. The Gemara in Bava Basra says that he wrote it using the collected wisdom and inspiration of ten elders including Adam, Avraham, Moshe, the three sons of Korach, and others.

This book of 150 chapters figures prominently in our daily, Shabbos, and holiday liturgy. The *pesukei d'zimrah* mostly come from Tehillim. The Hallel prayer recited on *rosh chodesh* and holidays comes from chapters 113 through 118.

It is customary, when someone is sick or in danger, to read sections of Tehillim out-loud, often as a communal recitation. Many chapters are read in private for personal needs including recovery of the sick, assistance in times of danger, or to give thanks for good fortune.

Chapter 119 of Tehillim is the longest of any chapter in Nach with 176 verses. As an aside, the longest *parsha* in the Torah (Nasso) has 176 *pessukim*, and the longest book of the Talmud is Bava Basra with 176 folios.

Mishlei – Proverbs:

This book is commonly attributed to King Solomon. The Gemara in Bava Basra credits its writing to King Chizkiyahu (Hezekiah) but still considers its proverbs to be those of Solomon.

It is composed of 31 chapters of wise sayings, aphorisms, and lessons. Its final chapter is the song of *Ayshes Chayil* which is recited at the Friday night Shabbos table.

Iyov – Job:

Job is the subject of much controversy. There are multiple opinions about which time period he lived in. There is even an opinion that he was not Jewish. The Gemara in Bava Basra ascribes the writing of the Book of Job to Moshe, although Job has alternatively been placed as a returnee from Babylon, one who lived in the time of the judges, and as having lived in the time of our Forefathers. There is also a view that he never lived and that his story is a parable.

There is a popular midrash that tells of Iyov, one of Pharaoh's advisors in the days of Moshe. When asked to comment on Pharaoh's plan to kill the Jewish babies by throwing them in the river, his co-advisor Yisro spoke openly against the plan. Another advisor, Bilaam, told Pharaoh to kill the babies. Iyov remained silent. For this, says the Midrash, he made himself susceptible to the punishments wrought against him by Satan in the Book of Job. Sometimes, remaining silent in the face of evil is more dangerous than evil itself.

The book opens with Iyov, a wealthy and blessed man, living an ideal life with his wife and 10 children in the land of Uz (could this have been the origin of the L. Frank Baum's Land of Oz in <u>The Wizard of Oz</u>?)

Satan makes a claim that Iyov, a man of G-d, would not be as righteous if he did not have as many blessings in his life. G-d gives permission for Satan to challenge Iyov, so long as he does not kill him.

Iyov loses his children and his wealth, and suffers terribly from physical ailments brought upon him by Satan. Iyov sits on a pile of ashes and laments his fate while his wife berates him, advising him that if he can't take G-d's judgement he should turn against G-d and end his suffering by dying.

Job's three friends (Eliphaz, Bildad, and Zophar) come to him, and the majority of the book is made-up of the conversations, challenges, and advice of these three and Iyov's responses. Finally, a young man named Elihu comes to Iyov in chapters 32-38 and angrily questions and challenges the advice of Iyov's friends. In the end, Iyov repents for having doubted G-d, and G-d blesses him with 17 children, tremendous wealth, and an additional 140 years of life.

This book speaks to our doubts in life. It shows the devotion of a man who has lost everything and his unwillingness to turn against G-d. Suicide is never an acceptable option and the advice of friends is often blasphemous and dangerous. Nevertheless, the advice of a young, faithful, and clear-thinking person can shake us back to reality.

Chapters 38 through 41 describe the appearance of G-d to Iyov and His message to him. G-d challenges Iyov to stand up, be a man, and to face the fact that it is G-d who controls the world. Iyov responds in chapter 42 with his understanding that the wonders of the world are concealed from him. His humility and his devotion lead G-d to shower him with blessings.

The Five Megillos -

1. Shir Hashirim – Song of Songs:

Composed by King Solomon, this song portrays the love between G-d and his people, Israel. It is written as an allegorical work describing the love between a man and a woman.

It is composed of 8 chapters. It opens with Israel, as represented by a woman, looking back at history and the experience of being metaphorically "kissed" (by G-d, having revealed the Torah). Her longing for kisses represents the longing of the Jewish People to be drawn-near to G-d.

Each chapter is tied to a different event in Jewish history – the exodus, splitting of the sea, wandering in the wilderness, dedication of the Tabernacle, and Israel during the first Temple, are each described in cryptic and poetic form. In Ashkenazic tradition, we recite Shir Hashirim on the Shabbos of Chol Ha'moed Pesach and some Sephardic communities read it every Shabbos afternoon between Pesach and Shavuos.

Shir Hashirim is often described as a love song and a conversation between the soul of man, the *neshamah*, and G-d, "her" lover.

2. Ruth:

The Book of Ruth is attributed to the prophet Shmuel (Ruth's story took place during the time of the judges).

It opens with Elimelech (a leader of the people), his wife Naomi, and their two sons, leaving Israel during a time of famine. Elimelech did not wish to share his wealth with others, so he fled to Moav.

Elimelech died, and Naomi's sons married Moabite women (Orpah and Ruth). Both sons died and Naomi decided to return to Israel. She tried to encourage her daughters-in-law to return to the houses of their parents, but Ruth would not be discouraged and remained with Naomi ("...for wherever you go I will go, wherever you live I will live, your people shall be my people, and your G-d will be my G-d. Where you die, I will die, and there I will be buried..." – Ruth 1:16-17).

The story continues with the return of Naomi to Israel and the reaping by Ruth in the fields of Boaz, a relative of Naomi's dead husband. In the end, Boaz and Ruth were married and had a son, Oved. Oved was the father of Yishai (Jesse) and from him came David (King David).

Ruth is Tanach's prime example of a righteous convert and her dedication to Naomi is considered by many sages to be the source of her blessing as the "mother" of the Davidic Dynasty from which the Mashiach will come.

It is important to note that both Boaz and Ruth came from non-standard ancestral lineage. Boaz was a descendant of Yehuda and Tamar (a story of a father-in-law and daughter-in-law's relationship) and Ruth came from Moav (dating back to the incestuous relationship between Lot and his daughter following the destruction of S'dom). In addition to this, Ruth was a widow and a convert. Maybe this can teach us something about the flaws inherent in putting too much attention on *yichus* (prominent lineage). The ancestral families of Ruth and Boaz are the progenitors of the Mashiach – you can't get any better than that!

We read this megillah on the holiday of Shavous, which is the time of year during which the grain harvest in the story took place.

3. Eicha – Lamentations:

This book is ascribed to the prophet Jeremiah (Yirmiyahu). He personally experienced the destruction of Jerusalem and the First Temple and the fulfillment of his prophecies. We read this megillah's five chapters on the fast-day of Tisha B'Av.

It is written in a style that exudes sorrow in short utterances that sound grievous. It is a lament (thus the title: "Lamentations") for the land of Judea and the city of Jerusalem and its Temple, destroyed by the Babylonians. It vividly describes the suffering and starvation of those who were besieged in Jerusalem.

This grief-stricken and heart-wrenching poetry is at the heart of our observance of Tisha B'av which is a day of remembrance for so many Jewish tragedies.

4. Koheles – Ecclesiastes:

The twelve chapters of this book authored by King Solomon, form the longest megillah. Ecclesiastes is from the Greek word for "preacher," which is a literal translation of the Hebrew word *"koheles."*

The author refers to himself as *Koheles Ben David*, a name that King Solomon took-on during a time of exile and punishment after having violated three laws. He had too many wives, too many horses, and collected too much money for his treasury. For that, he was banished from his kingship for a period that some say was three years.

This book describes the transitory nature of all physical beings and the vanities of our world. Koheles concludes that worldly pleasures disappear quickly and we should recognize the impermanence of our circumstances. These are the words of a the wisest of all men who came to the realization that the true nature of man does not change. It is pointless to pursue too much wealth in the face of a limited life span and the fact that we cannot take anything to the grave except for our good deeds.

This megillah concludes with two *pessukim* (12:13-14) that project the wisdom and final conclusions of King Solomon, who had immeasurable wealth: *"The end of the matter, after hearing all, is to fear G-d and keep His commandments, for this is the whole man. For G-d shall bring every work into His judgement concerning every hidden thing, whether it is good or evil."*

5. Esther:

This is the megillah with which most of us are familiar. We read it twice on the holiday of Purim. It is the last megillah and is attributed to Mordechai, although the Talmud ascribes its transcription to the *Anshei K'nesses Ha'gedolah* (of which Mordechai was a member).

This familiar story took place in the period between the two Temples and tells of the irrational hatred of our enemy (Amalek) and the efforts of Haman (a descendant of Agag, king of Amalek) to physically kill-off the Jews of Persia-Media. Esther, and her husband King Achashverosh, had a son (Darius II) who gave permission for the Jews to return to Israel and rebuild the Temple.

This megillah also carries a critical message of destiny and fate. When Esther was reluctant to go to the king (due to the fact that an uninvited visit could result in death), Mordechai said to her: *"Do not think that you can escape the king's house more than all the Jews. For if you hold your peace at this time, then relief and deliverance will come from another place, but you and your father's house will perish – and who knows whether you came to this royal estate for such a time as this?"*

Daniel:

The Book of Daniel was written by the *Anshei Knessess Ha'gedolah* (and is attributed to some of its members; Chaggai, Zechariah, Malachi, and Mordechai, among others).

Its first seven chapters are written in Aramaic (the prevalent language spoken by the Jews of Babylon), and the final five in Hebrew. It tells of the period of exile of the Jews under King Nebuchadnezzar. The story of three young men, Chananyah, Mishael, and Azariah being thrown into the fiery furnace and emerging unscathed is in this book as well as the story of the "writing on the wall." Belshazzar, the successor to King Nebuchadnezzar, held a banquet and used vessels taken from the Temple in Jerusalem. Suddenly, four words appeared on a wall of the banquet hall – *Mene Mene Tekel Ufarsin*. Nobody but Daniel could read the words which were written in ancient Hebrew script.

Daniel interpreted the message of the words as: *Your kingdom has been counted by G-d and it has come to an end. You have been weighed and found wanting. Your kingdom will be broken up* (and given to Persia). Belshazzar, despite the bad news, rewarded Daniel for his wisdom.

Later, accusations were brought against Daniel that he worshipped another god than the king of Babylon, he was thrown into a lion's den (*perek* 6). The next day, Daniel was alive, unscathed. The king threw Daniel's accusers into the den and they were devoured. Daniel prospered from that time forward.

The remainder of the book is filled with multiple visions and dreams and Daniel's prayers for redemption.

Ezra and Nechemia:

The books of both Ezra and Nechemia (Nehemiah) were originally one book and the Talmud credits their writing primarily to Ezra (who became known as *Ezra Ha'sofer* – Ezra the Scribe) with Nechemia having finished the books. Ezra is also credited with establishing a cycle of weekly Torah reading and formalizing much of our prayer service.

Cyrus of Persia conquered Babylonia and gave the Jews permission to return to the Holy Land. A group of *Kohanim, Leviim,* and around 40,000 others returned with Ezra and Zerubavel and began rebuilding the Temple in Jerusalem.

The 8th through 10th chapters document the leaders, families and clans that returned to Israel, along with a description of their journey.

Unfortunately, the Samaritans (a rebellious foreign sect that considered themselves Jewish but were rejected by main-line authorities) accused Ezra and the returnees of sedition against Persia and the work on the

Temple was halted until Darius II granted the right of the Jews to rebuild the Temple. It was completed around 20 years later.

The book of Nechemia, in 13 chapters, details his life from the time when the king of Persia permitted the Jews to return to Israel. He relates his story in the first-person, describes the difficult life in Jerusalem, and gives a personal account of the rebuilding of the walls of the city. He also documents the appointments of the *Kohanim*, *Leviim*, and Temple administrators. He established a system for guarding the city of Jerusalem and worked to re-establish the Temple service.

Nechemia is credited with abolishing the charging of interest, and worked to assure that the rich land owners returned property to the original owners. Together with Ezra, he worked to rebuild Torah life in the Holy Land. At the end of 12 years of service he returned to the Persian royal court but eventually returned to Israel to help establish new reforms.

Chronicles I and II (Sefer Divrei Ha'yamim):

The Gemara in Bava Basra credits Ezra with having arranged for the writing of this genealogy of Jewish history. It begins with the first man, Adam. Part 1 concludes with the coronation of King Solomon.

The second part of Chronicles documents Jewish history from King Solomon to the proclamation of King Cyrus allowing Jews to return to Israel.

In Chronicles, many Jewish leaders are listed under alternate names and there are multiple inconsistencies when compared to accounts elsewhere in Tanach. This book is written in a style that is designed for the delivery of a great deal of information for public consumption. It is not meant to be understood as linear or comprehensive. It is homiletical.

The books of Tanach document the history of our nation from creation to the return to the Holy Land and the rebuilding of the Temple following the Babylonian exile. There are no additional books in the official canon of Jewish writings.

We know some of the history of the 2nd Temple period from the Talmud, the Book of the Maccabees, from Midrashim, and from the writings of the Roman historian Josephus, but we have no sacred writings documenting the period following the rebuilding of the Temple.

Very few students of Torah take the time to study the books of Tanach. Unfortunately, today's Jewish educational culture has relegated the study of *Neviim* and *Kesuvim* to girls in seminaries and not to yeshiva students.

I once heard a teacher say that a Yeshiva that does not teach Nach is a "non-prophet" institution.

Take the time to study these sacred and revered works which have survived the test of time. The last of them (Chronicles) was written over 2500 years ago. The relevance of the themes in Tanach has not changed and the lessons taught to us by our ancestors (whether it be their persistence and devotion or their errors and stubborn behavior) still hold true.

As King Solomon wrote in Koheles: "There is nothing new under the sun!"

TRANSMISSION FROM GENERATION TO GENERATION
Torah, Halacha, Edicts, and Customs

A secret to Jewish survival has been our dedication to carrying-forward our traditions for thousands of years. Many of the laws and customs we follow are not specifically indicated in the Written Torah as given to Moshe. The Oral Law as transmitted by Moshe (as taught to him on Mt. Sinai) contains that which is not written in a Torah scroll. Jewish law is divided into three categories; Torah law (d'Oraisa), Rabbinic law (d'Rabbanan), and customs/traditions (Minhag).

Additionally, there is an oral tradition (much of which is documented in the Talmud) of laws and customs that go all the way back to the first man, Adam. As an example, The Talmud in Sanhedrin (56a) lists the seven laws given to the family of Noach (Noah). Our tradition additionally states that the first six of these laws were commanded to Adam. Ten generations later, the entire group of seven laws was transmitted to Noach and his sons.

These seven laws have become known as the שבע מצות בני נח – The Seven Laws of the Children of Noach.

Do not worship idols	(עבודה זרה)
Do not use G-d's name in vain – cursing G-d	(ברכת השם)
Do not murder	(שפיכת דמים)
Prohibition of forbidden relations	(גלוי עריות)
Do not steal	(גזלה)
Establish laws and a system of justice	(דינים)
Do not consume the limb of a living animal	(אבר מן החי)

The first law in the Torah was commanded to Adam and Eve; "Be fruitful and multiply." The first given to a Jew was the law of circumcision as commanded to Avraham. Later, just before the Exodus from Egypt, the Jewish People were collectively commanded to sanctify the new moon (establishing a perpetual calendar) and to keep Pesach (Passover). The Torah, as given to Moshe and subsequently written-down, is divided into five books and 54 weekly portions; *parshios*.

בראשית	שמות	ויקרא	במדבר	דברים
בראשית	שמות	ויקרא	במדבר	דברים
נח	וארא	צו	נשא	ואתחנן
לך לך	בא	שמיני	בהעלותך	עקב
וירא	בשלח	תזריע	שלח	ראה
חיי שרה	יתרו	מצורע	קרח	שופטים
תולדות	משפטים	אחרי מות	חקת	כי תצא
ויצא	תרומה	קדושים	בלק	כי תבוא
וישלח	תצוה	אמור	פינחס	נצבים
וישב	כי תשא	בהר	מטות	וילך
מקץ	ויקהל	בחקתי	מסעי	האזינו
ויגש	פקודי			וזאת הברכה
ויחי				

During the 40 years that the Jews wandered the Sinai Desert, the laws were transmitted to the Jewish nation by Moshe. The first were at Marah just after leaving Egypt and the Ten Statements (Ten Commandments) – עשרת הדברות were given at Mt. Sinai.

The Torah, as transcribed by Moshe (from G-d's "mouth" to Moshe's pen) contains 613 mitzvos, of which 248 involve positive actions and 365 are negative or prohibitive. All 613 are catalogued later in this book. The mitzvos are also divided into two further categories, the *chukim* and the *mishpatim* – those with no stated reason and those with a stated reason. For instance, we are commanded to keep Shabbos since G-d rested on the 7th day – that is one of the *mishpatim* since we are told the reason for the law. The laws of keeping kosher have no stated reason and are *chukim*.

Following Moshe's final descent from Mt. Sinai on Yom Kippur, he taught the nation the laws relevant to the construction of the Mishkan (the Tabernacle) and its related sacrifices. Later, he clarified the laws of Shabbos and its accompanying 39 categories of prohibited work, the laws of keeping kosher, observance of the holidays, civil law, etc.

The 39 categories of work prohibited on Shabbos (which are the 39 types of work used in constructing the Tabernacle and its furnishings), which are referred-to in the Talmud as *avos melachos*, are general "fathers" of categories that also include other prohibited actions on Shabbos that are not related to the Tabernacle. For instance, the general category of sorting which is called *"boreir,"* would, by extension, include a prohibition against taking a fruit and separating the seeds from its flesh.

These 39 *melachos* include sub-categories called *toldos*. Over the centuries, our sages identified many new things that they prohibited on Shabbos since they were deemed to be directly related to the original 39 prohibitions. Inventions such as electricity, telephones, televisions, computers and automobiles have led to new applications of law related to the original 39.

When Moshe was commanded at Mount Sinai to build a fence around mountain (Mt. Sinai), it was to prevent people from ascending too far and dying because they walked on holy ground.

Later, "fences" were built around Torah law. Our Rabbis have established the moving of such items as a pen or a computer on Shabbos as *muktzah* (separated or set-aside).

Why?

Because they established a fence (more commonly referred-to in rabbinic writings as a *s'yag* or a *geder*) around the law to prevent sin. For instance, we are so accustomed to writing that the very action of picking up a pencil may lead us to write, a violation of *koseiv*, the 32nd category of prohibited work on Shabbos. Rabbinic prohibitions are designed to prevent violation of Torah-level law.

Additionally, over time, seven positive "Rabbinic" laws were enacted.

1. Blessings before eating and drinking – Birchos Ha'Nehenin
2. The holiday of Purim
3. The holiday of Chanukah
4. The recitation of Hallel
5. The blessing for washing hands – ...*al ne'tilas yadayim*
6. Lighting candles for Shabbos (and *yom tov*)
7. Establishing an Eruv

There is a tendency to view "Rabbinic" laws as regulatory or preventative in nature. We often take many laws or customs for granted, especially those related to blessings. We don't stop to think of where the mitzvah of lighting candles came from or how the holidays of Purim and Chanukah were established (since they are not mandated in the Torah).

There are groups today that wish to abolish much of Rabbinic law, claiming that the reasons for these laws no longer apply. I find it difficult to believe that they would attempt to abolish the 7 <u>positive</u> Rabbinic laws!

The 39 Avos Melachos of Shabbos

1. Choresh – plowing	21. Koshayr – tying
2. Zoray/ah – planting/sowing	22. Mateer – untying
3. Kotzeir – reaping	23. Tofayr – sewing
4. Mameir – gathering	24. Koray'ah – tearing
5. Dosh – squeezing/threshing	25. T'zod – trapping
6. Zoreh – winnowing	26. Shocheit – slaughtering
7. Boreir- sorting	27. Mafsheet – skinning
8. Tochayn – grinding	28. Me'abed – tanning hides
9. Merakeid – sifting	29. Me'macheik – scraping
10. Losh – kneading	30. Me'sharteit – scoring holes
11. Ofeh (Bishul)– cooking	31. Me'chateich – cutting to size
12. Gozeiz – shearing	32. Koseiv – writing
13. M'labein – laundering	33. Mochek – erasing
14. M'napeitz – combing	34. Boneh – building
15. Tz'oveyah – dyeing	35. So'sayr – demolishing
16. Toveh- spinning	36. Mavir – igniting
17. Maysach- loom threading	37. Me'chabeh – extinguishing
18. Oseh bat neirin – loom work	38. Makeh B'patish – assembling /completing
19. Oreg-weaving	
20. Potzayah- cutting threads	39. Hotza'ah –transporting outside

The details of the construction of the Tabernacle and the categories of related work that are prohibited on Shabbos were totally dependent on precise, accurate, and effective transmission by Moshe to Yehoshua.

This is where things get complicated. The laws as given in the Written Torah (תורה שבכתב) are documented in cryptic form that often cannot be understood without further explanation. So much of what we follow today is a result of our study of the Oral Law in the Mishna and Gemara.

A simple example is the category of kashrus laws, which the Written Torah does not describe in much detail. How do we know how to kill an animal in a kosher manner? How do we know the details of the laws of not mixing meat and milk?

Another example is in the laws of holiday observance. The Torah commands us to take four species on the holiday of Succos and does not specifically describe the plants or trees from which we take them. How do we know what a *lulav* is? What about an *esrog*?

How do we know how many strands of *tzitzis* are on a *tallis*? How do we know what *tefillin* are supposed to look like?

This is the case with almost all of the laws in the Written Torah. We are not provided with much detail.

The details come from the Oral Torah (תורה שבעל פה) which literally translates as: "Torah that is by-heart." Our tradition states that there is a direct line-of-transmission from Moshe of the oral laws and their details. The following is the chain of transmission as detailed at the very beginning of Mishna Avos (which lists the basic principles and fundamental behaviors that should be followed by one who adheres to the Torah):

"Moshe received the Torah (from G-d) at Sinai and transmitted it to Joshua; Joshua to the Elders; the Elders to the Prophets; the Prophets to the Men of the Great Assembly."

Essentially, the Oral Law was transmitted from teacher to student (who became the next teacher) in a generations-long game of "telephone." Imagine the patience and precision with which these laws and their details had to be taught!

The Rambam, Maimonides, in his introduction to the Mishna Torah, catalogued the 40 generations from Moshe to the time of the compilation of the Talmud Bavli, a period of almost 1700 years. The following is his expansion of the short description in Mishna Avos of the chain of transmission of our tradition:

From Moshe through the book of Shmuel (2448 – 2884):

Moshe, Yehoshua, Pinchas, Eli Ha'Kohen, Shmuel Ha'navi, David Ha'Melech

From the period of the prophets (2924-3350):

Achiyah Ha'Shiloni, Eliyahu, Elisha, Yehoyadah, Zechariah, Hoshea, Amos, Yeshayah, Micha, Yoel, Nachum, Chavakuk, Tzefaniah, Yirmiyah, Baruch ben Neriah

From the Great Assembly to the time of the Mishna (3413 – 3728):

Ezra, Shimon Ha'tzadik, Antignus Ish Socho, Yosi ben Yoezer (together with Yosi ben Yochanan), Yehoshua ben Perachyah (together with Nital Ha'Arbeli), Yehuda ben Tabai (together with Shimon ben Shetach), Shemayah (together with Avtalyon), Hillel (together with Shamai). These last five "pairs" are known as the *Zvugim*.

The Tannaim (3768 – 3910):

Raban Shimon ben Hillel, Raban Gamliel Ha'zaken, Rav Yochanan ben Zakkai, Raban Gamliel (in Yavneh), Raban Shimon ben Gamliel, Rebbi (Reb Yehuda Ha'Nassi who compiled the Mishna)

The Amoraim (3979-4127):

Rav (with Shmuel and Rebi Yochanan who compiled the Talmud Yerushalmi), Rav Huna, Rabah, Rava, Rav Ashi

These are the forty generational leaders who faithfully passed the written and oral Torah from Mt. Sinai to the compilation of the Talmud.

As I documented earlier in the section on history, it became increasingly difficult to pass this information accurately following the destruction of the Second Temple. Rebbi, Reb Yehuda Ha'Nassi, took it upon himself to document the Oral Law in a work called the Mishna ("review").

Today, when we refer to the "Oral Law," we are usually referring to the Mishna (and the accompanying Gemara) both of which were compiled into the Talmud. "Gemara" is from the Aramaic word for "study."

Rebbi documented the laws in tremendous detail that encompass six volumes containing 63 sections. Because a chain of transmission had already been operating for almost 1500 years before him (since the revelation on Mt. Sinai), Rebbi chose to include not only the laws and their details, but he "showed his work." He documented the Rabbinic discussions that led to legal clarification and conclusions.

When students are asked to solve a complicated math problem, they are often told that they must "show" their work by detailing, in written form, the method by which the problem was solved. That is why Rebbi also detailed the discussions and arguments of the earlier Rabbis and teachers about these laws, showing how he "got there."

These earlier Rabbis and teachers became known as the Tannaim and they represent the Mishnaic and pre-Mishnaic teachers (such as Rabbi Akiva).

The six books or "orders" of the Mishna:

זרעים – Zeraim (blessings, tithing, gifts to the Mishkan, etc.)

מועד – Moed (Shabbos, holidays, etc.)

נשים – Nashim (marriage, divorce, vows, etc.)

נזיקין – Nezikin (damages, civil law, punishments, Avos, Sanhedrin...)

קדשים – Kadshim (sacrifices and related Mishkan and Temple laws)

טהרות –Taharos (ritual purity and impurity...)

Following the writing of the Mishna (keep in mind, there were still no printing presses and all written documents were scribed on parchment, with ink and a quill pen) came the period of the *Amoraim*, sages who learned the Oral Torah and taught subsequent generations. This invariably led to discussions and arguments about the accurate method or meaning of what Rebbi – Reb Yehuda Ha'Nassi, had written.

The Amoraim also sought to clarify much of the narrative of Tanach and other collected writings. They searched for the deeper meaning and hidden secrets in the text and sought to fill-in-the-blanks in the Tanach narrative. This developed into numerous works which collectively became the Midrash which often has counterpart stories in the Gemara.

About 100 years after the completion of the Mishna, scholars in Roman-controlled Israel compiled the Talmud Yerushalmi (the Jerusalem Talmud) as a further commentary on the Mishna. Almost 150 years later, Ravina and Rav Ashi, leaders of the community in Bavel, compiled all the work of the Amoraim who came before them and published the Talmud Bavli (the Babylonian Talmud). For the next 500 years, the Mishna and the Talmud as written in Israel and Bavel were transmitted by scholars in Spain, North Africa and across Asia Minor from Israel to Iran.

The next major period of Jewish scholarship and leadership was that of the Gaonim from the 7th to 13th centuries in Babylonia and Israel.

This was also a time when individual communities established customs based on their location and the influence of the surrounding population. In the 600's with the growth of Islam, Jewish communities under the rule of the Moors in Spain (and in North Africa and Asia under the Muslims) were deeply influenced by the culture around them.

The Jewish communities in other countries from Italy to Germany, France, and Russia were also influenced by European culture. There is no question that the customs, culture, and even the traditional foods of these disparate Jewish communities were deeply impacted by the non-Jewish population surrounding them. Every town and city had different laws and restrictions, often forcing their rabbinic leadership to enact case-specific rules. Many of these are carried forward to this day as customs – *minhagim*.

Around the time of the first Crusade (1096 CE), the period of the Rishonim (Rashi, Rambam, etc.) was marked by a growth in writing and commentary as scholars worked to disseminate the Torah. With their voluminous knowledge of the Talmud and Midrash, they were able to clarify much of Tanach. They also were able to reorganize and codify the Mishna and Talmud into separate books of law (such as the Mishna-Torah of the Rambam) that were concise and well organized.

Starting around 1500 was the period of the Achronim (the "Later Ones") which includes those scholars, commentators, and codifiers who worked to further elucidate Tanach and Jewish law. This enabled the general Jewish population to have more access to Torah and more clarification and commentary (especially after the invention of the modern printing press).

I am often asked by students: "How did we get from 613 Mitzvos to what seem like 6,130?" There are so many laws that have been restructured or enhanced by our rabbis over the centuries that it is easy to feel overwhelmed by halachic restrictions. There is no question that much of what we do today is the result of centuries of fences having been built around Torah law as a way of preventing modern culture from negatively influencing us. Many *takanas* or *takanot* (localized decrees established by rabbinic consensus) have been followed for so long that they have, de-facto, become treated as laws.

An example of one of these decrees is that Ashkenazim cannot eat rice or legumes on Pesach, whereas Sephardim can. Another would be that Ashkenazim cannot remove the sciatic nerve from an animal and then eat the meat from the hind-quarter. Sephardim, who have passed-down the tradition of how to properly remove the nerve, may eat that meat.

There are some decrees that apply to all Jews since they were established with a much larger consensus much closer to the time of the Roman conquest of Israel and the days of the Great Assembly (*Anshei Knesses Ha'gedolah*). An example would be that Jews who live outside of Israel are mandated to keep two days of Yom Tov on Pesach, Shavuos, and Succos.

There is no doubt that we have more "laws" than ever before. In reality, these are rabbinically imposed rulings meant to protect Jewish society from outside cultures. Even when times and circumstances change, it is almost impossible to counter these rulings. We do not have a unified Jewish court or assembly that would be able to change or eliminate any rabbinically established laws (partially because they would need to be greater in wisdom and in number to overrule those who enacted these laws).

Imagine a court in Israel saying that we will no longer have two days of Yom Tov. Some Jews would accept it and others would not. Too many would question the legitimacy of the court. In a world where we cannot agree on a standard for head-covering or a single standard of kashrus, how are we going to establish a unified Jewish court (Sanhedrin) that everyone will follow?

The truth is, that even with all of these laws and perceived restrictions, we have more freedom than ever before. We have Shabbos ovens, Shabbos lights, and a plethora of modern inventions and conveniences that work within the framework of *halacha*. Our ancestors could never have imagined our lives as Jews in a modern world. The availability of kosher products, groceries, and restaurants, is greater than at any time in our history. We have more of everything, yet there are those who continue to complain about the "fences" that have been placed around Torah law.

Why did G-d create the Oral Law? Why not just give us the Torah in full detail so that we would not need to clarify anything? Why not list all the specifics of the laws in the Written Torah? Why make us play the game of telephone for so many generations, resulting in such diverse rabbinic opinions?

The manner in which the Torah is written and the complex system of transmission of Oral Law are the keys to Jewish continuity. This has forced us, from the very day that Moshe descended from Mt. Sinai, to establish a system of teaching and transmitting.

Imagine if we had been provided with the Torah as an encyclopedic work filled with every conceivable law and detail. It would, in that scenario, include the Five books of the Torah, all of the books of Nach, and all of the laws as documented in the Talmud. Every story would have been written in full detail from the days of creation through the Book of Chronicles, including who, what, where, when, and why.

Every home could have a copy of this encyclopedic work with its tens of thousands of pages. All you would have to do is study this "Torah Encyclopedia" and you would know everything! You would not even need a teacher.

Instead, we have been blessed with the Torah that requires us to work tirelessly to try to understand and decode it. G-d created a nation of teachers, mentors, and students, and we are never done studying and searching for answers.

I remember the first time I played a video game called "Super Mario." I thought I had mastered it until a friend taught me the secrets hidden in the game ("cheat codes") and showed me the different combinations you could perform with the limited hand controls that were not documented in the instruction book. Suddenly, I realized that I wasn't very good at the game and had a lot to learn.

Likewise, in shiur in yeshiva, I would often think that I understood the Gemara. Invariably, someone would pose a question and the ensuing answer from our rebbi would completely change my perspective.

This is the beauty of the Torah and its secrets. We are never done studying and searching. Our teachers are never done teaching. We spend our lives seeking the answers to difficult questions and cannot settle complacently, believing that we know everything.

We have a Mesorah, a culture of transmission, that carries forward our customs and traditions. When you open a Torah scroll there are no vowels or cantorial notes. How do we know how to read the Torah? How do we explain the "crowns" above the words, the smaller or larger letters, and where does each *parsha* begin and end? Why do we read a specific *haftorah* on Shabbos and holidays and who established the portions we read?

Even though we have books that document these customs (such as the Tikkun familiar to any bar-mitzvah boy), they were originally transmitted from generation-to-generation in unwritten form. For example, the modern Tikkun emerged from the Aleppo Codex (which is on display in the Jerusalem Museum) dating back to the year 1000.

Many elements of our Mesorah (the transmission of our religious tradition) including individual community customs, remain unwritten. They are still passed from family and teachers to children.

The main body of our Oral Law is discussed and transcribed in the Mishna as documented by Rebbi. The ensuing discussions of the *Amoraim* and attempts at clarification of the meaning of the words of the scholars of the Mishna (the *Tannaim*) are documented in the Talmud.

Without studying these works, we cannot relate to the cycle of transmission that has built the Jewish People into such a unique, educated, innovative, and inquisitive force in the world. Our passion for study is a key to our survival.

The order of the Mishna is documented below along with the 63 separate tractates that fall under the 6 categories of the Mishna. Together, they form the *Shas* – (משנה) **סדרי** ששה which encompasses the entire Talmud.

Some say that the word "Gemara" (גמרא) contains the first letter of each of the four guardian angels who look after us as we delve into our studies. They are Gavriel, Michael, Raphael, and Uriel.

Today, when someone says that they have finished a cycle of "learning *shas*," it usually means that they have completed the entire Talmud. This is often achieved as part of a cycle of *daf yomi* (page-per-day) which takes over 7 years to complete.

A chart of the six orders of the Mishna and their related tractates is provided on the next page.

The six orders of the Mishna and the 63 Tractates:

Zeraim – זרעים	Moed - מועד	Nashim – נשים
ברכות	שבת	יבמות
פאה	עירובין	כתובות
דמאי	פסחים	נדרים
כלאים	שקלים	נזיר
שביעית	יומא	סוטה
תרומות	סוכה	גיטין
מעשרות	ביצה	קדושין
מעשר שני	ראש השנה	
חלה	תענית	
ערלה	מגילה	
בכורים	מועד קטן	
	חגיגה	

Nezikin -נזיקין	Kodshim- קדשים	Taharos –טהרות
בבא קמא	זבחים	כלים
בבא מציעא	מנחות	אהלות
בבא בתרא	חולין	נגעים
סנהדרין	בכורות	פרה
מכות	ערכין	טהרות
שבועות	תמורה	מקואות
עדיות	כריתות	נדה
עבודה זרה	מעילה	מכשירין
אבות	תמיד	זבים
הוריות	מדות	טבול יום
	קנים	ידים
		עוקצים

FUNDAMENTAL JEWISH CONCEPTS

I am amazed at the number of students, both young and old, who are surprised when taught Jewish concepts. Often, they will comment: "I had no idea that was a Jewish thing!" This chapter is focused on a review of a few key Jewish beliefs that are critical for all of us to understand.

In our daily morning prayers, there is a section called: *"Ani-Maamin"* – ("I Believe") and it contains 13 principles of faith as listed by Maimonides, the Rambam. They are documented, in short form, below. Each begins with the words: "I believe with perfect (complete) faith..." – אני מאמין באמונה שלמה....

One can reasonably ask: How can I be asked to say "I believe with perfect faith" when I have doubts?

One answer is that these 13 principles are aspirational. We spend our lives working, studying, and seeking to make a closer connection with our G-d. It is important for every Jew to accept these principles or articles of faith. We all, secretly, have doubts and questions. We don't necessarily witness G-d physically revealing Himself in front of us. Nevertheless, we aspire to reach the point where these principles become part of our very being and therefore, we recite them regularly.

1. (I believe with perfect faith) that the Creator creates and leads all creatures and that He alone made, makes, and will make, all things.
2. ...that the Creator is One, there is none other like Him, and that He alone is our G-d.
3. ...that the Creator has no physical attributes
4. ...that the Creator is first and last
5. ...that the Creator is the only One to whom to pray

6. ...that the words of the prophets are true

7. ...that Moses the prophet was our teacher and that he was the "father" of the prophets – those who preceded him and those who followed him

8. ...that the entire Torah now in our hands is the same Torah given to Moshe

9. ...that this Torah will not be changed nor will there be any other Torah from the Creator

10. ...that the Creator knows all the deeds and thoughts of humanity

11. ...that the Creator rewards those who keep his commandments and punishes those who violate them

12. ...in the coming of the Messiah, and though he may delay, I will daily await his coming

13. ...that the dead will live again at a time of the Creator's choosing

Our core belief is that G-d is singular and unique. We do not believe in multiple gods and do not establish intermediaries such as idols or elements of nature (sun, moon, trees, mountains, oceans, animals, etc.) as substitutes for G-d.

One of the fundamental principles of Judaism is the belief in the eventual coming of the Messiah - משיח (Anointed One) bringing the entire world into a new era. Before looking more carefully at this principle, it is important to discuss Judaism's views on death and the afterlife.

Judaism teaches us the concept of an immortal soul. That means that even after we die and our physical body and lifeforce, our *guf* (גוף) and our *nefesh* (נפש) are consumed, our soul, or *neshama* (נשמה) survives and its life continues.

This is where *gilgul* takes over. גלגול means "wheel" or "cycle" and is a deep mystical concept. We believe that our soul can cycle through multiple lives or incarnations while attached to different human bodies over time. Some would call this reincarnation, but in many cultures, reincarnation refers to a person being re-created into another being, not necessarily human.

Our sages teach that following physical death we enter a period during which we are judged for our past behavior. That period can be anywhere from a day to a year. This is viewed as a cleansing process. The survivors of the dead say the prayer of *Kaddish* for eleven months as a way of making a public pronouncement of faith on a daily basis to help the deceased through this period of judgement.

Why do we say this prayer for only eleven months? Why not say it for a full year? A traditional answer is that nobody wants to believe that their parent or family member was so bad that their soul requires a maximum twelve months of cleansing. Therefore, the Rabbis created a uniform timeline of eleven month for all Jews to say *Kaddish*.

Death is often called: *yetzias ha'neshama* (יציאת הנשמה), when our divine soul departs from our physical body. Our *ruach* (literally, wind or spirit) leaves us. Following burial and decomposition, our *nefesh* (vital spirit or lifeforce) finally departs. It is normal for those who survive the deceased to feel despondent and upset, but our tradition teaches that this world is only a portal into a greater World-To-Come and that the dead move to a level that we, here on earth, cannot understand or imagine.

Over 45 years ago, Rabbi Benjamin Blech told me the following story about life and death that resonates to this day.

Twins are being carried in their mother's womb. The temperature is perfect, their sustenance is provided, and they have everything they need to grow in total comfort. As the pregnancy progresses, both children move lower in the birth canal. The first one believes that he will eventually move to a better place. The second is a skeptic and cannot imagine any other world than the womb.

Their mother feels labor pains and the process of birth begins. The first one to be born is the believer. His twin hears screams of pain. His environment vibrates and contracts as he sees his brother, below him, being squeezed. Finally, the first boy is born. The skeptical twin, still inside his mother, hears a smack and then a cry and can only imagine the horrors of the world outside the womb as he exclaims: "I knew it! I was right!" In the meantime, the first child born is wrapped in a warm blanket and held in the loving embrace of his mother.

This is a metaphor for our world and the World-To-Come. We are comfortable here and can't imagine anything beyond what we know. If we are believers, we can anticipate a better world of peace, joy, and serenity.

The Rambam compares us, as earth-bound mortals, to those who are blind. Just as you cannot accurately describe colors to one who is blind from birth, so too we cannot conceive of the spiritual and loving joy of any world beyond this one. While we have faith that it <u>will</u> happen and that there <u>is</u> an afterlife, we should not spend significant time trying to figure out the exact details or the sequence of events that follow death.

Along with our belief in a World-To-Come, we have a belief that G-d will eventually bring the Mashiach – The Anointed One, to bring peace to the world and awareness of one true G-d. The Mashiach ("Messiah" in English) will be born of a human father and mother and will be a descendant of King David from the tribe of Yehuda. There will be no more wars, all Jews will return to Israel, the Temple will be rebuilt in Jerusalem, and persecution of Jews will cease as the world recognizes and accepts G-d's truth.

The twelfth core principle of Jewish faith that we recite every day at the end of davening is: אני מאמין באמונה שלמה, בביאת המשיח. ואף על פי שיתמהמה, עם כל זה אחכה לו בכל יום שיבא - *I believe with full faith, in the coming of the Messiah. And though he may delay, in spite of that I will await his coming every day.*

The era in which the Mashiach arrives will begin with a period of pain and suffering. The Gemara compares this to the pain of childbirth as a mother goes through labor. The birth of the Messianic era will be one of discomfort, pain, and suffering in the world. For centuries, Jews have speculated during times of trouble that the Mashiach's arrival was imminent. This first happened during the Jewish revolt against Rome. There have been many false claimants of the messianic title over time and it is not our job to speculate about the future or predict G-d's timeline.

Another of the fundamental beliefs of Judaism is that there will be an eventual resurrection of the dead.

This is the thirteenth of the Jewish Principles of Faith and reads as follows: אני מאמין באמונה שלמה, שתהיה תחית המתים, בעת שיעלה רצון מאת הבורא יתברך שמו, ויתעלה זכרו לעד ולנצח נצחים – *I believe with full faith, that there will be a resurrection of the dead at a time that will be pleasing before the Creator blessed be His name, and the remembrance of Him will be exalted for all time, for eternity.*

The 37th chapter of Yechezkel (Ezekiel) tells the story of the Valley of Dry Bones. It is a prophecy of the resurrection of the bodies of members of the Tribe of Ephraim who left Egypt early and died in the desert.

It is impossible to speculate about what this period of resurrection will be like. We have our hopes, dreams, beliefs, faith, and principles that point toward an indeterminate time in the future when G-d will bring the Mashiach and return us, as a People, to the Land of Israel.

We do not understand what <u>that</u> entails, let alone any other future event. *Emunah Sh'layma* – אמונה שלמה – full or complete <u>belief</u> is what we should be striving for.

THE TEN LOST TRIBES

The ingathering of exiles to Israel began in earnest with the early return of settlers to Ottoman Palestine in the late 1800's. It continues today with the Nefesh B'Nefesh movement and *Aliyah* (going-up, returning).

Following the initial conquest of Israel by Joshua and the subsequent kings of Israel, there were Jews who moved to other countries, usually to conduct commerce. They were joined, following the destruction of the First Temple, by large numbers of Jews exiled by the Babylonians.

Later, large numbers of Jews were exiled by the Romans following the destruction of the Second Temple in the year 69. Jews eventually made their way to far-flung countries where millions remain today. We, the Jews of *galus* (exile) who have not yet returned to Israel, are potential candidates for the eventual ingathering of the exiles.

There is a second group of exiles that includes those who were taken as captives from the Northern Kingdom of Israel by the Assyrians over a hundred and twenty years before the destruction of the First Temple. There is very little information available that can help us identify who their descendants are, but that has not stopped many researchers from trying to find them.

The Assyrians conquered the ten tribes of Yisrael in wars that took place between 574 and 556 BCE. They exiled everyone except for the tribes of Yehuda (Judah), Binyamin, and some of the Kohanim (priests) and Leviim (Levites) living in the area around Jerusalem. Where did they take the ten tribes? Where are they today?

In the 49th *perek* of B'reishis, G-d told Yaakov that his sons (the twelve tribes), will exist at אחרית הימים – the End of Days. We have a tradition that eventually, all twelve tribes will be united again.

When the Assyrians invaded the north of Israel, they transported the ten conquered tribes to *"Halah, the cities of the Medes, by the Habor and the river of Gozan"* as described in Melachim 2, *perek* 17, *passuk* 6. These Jews were known as Khumri, Ghomri, or Gimri, derivatives of the name of King Omri of Israel. They were also called "Iskuza," as derived from the name Yitzchak, Isaac. From them, a new people emerged and eventually migrated out of Assyria. Some say the Scythians of the Altai mountains of Southern Russia and the Cimmerians, Gauls, and Celts of Northwestern Europe came from them.

There were many explorers who claimed to have found remnants of these tribes. In the 9th century, Eldad Ha'Dani (Eldad of the tribe of Dan) appeared in Kairouan, Tunisia and claimed to be from the land of "Chavilah." There, he claimed, the tribes of Dan, Naftali, Gad and Asher remained.

The famous Jewish explorer Benjamin of Tudela (12th century), said that the Jews of Persia had evidence of remnants of Asher, Dan, Naftali and Zevulun living in Nissabur, a mountainous area of Afghanistan. Today, this is the territory of the Taliban.

In 1524, another Jewish adventurer, David Ha'Reuveni, appeared before Emperor Charles V and claimed to be an emissary of the Jewish tribes of Reuven, Gad, and half of Menashe.

In 1655, Rabbi Menashe ben Israel postulated that the Indians of the Americas were descendants of the lost tribes. The Spanish bishop Bartolomeo de Las Casas, who was a defender of the rights of the natives of the Americas was a vocal proponent of the idea that American Indians descended from the lost Jewish tribes.

Travelers to South America have, for centuries, provided evidence of native cultures following selective Jewish rituals. Some have found evidence of Jewish customs and observance among the Cajun of Louisiana and the Navajo of New Mexico.

The growth of Mormonism in the 1800's in the United States brought attention to their claim of having descended from Yosef and the tribe of Ephraim.

Genetic testing has now brought the power of modern science to this search. Some of the groups being studied as possible remnants of the lost tribes are the Lemba in Africa, Bene Menashe and Bene Israel in India, the Pathans (Pashtun) in Afghanistan, Beta Israel in Ethiopia, the Hmong of Laos, the Pashtun of Waziristan, as well as a few Indian tribes in the United States.

Some early missionaries who traveled to Japan claimed that the Japanese people descended from Jewish tribes. In 1919, Japanese representative Chinda Sutemi corresponded with Chaim Weizmann on behalf of the Japanese Emperor. He wrote: "The Japanese government gladly takes note of the Zionist aspiration to extend, in Palestine, a national home for the Jewish people and look forward with a sympathetic interest to the realization of such desire upon the basis proposed."

During World War II the Japanese provided asylum for the Jews of Shanghai (albeit, in a ghetto) and Harbin, as well as for thousands of Jewish refugees from Eastern Europe. They refused to comply with Hitler's call for Jewish extermination. Is it possible that either consciously or subconsciously, someone in a role of leadership in Japan held a belief that the Japanese descended from the lost tribes?

We anxiously await the future ingathering of "exiles" and the return of our lost tribes to the land of Israel.

THE JEWISH CALENDAR

In Egypt, just before the Exodus, we were commanded to celebrate the new-moon on a monthly basis and to establish a calendar.

The Jewish year follows a lunar cycle (the time it takes the moon to complete a cycle of travel around the earth) of 354 days, whereas most other cultures in their declarations of the seasons follow a solar cycle of 365 days. Our calendar is made-up of twelve months, except in leap years, which have an extra month (Adar 2).

The calendar of Hillel II was adopted around 359 CE to provide uniformity among Jewish people living outside of Israel, due to the degree of dispersion and the need for Jews everywhere to be able to observe holidays on the same days. The implementation of this calendar was the final act of the Sanhedrin (in exile) before disbanding.

Because we want our holidays to fall on the same Hebrew date every year and to be in the correct season (for example; Passover in the Spring, Succos in the Fall...) we have to declare a leap year seven times every nineteen years in order bring the lunar and solar years in line. The concept of the leap year and its complications is discussed in detail in the Talmud.

The Jewish year (this year, 2021 of the modern calendar, is the Jewish year 5781 from creation) begins on the first day of the month of Tishrei (the holiday of Rosh Hashanah). Our "historical" year dating from the Exodus from Egypt begins with the month of Nissan. During the year we observe the biblically mandated holidays of Rosh Hashanah, Yom Kippur, Succos, Shemini Atzeres, Pesach, and Shavuos.

Additionally, we observe two holidays that were not commanded in the Torah. Purim and Chanukah were proclaimed much later; Purim, in the years between the two Temples and Chanukah during the 2nd Temple period. The observance of these two holidays is tied to Rabbinic decrees.

The Jewish Calendar Months and Holidays

Tishrei - תשרי Rosh Hashanah/Yom Kippur/Succos/Shemini Atzeres

Cheshvan - חשון

Kislev - כסלו Chanukah

Teves - טבת

Shevat - שבט

Adar - אדר Purim (there is a second Adar in a leap year)

Nissan - ניסן Pesach

Iyar - אייר

Sivan - סיון Shavuos

Tammuz - תמוז

Av - אב

Elul - אלול

Additionally, we observe five fast-days besides Yom Kippur: T'zom Gedalia on the day after Rosh Hashanah, Asarah B'Teves on the 10th of Teves, Taanis Esther on the day before Purim, Shiv'ah Asar B'Tammuz on the 17th of Tammuz and Tish'a B'Av on the 9th of Av.

T'zom Gedalia: This fast day marks the date of the murder of the governor of Eretz Yisrael (Gedalia ben Achikom) who was appointed by the Babylonians following the destruction of the 1st Temple. The remnants of the population of Israel felt that they had lost their last chance at salvation and a fast-day was declared.

Asarah B'Teves: The beginning of the siege of Jerusalem by the Babylonians.

Taanis Esther: Based on the Purim story and honoring the request by Esther that the people fast before she sought entry into the King's throne room.

Shiv'ah Asar B'Tammuz: The date on which the Romans first breached the walls of Jerusalem in the year 69. This date marks the beginning of the "three weeks" (ending on the 9th of Av which marks the destruction of both Temples). It is also the day that Moshe descended from Mt. Sinai and broke the tablets, the day that the *Tamid* sacrifice ceased being brought (in the 1st Temple), and the day the pagan ruler Apostomus burned a Torah scroll.

Tish'a B'Av: (all of the following events fell on this day)

The spies returned to the Jewish encampment in 1312 BCE and gave their negative report to Moshe.

The 1st Temple was destroyed by the Babylonians.

The 2nd Temple was destroyed by the Romans.

The Bar Kochba revolt was crushed by the Romans and the city of Betar was destroyed in 135 CE by the Romans, after a 3-year siege.

The 1st Crusade was declared by Pope Urban II.

The Jews were expelled from England in 1290.

The Spanish Inquisition set this as the final day by which Jews in Spain had to convert to Christianity or they would be subject to death.

Britain and Russia declared war on Germany – World War I.

The first deportations from the Warsaw Ghetto to the death camp of Treblinka began on this date in 1942.

Days and Times

The days of the week are numbered beginning with Sunday:

Sunday is Yom Rishon (the first day), Monday is Yom Sheni (the second day), etc. Saturday, the "Day of Rest" is called "Shabbos" and is not numbered.

We also have unique terminology which identifies specific halachic times during the day. For the purpose of making time calculations, we divide the hours of sunlight in a given day into twelve equal parts, called **Shaos Z'manios.** In order to do this, we need to know the times of sunrise and sunset. First light is called **Alos Hashachar** – when the first rays of the sun appear on the horizon.

The next important time is **Neitz Hachamah** – when the sphere of the sun first appears (rising on the horizon).

The middle of the day is called **Chatzos**, sunset is called **Shekias Ha'Chamah**, and the first appearance of the stars is called **Tzeis Ha'Kochavim.**

Once it is completely dark outside, a new day begins. This is a unique element of Jewish law, that a day begins the previous night, not in the morning. Therefore, our first prayer every day is actually *maariv*, recited at night.

The Jewish calendar and the method of calculating when holidays fall, when to declare a leap year, how to calculate the beginning and end times of Shabbos, as well as how to figure-out what the daily times are (for saying *Shema*, when *shachris*, *mincha*, and *maariv* are, etc.), involve complex calculations.

Thankfully, today, we have the luxury of computer programs that can perform these intricate calculations with down-to-the-minute accuracy. We can also use printed Jewish calendars that are widely available. In the same way that today's computers can calculate the high and low tides of any body of saltwater in the world with accuracy, we can determine our halachic times. We know when to light Shabbos candles, when to make *havdalah* and when fasts begin and end. This is a luxury and convenience our ancestors did not possess.

In the days of the Temples in Jerusalem, there were experts who operated an office of celestial study that was overseen by the Sanhedrin. Witnesses would come to the Temple and give testimony as to when they saw the first sliver of a new moon. From there, the administration of the Temple would light fires and send signals around the country designating the new month.

Today, this no longer applies as we have complicated algorithms that help us establish, with infinite accuracy, our daily, Shabbos, and holiday times.

WHERE DID OUR STRUCTURED PRAYERS COME FROM?

Our tradition credits Avraham, the first of our forefathers, with initiating the practice of praying in the morning – *shachris* (from the word "*shachar*," morning).

Yitzchak initiated the afternoon prayer of *mincha* ("offering" or "tribute") and Yaakov, *maariv* ("bringing-on the evening").

There is also an opinion that our three daily prayers parallel the three fixed daily sacrifices that were brought in the Tabernacle and Temple.

We don't know what their form of prayer was or how it was recited, but the Gemara in Taanis (2a) tells us that prayer initially was עבודה שהיא בלב – "service that is from the heart." That same Gemara references the practice of prayer service by our ancestors and those special times when prayers were invoked, including times of disaster and drought.

"Prayer" is not a good description of our service or our conversations with G-d. Its roots are in the Latin word "precatio" which is translated as "entreaty" or "supplication" and implies begging for something from a higher-power.

The Hebrew word for prayer is *tefillah* – תפילה which has its roots in the word פלל – *executing judgement* or *thinking*. It is more closely identified as a process of accounting and contemplation and affords the one who is "praying" the opportunity to contemplate their actions, judge themselves, and speak to G-d.

After thanking G-d for the blessing of renewed life we receive every morning and after praising Him, only then do we ask G-d for further blessing. That is why our stance in prayer is opposite of that of many religions. We do not kneel or prostrate ourselves daily. We take an upright and respectful stance, as if standing before a judge.

Today, our offering of prayer is often called "davening" which comes from the Yiddish; "davennen" (a verb; *to pray*). It may also come from a source in Gemara Brachos (26b) which references our Forefathers as the source of prayer. The Aramaic "from our Forefathers" is "*D'Avuhun*" – which can be transliterated as "*Davennen*."

Rav Shimon Schwab says that when we "daven" we literally shake like a flickering flame since prayer is a combination of *ahava* and *yir'ah*, love and fear (of G-d). There is a constant tension between drawing close and retreating. This is what we call "shukeling," from the Yiddish word "to shake."

The actual structure of our *tefillos* is very complicated and has multiple inter-changeable elements depending on the day of the week. Shabbos and Yom Tov prayers have an even more complicated structure. Today, we have well-organized *siddurim* or *machzorim* that lead us through the entire service. The word *siddur* comes from "seder" (set order) and the *machzor*, used on holidays, comes from the Hebrew word for "cycle."

The first siddur that we know of was composed by Rav Amram Gaon in Sura, Bavel around the year 850. Rav Saadia Gaon followed (also in Bavel) and printed a siddur in Arabic. There were no modern printing presses in those days and everything had to be either hand-written or hand-pressed using manual processes.

I have visited centuries-old synagogues in Poland (dating back to the early 1600's) where the entire *tefillah* is painted on the walls (the synagogues of Tykocin and Lancut). You can go online and look at images of these famous shuls and the beautifully painted script of the prayers on their walls.

The contents of our prayer services have been composed over the course of over 2,500 years. The members of the *Anshei Knesses HaGedolah*, the Men of the Great Assembly during the times of the Second Temple, were instrumental in the design and structure of our liturgy. Ezra, following his return to Eretz Yisrael, began to exert influence on the order and content of daily prayer and initiated a regular cycle of weekly Torah readings.

Our prayers were organized in one common language, that of *Lashon Ha'Kodesh* (the "Holy Tongue"). Our tradition is that the 22 letters of Hebrew compose the original language as communicated by G-d to Adam. We view it as the language with which G-d created the world. Every letter has a meaning and a numerical value as well as spiritual significance. Its original calligraphic form is the same as what we see in a hand-written Torah scroll.

G-d created this world with words (i.e., "And G-d said 'let there be light.' And there was light.") The blueprint of the universe is drawn with words, not sketches. That is why we have to be so careful to faithfully maintain clarity and perfection in our transmission of the Torah.

Rashi indicates that until the time of the Tower of Bavel everyone spoke Lashon Ha'Kodesh, but G-d's punishment was that everyone from that generation was dispersed to many lands with multiple new languages.

Beginning with Avraham, *Lashon Ha'Kodesh* became the language of the Jews, with the traditional script (as in the Torah hand-scripted by Moshe) used from that time forward for all religious and ceremonial documents. We refer to this original script as *Ksav Ashuri,* although it is not clear why that name was used.

There is a debate among many scholars of the Mishna and Gemara as to whether the original calligraphic script of the Torah was *K'sav Ashuri* or *K'sav Ivri* (the "Writing of the Ivri"). The Gemara in Sanhedrin (21b) tells of Mar Zutra who claimed that K'sav Ivri was the original script, but later, the Gemara says that was not the case. Rebbi (Reb Yehuda Ha'Nassi) is quoted in the same Gemara on 22a as having said that it is called כתב אשורית (Ksav Ashuris) because (ש)מאושרת בכתב it is "the choicest" of all scripts.

The Jews who were taken in exile to Babylon were called *"Ivrim"* which came from the name of their language and script – *"Ivri"* – "Hebrew." Avraham had been known as *"Avraham Ha'Ivri"* because he came from "across" the water – the great rivers of Mesopotamia and the Jordan River.

The Book of Daniel tells the story of the writing on the wall which he interpreted for the king (the story of four words which appeared on a wall of the palace in Bavel, Daniel chapter 5).

Belshazzar, the king, held a banquet and used many of the vessels from the 1st Temple. Magically, four words appeared on the wall in the banquet hall – מנא מנא תקל ופרסין and the Jews in the room were asked to explain these words.

Nobody was able to read or interpret the words for the king. Our commentaries say that they were written in *K'sav Ashuris* which the Jews (who read and wrote in *K'sav Ivri* or in Aramaic) could no longer read (see table at end of chapter comparing the alphabets of Ashuris and Ivri). The prophet Daniel came forward and interpreted the words and told the King that G-d had numbered the days of the kingdom, had weighed them and found them wanting and the kingdom would be conquered and divided.

This story highlights the loss by the masses of the ability to read and write in traditional script. In fact, if you look at most ancient Jewish documents from archaeological digs, you will notice that the script used in them is usually *K'sav Ivri*. Only ceremonial documents as well as books of Tanach used in official services were written in *K'sav Ashuri*. The famous Dead Sea Scrolls found in Israel contain a mix of ceremonial, religious, and secular writings. Both scripts (*K'sav Ivri* and *K'sav Ashuri*) were used, depending on the type of document. If you look at the first Tikkun, the Aleppo Codex from around the year 1000 (on display at the Jerusalem Museum), it is written in *K'sav Ashuri*, just like our Torah scrolls.

From the time of the 2nd Temple to today, the design and content of our prayer services have been a work-in-progress. Many elements were added throughout the periods of the *Tannaim, Amoraim,* and *Gaonim*. Even today we have new prayers that have been constructed and added to our siddurim such as the prayer for the State of Israel.

Where did the details of *tallis* and *tefillin* come from? Were they commonly used by our ancestors?

This is another example of the Oral Law providing us with details that are not written in the Torah. The key reference to *tallis* in the Torah is in the *Shema* where we are commanded to make *tzitzis* (fringes) on the corners of our garments and to include a strand of *techeles* – that we should see them and remember all the mitzvos. The laws of *tefillin* are even more general, with the command in the first paragraph of the Shema (and a second reference in the next paragraph of Shema): ...(וקשרתם לאות על ידיך והיו לטטפת בין עיניך "and you shall bind them as a sign on your hand and they shall be an emblem between your eyes"). No details are given. What are we to wrap around our hands? What material are they made of? How are they to be shaped? Without an oral tradition we are left with too many questions.

The English word for *tefillin* is "phylacteries," a derivation of the Greek word for amulets or charms. This highlights the simplistic and superstitious nature of the Greeks and their lack of understanding of our laws.

All the details relating to the *tzitzis* and *tefillin* are given as part of the Oral Law and are described in detail in the Mishna and Gemara, just like the laws relating to *mezuzah*, also cryptically referenced in the Shema. There is ample archaeological evidence dating back to the 2nd Temple period of both *tallis* and *tefillin*. They were discovered in the digs at Masada and Qumran (with a very dry climate that may have slowed the decomposition of their natural materials).

Today, particularly because of the chain of observance and communication dating back to the period of the Rishonim (such as Rashi, Rabbeinu Tam, etc.) we have a very clear tradition for how to fulfill the mitzvos of *tallis* and *tefillin*.

Our current customs relating to the details of our communal prayer services have unquestionably been colored by our interaction with multiple cultures over the last two thousand years. Nevertheless, the essence of the laws and our observance of them remains the same. We have added and modified, yet have remained faithful to the letter-of-the-law as dictated by the Torah and our Oral tradition.

The next page shows examples of both K'sav Ivri and K'sav Ashur.

116

Ivri Ashuri

TRADITIONAL JEWISH DRESS

No matter what country a Jew originates from there are still elements of our clothing that bind us together.

The earliest biblical reference to clothing (other than a fig-leaf or animal skins) is the *kesones* or the *me'il*, a type of tunic, robe, or upper body covering.

Tanach also uses the term *simlah* or *salmah* which refers to an outer garment, either square or rectangular. A Jewish man's garment as depicted in ancient Assyrian or Babylonian monuments, wall-reliefs, or obelisks often had fringes.

The *ezor* or *chagor*, although they are translated as "belt," are thought to represent a type of undergarment that "bound" the body, somewhat like underwear.

Shoes were generally sandals, *na'alayim*, made of leather, skins or fabric, and sometimes wood.

The Torah is very specific in describing the unique clothing of the High Priest and elements of the dress of Kohanim, but does not say anything about the dress of commoners.

The oldest visual reference to Jewish dress is the Obelisk of Shalmaneser III that stands in the British Museum in London. It dates to 842 BCE, a time when King Yehu was sending gifts of tribute to Assyria. A carving on that stone obelisk depicts Jewish porters carrying the king's gifts and each is wearing a *kesones* and a fringed *simlah*. Their clothing appears different from that of the Assyrians, with fringes, upturned toes on their sandals, and head coverings.

Although there are no references in the Torah to head-dress, the earliest Assyrian carvings show Jewish prisoners wearing head coverings. Jewish men were usually depicted with beards. Later carvings by the Babylonians (such as the relief of Sannechariv capturing the Judean city of Lachish in 700 BCE) show the male Jewish prisoners with no head covering, but the females with their heads covered by cloth extensions of their *simlah*.

The Torah references four specific elements relating to Jewish dress.

1. *Tzitzis* – fringes on our 4-sided garments as commanded in the Shema.
2. *Pe'os* – locks of hair on the side of head – Va'Yikra 19:27 ("...and the corners of your head you shall not round and the corners of your beard you shall not destroy") Early Persian stone reliefs dating to 600 BCE show Jews with *pe'os*.
3. *Shaatnez* – mixing wool and linen (Devarim 22:11) which does not apply to our *tzitzis*.
4. *Tefillin* (as commanded in the *Shema*)

There is no direct reference in the Torah to the law that women should cover their hair, but the Mishna in Kesuvos describes it as an ordinance. The Gemara in Kesuvos 72a says that it is a *minhag* – custom. We know from the book of Ruth (3:15) that Ruth wore a shawl or scarf; a *mitpachat*. The Torah, in its description of the laws of a *sotah*, says that when a married woman suspected of infidelity was brought before the *Kohen* she had to "uncover" her hair. This is taken as an implication that married women would normally cover their hair in public.

Today, a shawl or scarf used to cover a woman's hair is still called a *mitpachat* or is referenced by its Yiddish name, *tichel*.

The Gemara in Sanhedrin (112a), Nazir (25b), and Eruchin (7b) references women having worn wigs in Talmudic times. Today, a wig is often called a "sheitl" or "shaytl" (Yiddish) from the German word for "crown of the head."

There are no references in the Torah to men covering their head except for the Kohanim performing their duties in the Mishkan. Nevertheless, the Talmud says (in Aramaic) that when one gets up in the morning and puts a covering on his head - כי פריס סודרא על רישיה (Brachos 60b) he recites a bracha.

The Shulchan Aruch outlines strict laws regulating the wearing of a covering over our head. It is not clear whether this was a carry-over from medieval regulations that required Jews to wear specific types of hats in public. It is also not clear whether the biblical laws that applied to the priests also applied to the masses and whether common folk wore head coverings. Yet even with the lack of much detail on this subject, it is clear from archaeological evidence that as far back as the 1st Temple period, Jews dressed differently and usually covered their heads (as seen on ancient wall carvings and on obelisks and stelas).

For many centuries of exile, Jews have been required to dress uniquely as a way of clarifying their identity. In the 800's, "dhimmis" (those who lived in Islamic countries but did not believe in Islam) were required to wear a yellow mantle (which was called a "tailasan"). Later, that was reduced to wearing two overlapping patches or badges of yellow cloth.

In Egypt in 1004, Caliph al-Hakim required Jews to wear a necklace made out of a block of wood carved into the form of a golden calf.

In the 14th century, Jews in Israel who were under the control of the Mamelukes were required to wear yellow clothing in public.

Throughout Europe, from the Dark Ages through the Middle Ages, Jews wore distinctive dress. Sometimes it was a badge (in Spain it was yellow, in Italy it was blue). In Germany, Jews were distinguished by unique pointed hats, and in 1434 were required to wear yellow badges. It was no accident or circumstance that led the Nazis to require Jews to wear yellow badges in the shape of a Star of David.

In Eastern Europe Jews wore a special hat and a red badge (as required by the Council of Ofen in 1279).

Polish and Russian non-Jewish gentlemen wore long black jackets and fur-trimmed hats in the Middle Ages until almost the 17th century. In the late 1600's the "upper class" began to adapt to Western clothing which was determined to be more fashionable. The earlier traditional dress was then adopted by Jews, and by the next century, was considered to be uniquely Jewish dress.

The traditional Jew of that time wore a *yarmulke* (Yiddish, from the Polish "jarmulka" – skullcap, or the Latin "almutia" – hood).

The Gemara in Shabbos (156b) tells a story of the mother of Reb Nachman bar Yitzchak who instructed him to always cover his head out of fear of G-d. The Gemara uses the words, in Aramaic, אימתא דשמיא which in Hebrew are יורא מלכה ("fear of The King"). Some say the word "yarmulke" is a transliteration of *"yoreh Malkah"* – *fear of The King*.

Also worn were the *spodik* or *shtreiml*, fur-brimmed hats previously fashionable among Polish and Russian nobles. Today, many sects of Chassidim wear this traditional dress as a way of celebrating Shabbos, holidays, and special occasions.

If you visit the Jewish museum in Hong Kong (at the Jewish Community Center), you will see a display of traditional Jewish dress of Sephardic or Oriental Jews from North Africa and India who founded that community. The patriarchs of the Kadoorie and Sassoon families wore flowing robes that resembled those of caliphs in Arab countries or the shahs of Iraq and pashas of India. Their Shabbat and holiday outfits were royal, colorful, and bejeweled, and stood in stark contrast to the dark and drab clothing of Eastern European Chassidic leaders.

Today, our "traditional" dress continues to evolve. For some, a white shirt and a knitted kippah are the standard on Shabbos. For others it may be a suit, tie, and black hat. The important thing is that we continue to stand-out as Jews and maintain our tradition of wearing that which identifies us as unique, preserving our identity as Jews.

KEEPING KOSHER

Let's be a clear about one thing regarding kashrus from the outset. All of the laws of keeping kosher are *chukim* – they are ordinances that have no reasoning provided in the Torah. We observe these laws because we are commanded to do so. There is no rationale given by G-d and we are not meant to speculate about the reasons for keeping these laws.

What is Kosher?

The Hebrew word כשר (kasher, kosher) means that something is fit, clean, proper, and lawful. The only use of this word in Tanach is in the Book of Esther (8:5). When Esther made a request from the King that he grant her wish to countermand the evil decree of Haman. She said: ...וכשר הדבר לפני המלך... ("...and if this proposal seems *proper*..."). In Koheles the root word כשר is found twice but has a different meaning in both cases.

The term "kosher" is the opposite of *treif* or *treifah* (which refer to that which is "torn" from an animal or is otherwise deemed unfit for consumption due to defects such as lesions or growths). The Gemara in Chulin is our source for many of the laws of kashrus.

Kosher food is not blessed by a rabbi. It is simply food that has been deemed permissible for Jewish consumption. Let's look at the main categories of that which can and cannot be eaten.

1. Animals: The Torah is very specific in requiring that animals must chew their cud and have split hooves to be kosher. This includes cattle, buffalo, deer, antelope, sheep, goats, etc. Excluded are those with only one of these two signs (such as pigs which have split hooves but do not chew their cud, or camels, which chew their cud but do not have split hooves). Wild animals are thus excluded

as well (lions, tigers, bears). Kosher animals may only be consumed after they have been ritually slaughtered, which includes having their trachea, esophagus, jugular vein and certain nerves severed in one motion by a *shochet*, one trained extensively in ritual slaughter. The Torah in Devarim 12:21 says that we may eat from the cattle "...as I have commanded you." But where are those commandments? That is where the Oral Law takes over.

2. Birds: There is no formula by which birds are deemed kosher. The Torah does not list the kosher birds such as chickens, ducks, pigeons, doves, geese, and quail. Instead, it lists those birds we cannot eat. The list, by implication, seems to categorize the kosher birds as ground-feeders and excludes the predatory birds such as crows, hawks, vultures, and eagles. The non-kosher birds are detailed in the Torah in Va'yikra 11:13-23 and Devarim 14: 11-20. Kosher birds must also be killed using the method of *shechita – ritual slaughter*.

3. Fish: The Torah says that we may eat a fish so long as it has both fins and scales. Shellfish, turtles, octopus, squid, sharks and many others may not be consumed. In Bamidbar 11:22 Moshe was speaking with G-d and referenced the "gathering" of fish, from which it is derived that fish do not require ritual slaughter.

4. Rodents, lizards, snakes, snails, insects: All living creatures that crawl or creep on their bellies, swarm, or are "winged swarming things" are also not fit for our consumption.

5. Blood: The consumption of blood is also forbidden in the Torah. The preparation of kosher meat of animals and birds requires that we soak the meat and then salt it to draw-out as much blood as possible. The kosher salt used in gourmet kitchens is really "koshering salt." It is coarse grained sea salt that is thick enough to absorb blood, but is not so fine-grained as to be absorbed into the

meat. It is fascinating that for many centuries our enemies have used blood libel against us. This began in the Middle Ages and continues to this day. The claim is made that Jews, in the process of making matzoh for Pesach, kill Christian children and use their blood in the recipe. They also spread the lie that the wine we use at the seder contains the blood of Christians. We are specifically prohibited by the Torah from consuming blood or using it in our cooking. Nevertheless, as postulated by Hitler in his book Mein Kampf (1925), it is easier to get the public to believe a big lie since "...someone could not have the impudence to distort the truth so infamously."

6. Meat and Milk: The Torah specifically mandates that we not mix meat and milk. Although the written commandment is that we not cook a "kid goat in the milk of its mother" (Shemos 23:19, Shemos 34:26, Devarim 14:21) the Oral Law provides clarity and details the specifics of this commandment. Milchig or *chalavi*, refers to dairy products. Fleishig or *b'sari* is meat. Pareve (fruit, vegetable, grain or synthetic-based) is neutral.

Here are some important terms from the world of kashrus that it is important to know.

Glatt Kosher: The word "glatt" is Yiddish for "smooth" (the Hebrew word is *chalak*) and refers to a standard and process by which a *shochet* removes the lungs of an animal and checks that there are no lesions or adhesions on the surface which would render the animal unfit or *treif*.

Chalav Yisrael: Milk that is produced under the supervision of a Jew. Since there was an ancient practice for farmers to add the rich milk of camels and pigs to the goat or cow's milk they were selling to the public, it became customary in many places for Jews to require supervision of milk products.

Yayin Nesech and Stam Yaynum: This refers to two separate prohibited categories of wine consumption. Yayin Nesech is wine that is produced and used specifically for idol worship or non-Jewish religious practice. An example of this would be the wine that is produced for Christians to use in their religious ceremonies. Ironically, most churches in the United States today use kosher wine for their communion service, since it is more readily available and cheaper than sacramental wine. If you Google "sacramental wine brands" you will find that the non-kosher Rossi, Mass Wine, Louis Jadot, etc. are listed alongside the kosher Mogen David, Carmel, and Manischewitz brands.

The second term, Stam Yaynum, refers to the general prohibition against drinking wine with a non-Jew, or allowing that person to serve us wine.

The Talmud says that a person's true character can be seen through three things. One of these is what a person does when drunk. We must make every effort to control our interactions with others when under the influence of alcohol. Our sages say that drinking wine with non-Jews leads to comfortable socialization and eventually, sin.

Kosher Philosophy: The Rambam (Maimonides) classifies kosher animals as plant-eaters. Our commentaries say that during the short stay of Adam and Eve in the Garden of Eden, every creature was a vegetarian. Once they were exiled from the Garden, everything changed. Since we are permitted to consume only those animals and birds that eat grains and plants, perhaps that provides a hint to the development of our temperament and the effort to control our blood-lust.

Jews are not natural warriors. We have been viewed for millennia by our enemies as scapegoats or sheep and not as lions or eagles. We are commanded not to be cruel to animals or to savagely rip meat from them. Instead, we try to prevent *tza'ar ba'alei chayim* – causing pain to living creatures.

ORTHODOX, CONSERVATIVE & REFORM JUDAISM

It is important to remember that prior to the 18th century, there was only one denomination of Judaism. Although there were differences in rituals and customs (between Ashkenazic and Sephardic Jews), these differences did not define their adherents. The basic laws and concepts were viewed in the same way. In any given Jewish community, there were always varying levels of observance and some who were more devout than others. Nevertheless, there was no formally established difference of opinion about the authenticity of Torah law, the basic practices (such as kashrus or Shabbos) and the laws surrounding them.

The word "orthodox" comes from the Latin words "ortho" (correct) and "dox" (faith) and refers to something done in a manner that is faithful to its past.

Reform Judaism emerged from the Haskalah movement of so-called "Jewish enlightenment" in 18th century Germany. Intellect (the Hebrew word *sechel* is the root of the word *haskalah)* was cherished above tradition. In 1810, in Seesen Germany, the first Reform congregation was established. The essential belief in a singular G-d and His authorship of the Torah was rejected. The tenets of Reform Judaism were re-defined multiple times (as at the Pittsburgh Platform of 1885 when the eating of non-kosher food was defended). Early Reform scholars held that the rituals of Judaism impeded the ability of Jews to bring about "universal morality." They re-defined Biblical laws and made them non-binding. Reform Jews, by definition, believe they have the right to decide whether or not to subscribe to any particular religious belief or practice.

Conservative Judaism began as a movement following the teachings of Zechariah Frankel, who established the Jewish Theological Seminary in Breslau, Germany in 1854. It grew out of multiple disputes with the positions of the German Reform movement. Rabbi Solomon Schechter, who came to the United States in 1902, was the one who built the modern Conservative movement.

Schechter did not believe in rejecting the Torah as a way of keeping Jews from leaving the fold. Basically, the Conservative platform says that Torah laws and rituals are to be kept, but rabbis are free to innovate in areas of Jewish practice (e.g. driving on Shabbos is viewed as permissible, a microphone may be used in a synagogue on Shabbos, etc.). The Torah is viewed as "divinely inspired" but not as having come through direct divine revelation.

Orthodox Judaism does not have a clear definition and is not, per se, a "movement." It is simply a way of describing those Jews who follow the laws and traditions from Sinai and who believe that G-d gave us the Torah. Included under the title "Orthodox" (or "Ultra-Orthodox") are numerous Chassidic groups. It does not matter if you are Ashkenazi, Sephardi, or Mizrachi (eastern or oriental) – if you follow Torah-law you are categorized in this manner.

Within the world of Orthodox Judaism there are sub-groups or movements that also define themselves based on multiple levels of synthesis with the modern world. This would include "Modern Orthodox," the "Yeshiva Movement," the "Black Hat Movement" and others. Also included are multiple Chassidic groups including Satmar, Lubavitch, Ger, Viznitz, Belz, Breslover, Bobover, Skver, Tsanz, and many others.

Nevertheless, in all these groups there is a common thread that following Torah law is paramount. Customs may differ and there may be different views on adapting to society around us, but keeping kosher, keeping Shabbos and the holidays, keeping the mitzvos – these have not changed.

In today's unique environment, there has been a "boutique" re-definition of Jewish movements. Now there are reconstructionist synagogues as well as Kabbalistic, meditative, cultural, environmental, tikkun olam, and more.

The growth of the Reform and Conservative movements from the 1960's through the late 1990's in the United States has resulted in tremendous pressure to change the standards of many Jewish laws. The question of "who is a Jew" and the definition of marriage, the procedures involved in Jewish marriage and divorce, as well as the structure of our prayers and the custom of separating men and women in synagogue – all of these have emerged as new sources of conflict.

In Israel, where the Chief Orthodox Rabbinate oversees governmental standards of marriage and divorce and effectively decides who is a Jew, there is increased pressure to make changes and loosen standards. Even Israel's requirement that conversions be done according to Orthodox tradition has come under fire.

Orthodox and Conservative Judaism require matrilineal descent for one to be declared a Jew. That means that your mother must be Jewish (either by birth or proper conversion) in order for you to be a Jew. Reform Judaism has now taken the position that patrilineal descent is acceptable – if your father is Jewish then you are. Conservative Judaism traces matrilineal descent to the time of the *Tannaim* of the Mishna, around the time of the destruction of the 2nd Temple. Orthodox Judaism considers it an element of the Oral Law given at Sinai.

Recent years have seen the expansion of "boutique-ization" with the building of synagogues and movements that reflect one's own preferences, desires, and proclivities. For many, selecting their "brand" of Judaism is like ordering coffee at Starbucks. They want it "their way."

The Reform, Conservative and Reconstructionist movements, their schools, attendance at synagogue services – are all experiencing an exodus.

Maybe it is time to drop the labels and go back to just being "Jews." We must be willing to accept our shortcomings, admit when we are lazy, and not be afraid to recognize that there are things we do that are wrong and that we often lack discipline. We need not adopt any specific movement to justify our actions.

When an individual tells you that they **are** a _____ Jew (feel free to pick a denomination or type), they are actually declaring what they are **not**. If I tell someone I am "Modern Orthodox" I am essentially saying that I am not Yeshivish, Chassidic, Reform, Conservative, etc.

If someone asks you to define what kind of Jew you are, try simply saying: "I am a Jew." No other labels are necessary. It did not matter in the desert, in the ancient land of Israel, during the Inquisition, and certainly not in the barracks or gas chambers of Auschwitz!

Today, our re-definition of peoplehood based on religious affiliation separates us more than ever. It is time to return home, get back to our roots, and drop the labels.

Who are You? What are you?

"I am a Jew!"

FUNDAMENTAL MISHNAIC & TALMUDIC CONCEPTS, ADAGES, & PRINCIPLES

This is an introduction to a few Mishnaic and Talmudic principles that cannot be fully understood or mastered without in-depth study. This chapter is meant to provide exposure to these concepts.

העוסק במצוה פטור מן המצוה – *One who is engaged in performance of a commandment is exempt from another commandment.*

This is an important basic concept in the Mishna and Talmud that relates to our performance of Mitzvos. A Mishna in Sukkah (25a) says that if a person is on his way to perform a mitzvah (for example, delivering funds to a charity) he is exempt from having to sit in a sukkah.

This is a very complicated concept that raises numerous questions. How does it apply to Torah law vs. Rabbinic law? Does involvement in any mitzvah exempt one from performance of others? What is the rationale for this ruling? Why do we interrupt our study of Torah to attend a minyan and daven?

גדול מצווה ועושה ממי שאינו מצווה ועושה – *One who performs a mitzvah having been commanded to do so is greater than one who performs a mitzvah without having been commanded to do so* (Kiddushin 31a). This concept is also in Bava Kamma (38a, 87a) and in Avodah Zarah (3a).

Who gets more "credit" from G-d, someone obligated to perform a mitzvah or someone who does a mitzvah simply because they want to? On the surface, the above ruling appears counter-intuitive. Isn't it better to "want" to act?

If your parents ask you to clean your room or help in the kitchen, isn't it better to want to help rather than complain and do it begrudgingly? This adage does not appear to take into account a scenario where you grumble and initially resist, but nevertheless, follow your parents' orders.

What is better, to observe the laws because we are commanded to or to follow the laws because we enjoy doing them?

Tosafos says that a person who is commanded to do something has a more difficult time following-through because his evil inclination will try to discourage him from doing that which was asked. Alternatively, if you volunteer to do something you are making a proactive choice that helps you resist the evil inclination.

This adage appears to take into account the fact that we are naturally resistant to being <u>ordered</u> to do anything. We want to exercise our free choice and do it without being judged. Are we soldiers in boot camp who must do everything our drill sergeant orders us to do?

In fact, this ruling recognizes that our performance of G-d-given commandments reflects a higher level of observance because it continually tests our dedication and resolve, encouraging self-discipline and proper behavior.

לפני עור לא תתן מכשל – *Before the blind, do not put a stumbling block.*

We are specifically commanded in Va'Yikra 19:14 not to put an obstacle in front of a blind person and the Talmud opines that if one violates this they are to be excommunicated from their community. This prohibition is not just literal. Obviously, placing an object in front of a blind person, tripping them, causing discomfort – these are not ethical acts.

This law is expanded-upon in the Oral Law which goes far beyond the literal translation of the commandment. We understand this commandment as a prohibition against misleading an individual by purposely giving them bad advice or by facilitating a sinful act when they lack the means to commit that sin.

There is another element to this law, which we call "theft of the mind," or גניבת דעת. The Talmud in Chullin (94a) says that we are forbidden to mislead people. By misrepresenting something or deceiving someone, we are violating the law. This prohibition applies to advertising, sales, and general treatment of others.

Imagine the following scenario. I bought a car built in 2000 with 60,000 miles on the odometer for $5,000. I then rolled-back the miles, fixed it up and repainted it. I then advertised it as "A Classic, Good-as-New, Lightly-Used, $25,000!" and showed in the ad that there were only 5,000 miles on the odometer. Not only am I lying but I am misrepresenting the condition of the automobile and deceiving a potential buyer.

There are many questions one can ask about the application of these laws. For instance, are manufacturers that design products with planned obsolescence violating this law? Today, most companies that build washing machines, dryers, kitchen appliances, televisions, etc., design these products with a limited life-span. When I was a child, my parents bought Maytag appliances. Some of them are still operating, fifty years later. Today, it is common for many products to stop working right after their manufacturer's warranty expires because they are designed and manufactured with built-in obsolescence.

Are we told when our cellphones, computers, automobiles, and other high-tech products will experience their expiration date? The deception that is rampant in the world of advertising is a violation of these precepts as well. We, as the consuming public, are figuratively a "blind man" and we are taken-advantage-of on a regular basis by those who deceive us and commit "theft of the mind."

There is also a tendency on the part of mean-spirited individuals to give bad advice to others. Some people cannot stand to see others profit or do well. Sometimes, we look at others who are doing good deeds and it bothers us, since we cannot see ourselves taking the time to do the same thing. Is this envy or jealousy? Others will try to trip-up their friends or acquaintances by misleading them. That is a violation of this category of law as well.

אם אין אני לי מי לי? – *If I am not for me, who will be for me?* (Avos 1:14).

This is an important adage of Hillel, one of the early *Tannaim*. In the same Mishna as the above quote he continues with: וכשאני לעצמי מה אני? ואם לא עכשו אימתי? – *And if I am for myself, what am I? And if not now, when?*

This Mishna is a classic example of the theory of living life in balance. On one hand, Hillel is telling us that we must think of ourselves first. We have to provide for ourselves and our families before helping others. But that must be balanced with the second precept. If we are only for ourselves, who or what are we? He points-out the danger of being self-centered or selfish and leaves the question open. If one does such things, who or what are they? He does not answer his own question since it is obvious that one who is only for himself holds no value (what my grandparents used to call a "good-for-nothing").

The third element of this Mishna, *"And if not now, when?"* has a direct connection to the first two statements. It is easy to be consumed by our careers and our responsibility to take care of our families. Even when we help others and recognize that we should not be selfish, there is a tendency to become consumed with that pursuit and ignore other things including Torah study and prayer. Some say that there is never a "good" time to do anything. Why do today what you can put off until tomorrow?

Hillel is telling us that we must live in the "now." The future is uncertain. We must live our lives by balancing our personal needs and those of our community, while still managing to keep moving forward and working diligently to build and improve. Don't put things off and don't say: "When I retire and have time, then I will do it." "When I make more money, then I will do it." "When my kids are out of the house, then I will do it."

As I write this, the world is consumed by the continuing effects of the 2020 - 2021 global Coronavirus pandemic. In some communities there is a breakdown of social order and people are rioting, ignoring new safety protocols. Yet, in most others, people are making sacrifices and caring for their neighbors. Hillel's wisdom is as relevant now as ever and can be seen in this, his most famous adage which many have called: "The Golden Rule."

The Gemara in Shabbos (31a) tells the story of Hillel, who was approached by a gentile who wanted to be taught the entire Torah while "standing on one foot." In other words, he wanted to be taught, in a very short and concise way, the key to the Torah. Hillel responded with the following: דעלך סני לחברך לא תעביד. זו היא כל התורה כולה which is translated as: "*What is hateful to you do not do to your friend; This is the whole Torah.*"

מתוך שלא לשמה בא לשמה – *What is not done for its own sake will come to its own sake.* In other words: *Good intentions will follow good actions.*

Our sages explain that it is not easy for us to be completely motivated "for the sake of heaven." As humans, there is always an element (as described by Reb Chaim of Voloshin in Nefesh Ha'Chayim, Perek 3) of שלא לשמה (done without the right intent) in our observance. Nevertheless, our belief is that as we continue to observe the mitzvos we will grow to do them for their own sake. This is considered a higher level of observance but one which is not easy to reach.

Some say that when we observe the Torah's laws, our actions are more important than our motivation, but when we <u>learn</u> Torah, the purpose of that learning is to lead us to <u>action</u>. If one is only going to learn Torah without applying that which they have learned to daily life, then it is only an exercise of the intellect.

It is difficult to do things for the right reason. We all have competing desires and are motivated by different social, intellectual, and practical pressures. This adage is coming to teach us the importance of striving to do things for their "own" sake and not for "our" sake. It involves a lot of faith and belief and is a major challenge every day.

הוי זהיר במצוה קלה כבחמורה שאין אתה יודע מתן שכרן של מצות – *Be as scrupulous in performing a minor mitzvah as a major mitzvah, for you cannot know the rewards of mitzvos* (Avos 2:1).

Most people are surprised to learn that there are only two laws in the Torah attached to a specific reward for their performance.

The first is in the command to honor our father and mother (where it states the reward of long life).

The second is in the command to shoo-away a mother bird when you collect her eggs or hatchlings. Again, the stated reward is that of long life.

The command to honor our parents is one which is very difficult to perform. It requires constant care and respect and continues to the day we die. We must speak respectfully of them even when they have passed.

The command of *shiluach ha'kan*, to send away the mother bird, only requires a flick of the wrist, the bird flies away and the commandment is fulfilled.

By associating these two mitzvos, one difficult and one simple, the Torah is sending us an important message. We should not assume to understand G-d's system of reward.

The Mishna in Avos is teaching us to follow the Torah without prioritizing mitzvah performance. Modern society tries to attach ethical priorities to our actions and even within Jewish groups there are those who attempt to make *tikkun olam* (repair of the world), the cornerstone of a Jew's obligations. Many of these same people attach little to no importance to keeping kosher or observing the laws of Shabbos.

This Mishna teaches us <u>not</u> to prioritize mitzvah performance based on a perception of potential reward.

תדיר ושאינו תדיר, תדיר קודם – *The frequent takes precedence over the infrequent* (Gemara Brachos 51b).

This is an important rule in establishing many of our customs and the structure of our liturgy. For example, when one says the *Birkas Hamazon* after eating, if it is Shabbos, we add the special sections for that day. If it is Rosh Chodesh which only happens once a month, then we add the *Ya'aleh V'yavoh*. The same holds true for our Shabbos and holiday davening – that which is more common is said first.

That is also why we put on our *tallis* <u>before</u> putting on our *tefillin* – the tallis is put on <u>every</u> day. Therefore, it comes first.

לכתחילה – בדיעבד – *Le'chatchilah – Initially or optimally. B'dee'eved – Having been done already, after the fact,* or *under duress.*

There is a concept in Jewish law that although mitzvos should be fulfilled in a preferred way, there are times when they are performed or based on a lower standard that was not originally anticipated.

There are many laws and customs governing the laws of lighting candles on Chanukah. While they should be performed in an optimal way (and even with *hiddur mitzvah* – in a glorified and more beautiful way), the same laws can be fulfilled, after the fact, in a much simpler way.

Imagine fulfilling the laws of Pesach in a barracks in the Holocaust, with ersatz matzo and marror. What about lighting the wicks of the Temple Menorah in the days of the Maccabees with insufficient oil? What about praying when under conditions of duress? Yes, optimally we would prefer to do things in a better way, but sometimes that cannot be done.

There is a further application to this concept. Sometimes, when performing a mitzvah, we make a mistake and do something wrong. In cases such as these, there are times when we look back retroactively and rule that it is permissible. We sometimes apply this to kashrus when it comes to those rulings which may damage the availability of kosher meat to the community. By making certain assumptions or waiving stringencies, we can, after the fact, rule that the products are permitted.

Another example is that a person who is counting the omer (the 49 days from Pesach to Shavuos) and counts too early (before dark), can have the counting accepted after-the-fact.

The danger in applying the concept of "after-the-fact" (known in legal parlance as "ex-post-facto") is that it often becomes our fallback position. That is why we do not proactively state that things can be done at a secondary level. Instead, our rabbis rule that mitzvos must be done a certain way, by a certain time. If, on the other hand, there are extenuating circumstances, we can sometimes look back at that which has been done and rule that it was permissible.

מצוה הבא בעבירה – *A mitzvah that is fulfilled through a transgression.*

The Gemara in Sukkah (30a) discusses the case of an individual who uses a stolen Lulav to fulfill the mitzvah of bringing the *arba minim* (*lulav, esrog, hadassim, aravos*) on Sukkos. The case is ruled as a being a mitzvah that is fulfilled through stealing, and represents a violation of Torah law. The same ruling would be applied to a person who stole matzoh for Pesach or gave stolen funds to charity.

Performance of a good deed does not give one permission to break the law.

מצוה גוררת מצוה – *Performance of a mitzvah leads to another mitzvah* (Avos 4:2).

This adage, as pointed out by Ben Azzai, teaches us that the reward for doing a mitzvah is the opportunity to perform another, leading to positive deeds and good behavior. Alternatively, we can apply this formula to negative mitzvos. Doing a sin will lead to another sin and can begin a chain-reaction of destructive behavior.

זריזין מקדימין למצות – *The zealous perform mitzvos without delay.*

The Gemara in Pesachim (4a) teaches us the principle that it is preferable to do a mitzvah at the earliest possible opportunity. We know that Avraham awoke early to fulfill the mitzvah of bringing Yitzchak as an offering to G-d. This is one of the sources for our custom of performing a circumcision early in the morning.

Some say that this concept is an application of *hiddur mitzvah*, performing a mitzvah in an enhanced way. Others say that we do mitzvos as soon as we can so we do not delay and possibly lose an opportunity.

המוציא מחברו עליו הראיה – *One who seeks to take from his fellow, the burden of proof is on him* (Gemara Bava Kama 46a).

This statement has been adopted in most legal systems as a fundamental rule. If a case (e.g., someone says you owe him money) is brought against you it is the responsibility of your accuser to establish his legal position and bring evidence of his claim.

There is a relationship as well between this rule and the Western legal concept of "presumed innocent until proven guilty." In other words, the burden of proof is on the plaintiff.

Unfortunately, in today's "woke" world and our "cancel culture," just the appearance of an accusation can render an individual guilty or unworthy of favorable consideration. Nevertheless, Jewish law does not accept such accusations as truth, whether in civil or capital cases.

In practical terms, especially in monetary cases, it is possible that the defendant (the accused) admits that he has partial or minimal responsibility (מודה במקצת). If a claim is brought that you owe someone $10,000 and you admit that you owe them money, but you state that the amount is actually $1,000, the law treats this differently.

דבר שלא בא לעולם – *A thing not yet in existence.*

In our halachic system we transfer ownership by making a *kinyan*, effecting a transaction. For example, if I sell you my car for "consideration" which may be a large sum of money, you and I are parties to the sale and your purchase is acquired through a *kinyan*.

The Talmud poses the following question: Can one transfer ownership of an object by pledging to pay with a non-existent item? For instance, can you offer a seller money from the sale of fruit that has not yet grown? Can you offer water that is not yet in storage?

An interesting question: Did Eisav have the right to sell his birthright to Yaakov? After all, it was not yet his – it would not have been his to sell until his father, Yitzchak, had died.

An important element to consider is that we live in an uncertain world. As certain as it is that the sun will rise tomorrow morning, it is just as uncertain that one's crops will be healthy and ready to harvest on time. Will the check come in the mail? Will stocks continue to rise? Will gold stay above $1,800 an ounce?

Halacha takes into consideration that we should not promise that which is not yet ours. We should not write checks that can't be cashed.

THE WHAT & WHY OF ANTISEMITISM

It is important to define the word "antisemitism" and look at the history of this terminology. Most dictionaries define it as hostility, prejudice, or discrimination against Jews.

In 1879 Germany, a political agitator named Wilhelm Marr used the term "antisemitismus" to replace the word "Judenhass," Jew hatred. Since Jews are the descendants of Noach's son, Shem, we are often referred-to as "Semites."

Throughout history, Jews have been viewed as outsiders by other nations. The self-imposed separation of Jews from general society began in Goshen, in Egypt, following the descent there by the 70 members of the family of Yaakov. The Midrash says that in Egypt they did not change their Hebrew names, their language, or their unique dress. In the opening of *parshas* Sh'mos, we are told of the fear of the Egyptian leadership that the Jews would grow too powerful. Back then we were known as *B'nei Yisrael* – the Children of Israel (Yaakov).

Later, we became known as the *"Ivrim,"* those who came from "across" the river. Some say this hearkens back to Avram (before his name was changed to Avraham) having come to the land of Canaan from the other side of the Euphrates River (see reference in Bereishis 14:13 to Avram the "Ivri"). The later crossings of the Yam Suf (Reed Sea) and the Jordan River following the exodus from Egypt cemented the reputation of the Jews as "those who crossed."

Another opinion is that Avram had a close association with Ayver, the grandson of Shem and that the name "Ivri" originated with him.

Jews have been projected with negative stereotypes for thousands of years. This appears to have been a result of Jews separating from surrounding cultures and remaining steadfast, believing in a singular G-d. The Midrash Tanchuma says that the Roman emperor Hadrian asked Rabbi Yehoshua: "Is one sheep greater than seventy wolves?" In other words, are the Jews (the sheep) greater than the 70 nations of the world? There is an opinion that Hadrian was asking a rhetorical question, making a statement about the inner-strength and stubborn nature of Jews.

For those Jews who are traditional, antisemitism is not a great mystery. A Jew understands his role in the world as a messenger of G-d whose job it is to live an exemplary moral life. When you look at yourself as a priest of a holy nation, you know that you are going to stand out with a target on your back.

A message that we are "the chosen people" can belittle those who live around us. That is why the Torah makes it a point to say that it was the Jews who said to G-d: "We will do and we will hear" (נעשה ונשמע). This statement is quoted in the Torah in the parsha of Mishpatim, Perek **24**, Passuk **7** of the book of Sh'mos– keeping the Torah requires a 24-7 commitment!

It is critical that we project a message that we are the ones who chose G-d and agreed to accept severe restrictions. Instead of showing how special we are, perhaps we should let others know of the sacrifices we make every day to maintain our identity as Jews. As Rabbi Blech taught me: We are not "The Chosen People." Instead, we are "The Choosing People." That choice is accompanied by many challenges.

What is the secret to societal resentment and hatred of Jews? Some answers to this question are as crazy as the question itself. The Germans said that we controlled all their money, yet hated us as poverty-stricken shtetl dwellers. We were hated as communists, yet accused of being money-grubbing capitalists. We are hated for being too religious yet accused of being agents of Satan. We are hated as victims yet loathed as victors.

The Greeks and Romans, with all their pagan worship, considered Jews to be impure. The early Christians blamed the Jews for killing their "savior" yet the New Testament clearly describes the Roman execution and a soldier name Longinus who stabbed Jesus to hasten his death so he could be taken down from the cross before sunset and buried.

In Russia, a book was published in 1903 (as a hoax) called: <u>The Protocols of the Meetings of the Learned Elders of Zion</u>. It purported to detail a Jewish plan for global domination. In the 1920's Henry Ford (a notorious anti-Semite) purchased 500,000 copies for distribution in the United States. This book continues to be cited, especially in Arab countries, as proof that Jews actively plot to take over the world. Its claims, much like those of the blood libels of the Middle Ages, are so preposterous that they are believed by many. After all, who would make up such stories if they were not true?

Do you think that antisemitism stopped with the defeat of the Germans in World War II? As descendants of Amalek, they sought our destruction, but we did not completely defeat them or their spiritual disease of Jew-hatred. During the war, it was more important for them to keep the trains running and delivering Jews to the concentration camps, then to ship military supplies to the Eastern Front in Russia. Their hatred was so all-consuming that they literally destroyed themselves in an effort to destroy us! <u>That</u> is the spirit of our eternal enemy, Amalek, and it is still alive!

Do you think things have changed today? Europe has become less religious than at any time in history, yet its antisemitism has reached more dangerous levels than at any time since World War II. In Japan, there are popular antisemitic comic books. Throughout the Arab world, Jews are reviled as "Zionist oppressors."

The world has always had its excuses for hating Jews and there are many theories why. There is the Jealousy Theory, the Scapegoat Theory, the You Killed our God Theory, and many others. Every country we have populated has benefited from our loyal service and accomplishments, yet we have been hated as separatists, communists, capitalists, killers of gods, worshipers of the devil, well-poisoners, and murderers.

The answer to antisemitism for many Jews has been assimilation. But that only makes things worse. Whenever Jews have tried to assimilate into surrounding cultures the results have been catastrophic. There is a claim made by our detractors that Jews are a race. Even in the face of physical evidence that there are white Jews, black Jews, oriental Jews, etc. the claims have not stopped. Even the assimilated population of Jews of Germany were seen as genetically inferior to Germanic Aryans.

There are literally hundreds of reasons given for antisemitism (see <u>Antisemitism, a Historical Encyclopedia of Prejudice and Persecution</u> by Richard S. Levy). The harsh reality is that this type of hatred is a disease that adapts to different social and historical environments.

There is a rabbinic tradition that the word "Sinai" derives from the root of *sin-ah*, hatred. Even in English, the first three letters of "Sinai" spell "sin." Our detractors look upon us as sinners.

I once heard an interesting explanation for antisemitism from a Breslover Chassid who said that the message of G-d giving us the Torah at Sinai is: "The Jews have the Torah. I have given them The Truth and everything I am telling them is true." Isn't that enough reason for others to be jealous of us, hold us to a higher standard, or hate us?

Even when our enemies do not actively seek our destruction, we have an internal enemy – our own people. Why is it that so many non-observant Jews harbor ill-will towards traditional Jewish observance? Is it the fact that they don't want to hear the truth?

This reminds me of the famous line from <u>A Few Good Men</u>, a Hollywood movie. Tom Cruise said to Jack Nicholson: "I want the truth!" Nicholson responded: "You can't <u>handle</u> the truth!"

Does traditional adherence to Jewish law remind some of a truth they don't want to hear?

Precisely the very contributions we have made to society; our principles, our values, and our laws, are the root cause of antisemitism. Isaiah prophesied (Isaiah 42:6) that G-d is sending us a message that we are to be a "light unto the nations' (אור לגויים).

That is our job and our destiny. It is difficult and often painful, but it is why we are here!

The world will say: "Oh no, we don't hate Jews. We hate the State of Israel and its oppression of the Palestinians." Unfortunately, this statement is often made by our fellow Jews!

The reality is that we cannot comprehend the current war against Israel without understanding the war against Jews that has been perpetuated for thousands of years by Europeans. It all boils-down to antisemitism. If you lived in Germany in the 1930's you would see protestors carrying signs telling Jews: "Get out! Go to Palestine!" Today, their descendants carry signs saying: "Jews, Get out of Palestine!"

Our world is filled with hypocrites who cannot recognize, comprehend, or correct their double standards.

Our only protection is to come together as Jews and to unite in our support of Israel and our People. We cannot and will not make the rest of the world happy. Let's do what is right in the eyes of G-d and let the Master Planner take care of the rest. Our world today is upside-down. Let Him turn it right-side-up when He is ready and we are deserving!

Rav Chaim of Volozhin said: "If the Jew does not make kiddush, the goy will make Havdalah!"

THE TRADITIONAL ROLES OF MEN & WOMEN

There is a rabbi in Israel who often speaks to Birthright and NCSY tour groups and poses the following question, first to the girls: "How many of you have platonic male friends?" Most of the girls raise their hands.

He then asks the boys: "How many of you have platonic female friends?"

Very few if any hands go up.

Why is this?

The reality is that no matter how much society tries to teach us that boys and girls are the same, we are very different. There are those who want to spread a culture of gender-fluidity and reject historical perceptions of male and female identities. It is not culturally sensitive today to assume that someone is a boy or a girl and gender activists have now defined as many as fifty-two gender identities.

My youngest grandchild was born in September of 2020, and the hospital asked my son and daughter-in-law what they wanted to put for "gender" on the birth certificate. Even the knitted cap that the hospital put on the baby to provide warmth, came with three choices: light blue for boys, pink for girls, or white for gender-fluid or "undecided."

Modern society may promote new standards, definitions, and assumptions, but we have been around for thousands of years and, as King Solomon said in Koheles (Ecclesiastes): "There is nothing new under the sun." Our world has not changed and people have not changed. We may have modern conveniences and inventions that provide physical comfort, but the basics chemistry and tension between man and woman as related to sexuality, remain the same as they always were.

The Torah's view of men and women is very different than that of modern or western society. Gender roles are more clearly defined based on the physical and spiritual gifts of each. Men are more physical and women are more spiritual. While men often take-on the role of hunter-gatherer, women are more emotional, nurturing and caring.

Unfortunately, the very act of writing these words today is viewed by some as a form of heresy and challenges modern perceptions of gender identity. Nevertheless, the Torah makes it abundantly clear that the human world is limited to only two genders, man and woman.

G-d does not ask who you "think" you are or what you "identify" as. Some may see this as insensitive, unfair, or phobic. G-d does not ask whether you suffer from gender dysphoria and see yourself as being of a different gender than that of your birth. The Torah does not define individuals based on their sexual proclivities. Instead, it defines conditions and prohibitions that make it clear what is (and what is not) acceptable human behavior.

The Torah describes the creation of man and woman in *B'reishis* and identifies homosexuality (*Vayikra* 18:22, 20:13) as a *toevah* – something abhorrent to G-d. The Talmud further references an "androgyne," someone who has physical signs of being both a male and a female. There are no other categories of human sexuality in the Torah. There are many illicit relations documented in the Torah such as incest, and many prohibitions against relationships that may lead to physical sin.

One of the most common questions posed to challenge Torah law is: "If G-d created me this way, what is wrong with it?" For example, why would He create homosexuality if He considers it abhorrent.

G-d created a very complex world filled with many wonders and challenges. There is a Chinese proverb that says: "Don't thank G-d for creating the tiger. Thank Him for not giving the tiger wings." Every creation has a unique design and purpose and is part of a grand vision. Every animal has its own unique abilities and limitations.

As humans, we have an additional element of free choice which brings something new to the table. We have temptations thrown at us every day. The Torah is a guide through this intricate minefield. The fact that G-d created such a diverse world does not necessarily give us permission to use or abuse every element within it. Are we free to assume that everything in this world was put here for our enjoyment?

Should one be free to marry or mate with anyone or anything that G-d created? Modern society has re-defined marriage based on a simple philosophy that you should be able to marry anyone you love. Is it then permissible to marry your brother or sister? How about your mother or father? How about your pet? As ridiculous as this may sound, it is a logical extension based on today's progressive redefinition of marriage.

Adam and Eve and the creation of our subjective world:

Let's go back to the very beginning and the creation of the first man and woman, Adam and Chava (Adam and Eve).

In the Garden of Eden, the world operated with the absolutes of אמת ושקר – *emmes* and *sheker* (truth and falsehood). Following the sin of Adam and Chava when they ate fruit from the Tree of Knowledge, they brought something new into the world. The full name of the tree was: עץ הדעת טוב ורע – The Tree of Knowledge of Good and Bad. The Torah tells us that when they ate from that tree, their eyes were opened.

An entirely new mindset consumed Adam and Chava as they brought the knowledge of "good" and "bad" into their world. Once they ate from the fruit of the tree, they suddenly realized that they were naked. In the perfect world of *emmes* and *sheker*, they were like the animals and had no shame. But now, they were in an entirely different world where things could be viewed in a subjective way and G-d had to exile them from the Garden.

The Rambam in <u>Moreh Nevuchim</u> discusses this concept and says that after eating from the tree, Adam and Eve went from an absolute objective reality to a subjective perception of reality.

Today, we operate in a subjective world where some things seem good to some people and bad to others. Humans are free to view things differently, to disagree, and to be motivated in different ways.

The punishment of man and woman:

Following the sin of eating from the tree and banishment from the Garden, man and woman were assigned new roles by G-d. The Garden of Eden is symbolic of an ideal or utopian world that awaits us at the End of Days. The exile of Adam and Chava into a new world is all part of G-d's plan for humanity.

The following is the curse of woman (as stated in B'reishis 3:16): הרבה ארבה עצבונך והרנך בעצב תלדי בנים, ואל אישך תשוקתך והוא ימשל בך – *I will greatly increase your suffering and your childbearing, in pain you shall bear children, and to your husband shall your craving be and he shall rule over you.*

The following is the curse of man (as stated in B'reishis 3:17,18,19): כי שמעת לקול אשתך ותאכל מן העץ אשר צויתך לאמר לא תאכל ממנו, ארורה האדמה בעבורך בעצבון תאכלנה כל ימי חייך. וקוץ ודרדר תצמיח לך,ואכלת את עשב השדה. בזעת אפיך תאכל לחם עד שובך אל האדמה כי ממנה לקחת כי עפר אתה ואל עפר תשוב – *Because you listened to the voice of your wife and you ate from the tree about which I commanded you saying "You shall not eat of it," cursed is the ground because of you; through suffering you shall eat all the days of your life. Thorns and thistles, shall it sprout for you and you will eat the herbage of the field. By the sweat of your brow you shall eat bread until you return to the ground from which you were taken. For you are dust, and to the dust you shall return.*

Let's analyze these two punishments or curses. Man and woman were punished with mortality – they would not live forever. Life would be accompanied by pain and toil. Woman would be subservient to her husband and he would have to work tirelessly.

These punishments must be understood within a framework of G-d's design for our world. Man was assigned a role of farmer, worker, gatherer, etc. In order to rise above this level, he would have to work hard and then, utilizing his brainpower, develop and improve the world. If he were to use just the sweat of his brow, he would eat bread. But, as my paternal grandfather used to say, if he used his brain, he could go beyond that and "eat cake."

Woman was assigned a role of child-bearing and rearing. Traditionally, it was the woman who took care of the home and raised the children, but that is not to imply that a woman must limit her attentions to that area.

It is difficult to explain the specific meaning of "...and he shall rule over you." Perhaps that could be compared to a king who rules over his people yet has a tremendous responsibility to care and provide for them. The curse of woman, that her husband will rule over her, is one of subordination, but not one of oppression or slavery. Our sages almost universally teach that a man's respect for his wife must be greater than that which he desires for himself and he must provide for all her needs, both physical and emotional.

Women and spirituality:

There are many generalities that apply when looking at the differences between men and women. Women have a greater need for developing relationships and have within them the necessary skill for that. Women seem to understand men, but men do not understand women. Women are a mystery and exist in a world that men cannot tune into. Men tend to wear their emotions on the outside, while women are much more focused on their inner emotions.

Our sages, postulate that man, who was created from the dust of the earth, is a more physical and animalistic creature. The divider that we put in a synagogue between men and women (*mechitzah*) is a reflection of a simple reality; men cannot spiritually focus while in the presence of women.

The first woman, Eve, was made from an already existing being (Adam), not from the dust. Women, therefore, have a distinct advantage. They have a greater inner spirituality and do not require all of the physical limitations that the Torah puts on man. Women are more "complete."

It is fascinating that as you study Tanach you are hard-pressed to find stories of Jewish women openly challenging G-d. All of the stories of rebellions against G-d are those of men complaining and taking action. It is the women who are portrayed as those with better judgement, patience, understanding, and belief.

When we recite our morning prayers, one of the things women thank G-d for is that He created them כרצונו – according to his *ratzone* – more accurately translated as: "Blessed is G-d, King of the world, who made me <u>like His will</u>." Women are a reflection of G-d's will, his *ratzone*. They have the emotional, nurturing, caring, and spiritual qualities that are a direct reflection of Godly attributes.

A woman's perspective is usually more intuitive than that of a man. I recently read the following that highlights this fact:

An English professor wrote the following words on a chalkboard and asked his students to punctuate the sentence correctly:

"A woman without her man is nothing."

The males in the class wrote: **"A woman, without her man, is nothing**."

The females in the class wrote: "**A woman: without her, man is nothing**!"

Two entirely different meanings – perspective is everything.

Modesty:

We are commanded to be humble in the face of G-d and to carry ourselves with dignity and self-respect. Both men and women are bound by Torah law that demands a degree of modesty in both dress and behavior. The emphasis that society has placed on the projection of overt sexuality in our dress (or lack thereof) is unfortunate. Even the way we speak or otherwise project ourselves is regulated.

Many great nations and societies have fallen because of decadence, licentiousness, and moral degradation. As Jews, it is our mission to live respectful and dignified lives that set an example for all those around us.

JUDAISM VS. OTHER RELIGIONS

Many Jews are woefully unprepared to discuss comparative religion. It is common to be challenged on a college campus or in some social environments about the basis of one's belief.

A fundamental misunderstanding of the close relationship between Judaism, Christianity, and Islam, has contributed to friction on college campuses and Jews are generally unprepared to deal with this.

Additionally, many Jews who are not traditional have tried to replace Judaism with ideologies and practices that run contrary to Jewish beliefs.

Therefore, it is important to be educated about Judaism and to understand the claims of those who believe in other gods. Only then will we have the tools to refute them.

It is important to note that Judaism is not, per-se, a "religion." If a Christian rejects the tenets of their religion, he is not a Christian. If a Muslim rejects Allah or disrespects Mohammed, he is not considered a member of the Muslim religion.

Jews, on the other hand, are always Jewish. You can reject G-d and not follow any of the commandments, but if you are born from a Jewish mother, you are always a Jew. No matter what political views you hold or how hard you try to reject your Jewish heritage, you are still a Jew. Even if you convert to another religion, you are still Jewish.

Bernie Sanders is Jewish. Andrew Klavin is Jewish. Karl Marx was Jewish. Being an atheist, agnostic, or non-believer, does not change your status as a Jew.

Israeli Prime Minister Golda Meir was famously asked if she believed in G-d. She responded: "I believe in the Jewish People and the Jewish People believe in G-d."

Jews are members of a "People." The shared heritage and descendants of those whose souls were at Mt. Sinai, defines "The Jewish People." Jews cannot escape, no matter how hard they try, the gravity that pulls us towards G-d as we try to understand or explain an invisible force that tugs at our souls.

But that does not stop others from trying to convert or destroy us, whether it be physically or religiously.

The Torah warns us that there will come a time when self-proclaimed prophets may arise who will perform miracles and ask us to follow them. We are directed to reject them. It is critical that every educated Jew learn this section from Devarim, *perek* 13, *pesukim* 2-4.

כי יקום בקרבך נביא או חלם חלום, ונתן אליך אות או מופת. ובא האות והמופת אשר דבר אליך לאמר, נלכה אחרי אלקים אחרים אשר לא ידעתם ונעבדם. לא תשמע אל דברי הנביא ההוא או אל חולם החלום ההוא, כי מנסה ה' אלקיכם אתכם לדעת הישכם אהבים את ה' אלקיכם בכל לבבכם ובכל נפשכם.

If there should stand up in your midst a prophet or a dream-diviner, and he will produce for you a sign or a wonder. And the sign or the wonder comes about, of which he spoke to you saying, 'Let us follow gods of others that you did not know and we will worship them.' Do not listen to the words of that prophet or dream-diviner, for the Lord your G-d is testing you to know whether you love Hashem, your G-d, with all your heart and all your soul.

The Torah recognizes the reality that over time, we will be challenged by proponents of other religions who will try to convince us of the truth of their beliefs. We must be prepared for such confrontations and not just hide in a cloistered environment, trying to avoid such people. One of the dangers of such challenges is that they could lead us to question our own beliefs if we are not fully prepared to answer our detractors. We must understand the foundations of the world's major religions.

Let's take a look at some of these religions. Keep in mind that Judaism is the <u>only one</u> of these that is based on the revelation of G-d's law to the <u>masses</u> – to the entire Jewish nation at Mt. Sinai. The other religions are based on the vision of a single individual and their claims of <u>personal revelation</u>.

Out of approximately 7.8 billion people on our planet, here are the number of adherents to the major religions:

Christians: 2.3 billion

Muslims (Islam): 1.9 billion

Hindus: 1.1 billion

Agnostics and Atheists: apx. 1 billion

Buddhists: 506 million

Shinto's, Jains, Zoroastrians, Satanists, Pagans: apx. 500 million

Chinese Traditionalists and Taoists: 394 million

African Tribalists: 100 million

Sikhs: 23 million

Mormons: 16 million

Jews: 14 million

Jews represented 0.00179% of the world's population (apx. 14 million of 7.8 billion) in the year 2021!

Christianity: The first Christians were Jews who lived during the Roman occupation of Judea in the 2nd Temple period. A man arose who some believed was the messiah, the "anointed one," named either Yeshua or Yehoshua. His name, as cited in the later Greek and Latin translations of the New Testament (the Codex Sinaiticus is the earliest copy from the 1st or 2nd century) was changed to "Jesus Christos," ("Jesus the anointed one").

He lived during a time of war and societal instability. Jewish leadership in Jerusalem was threatened by the large crowds Jesus was influencing as well as by his radical and zealous teachings. He was turned over to the Romans as a rebel. He was arrested after a Passover Seder attended by his apostles (as depicted in Da Vinci's famous painting, The Last Supper). The Romans put him on trial for sedition and he was found guilty and crucified, a common Roman death-sentence at that time.

The Gospel of Mathew (one of the twelve apostles, whose real name was Levi) says that after putting Jesus to death, Pontius Pilate (the Roman leader in Judea) literally "washed his hands" in front of the Jewish crowd and declared himself innocent of having shed his blood. The Jews, according to Mathew, responded: "His blood shall be on us and our children." This gospel has led to over two thousand years of persecution and killing of Jews!

Jesus was buried in a cave in Jerusalem. According to Christian teaching, when his mother went to visit his grave, she saw that the rock covering the entrance to his burial tomb had been moved aside and his grave was empty. His apostles believed that he had been resurrected and had ascended to heaven from the crest of the Mount of Olives.

Keep in mind that Jesus was not a Christian. He was a Jew who preached a return to zealous performance of Jewish practice and some say he was either a member of the Essenes or the Pharisees. He had twelve main followers called "apostles," including Judas, who betrayed Jesus to the Romans (which is the basis of the Christian claim that the Jews killed Jesus).

His two most influential followers were Shaul of Tarsus (Paul) and Shimon bar Yonah (Peter). They both claimed to have had personal revelations from Jesus and were influential in the writing of the New Testament. For Christians, the New Testament succeeds the Torah and literally overrides its teachings. This led to negating most Torah laws including Shabbos and holiday practices, *tallis*, *tefillin*, kashrus, and much more.

Christian theology teaches the primacy of the Trinity, a 3-part god, with "the Father, the Son, and the Holy Ghost" directing the world. Christians teach that Jesus is the son of G-d and that he died for our sins. They claim that one can be forgiven for their sins simply by confessing them and believing in Jesus.

To us as Jews, Christianity contains elements of *avodah zarah* and its practice is tantamount to idol worship, mainly because of its belief in the Trinity.

Islam: It is important to note that Islam began in the 600's of the modern calendar, almost two thousand years after the Jewish nation first settled Israel.

Muhammad was born in Mecca (Saudi Arabia) in 570 CE. Originally, he was a Hanif, a pre-Islamic Arab. The Hanif recognized their having descended from Avraham's son Ishmael and were rigid monotheists, but they had no formal unifying religion to bind their multiple tribes and family clans.

In 610 Muhammad claimed to have received a series of divine revelations from the prophet Gabriel. The written form of this revelation is the Qur'an (Koran), which Muslims claim is the word of the One (G-d). Muhammad won-over a group of dedicated followers and a new religion took root. In 622 he migrated to the city of Yathrib (Medina, in Saudi Arabia).

He saw Islam as a return to the faith of the "prophets" Adam, Noach, Avraham, Moshe, David, Shlomo, and Jesus. He died in 632 and was succeeded by a militaristic caliphate that expanded a series of conquests begun by Muhammad that converted the lands from Pakistan to Morocco and Spain to Islamic control.

The basis of Islamic doctrine is found in the Qur'an which was only in oral form during the life of Muhammad. It was written during the Caliphate of Abu Bakr in the ten years following the death of Muhammad. It contains 114 surahs, or chapters.

The Arabic word for the religion is "Islam;" submission and unwavering obedience of G-d's word. Islam advocates five key pillars of faith.

1. Shahadah: confession of faith
2. Salat: Prayer – believers must pray five times a day
3. Sawm Ramadan: the fast during the month of Ramadan
4. Zakat: giving of charity, 2.5% of one's wealth
5. Hajj: a pilgrimage, at least once in a lifetime, to Mecca.

Islamic religious law is called "Shari'ah."

It also calls for its adherents to follow six articles of faith.

1. Tawhid – Monotheism (belief in only one G-d)
2. Belief in Angels
3. Belief in Prophets and Messengers
4. Belief in Holy Books

5. Belief in a Day of Judgement
6. Belief in Predestination – if G-d wants it to happen, it will happen.

Jews are allowed to enter an Islamic place of worship since the Islamic religion is strictly monotheistic and rejects the Christian Trinity. G-d is called "Allah" and "The One True G-d."

Hinduism: Hinduism is over 4,000 years old and is the world's third largest religion behind Christianity and Islam. Over 95% of its followers live in India. The religion has no specific founder and it is difficult to trace its early history. Most scholars trace its beginning to a period between 2300 BCE and 1500 BCE which would put its founding into the period between Noach and Avraham.

The primary texts of Hindus are the Vedas, composed around 1500 BCE as a collection of verses and hymns written in Sanskrit. Their belief is that these contain the revelations received by ancient saints and sages and that the Vedas transcend time.

Hindus revere many gods and goddesses (they believe that there are 33 million gods) in addition to Brahman, who is believed to be the supreme "god force." Most Hindu families choose to worship one god as their primary deity or "personal god."

Their two key symbols are the om and the swastika. The om symbol is composed of three Sanskrit letters representing sounds that are sacred and used in meditation and chanting. The swastika is a sign of good fortune in Sanskrit. This symbol is seen on many Hindu temples and is prevalent in India (and was appropriated by the Nazis in the 1930's).

Hindus believe in the doctrine of Samsara, the continuous cycle of life, death, and reincarnation. They also believe in Karma as the universal law of cause and effect.

All creatures are believed to have a soul and the goal for all creatures is to reach a state of "moksha" or salvation, ending the cycle of rebirth and becoming part of the "absolute soul." All creatures are revered. Therefore, most Hindus do not eat beef or pork (a large percentage are vegetarian). The majority of Hindus live in India, Nepal, Bangladesh, and Singapore.

Buddhism: This religion was founded in the late 6th century BCE by Siddhartha Gautama, the warrior son of a king in Lumbini, near the foothills of the Himalayas in Nepal. It began as an outgrowth of Hinduism with Siddhartha taking on a role as the first "Buddha;" the "Enlightened" or "Awakened."

He claimed to have taken a series of four celestial chariot rides where he saw from above, human suffering such as old age, illness, and death. He claimed to have realized that the pleasures of the earth are transitory and only cover up human suffering. He is said to have meditated until he reached nirvana (enlightenment) which provided him with the answers to the causes of suffering and a permanent release from it. He began to teach this to others and expanded by teaching his Four Noble Truths. When understood and followed, these are supposed to help one to achieve nirvana, a state of enlightened awareness bringing peace and joy to the adherent.

The "Four Noble Truths" of Buddhism

1. Dukkha: Life is suffering. Pleasures don't bring lasting happiness.
2. Wanting and craving lead to inevitable suffering
3. Suffering has an end

4. The Eight-Fold Path and the Middle Way (practices that lead to righteousness)

Buddhism has grown into a spiritual practice that focuses on personal spiritual development and the acquisition of deep insight into the true nature of our universe. There is no belief in a personal god, but a strong belief that change is possible through belief in morality, meditation, and acquired wisdom. Buddhism also teaches a belief in reincarnation and the existence of multiple Buddhas over time.

There are over 500 million followers of Buddhism in the world, primarily in Cambodia, Thailand, Laos, Myanmar, Tibet, China, Korea, Taiwan, Sri Lanka, and Japan.

Sikhism: Sikhism is the fifth largest religion in the world, with most of its followers living in the Punjab State in the north of India. It was founded in 1469 by guru Nanak (Guru means teacher or master) in Punjab. He and his nine successors shaped its core beliefs. The word "Sikh" means "disciple" or "learner" in Punjabi and their name for the religion is "Gurmat," meaning "the way of the guru." Their community of believers is known as Panth (Path).

Sikhism teaches that Nanak and his nine successors were the ten human gurus and were inhabited by the same spirit. Upon the death of the 10th, guru, Gobind Singh in 1708, this spirit transferred itself to the sacred scripture of Sikhism, the Adi Granth (First Volume).

Sikh's claim that their tradition is separate from Hinduism. Nevertheless, Nanak was raised as a Hindu and was a worshiper of the Hindu god, Vishnu. He taught that devotion to god is an essential liberation from the cycle of life, death, and rebirth, in which all humans are trapped.

Meditation and yoga are key elements of religious practice that seek to help one ascend spiritually to a state of ultimate bliss.

Mormonism: Born in Vermont in 1805, Joseph Smith claimed (in 1823) to have been visited by an angel name Moroni who revealed to him an ancient Hebrew text that had been lost for 1,500 years. This holy text was supposedly engraved on gold plates relating a story of ancient Israelites who came to America. Smith claimed to have unearthed these plates (which he called the "Urrim" and "Thummim"- after the insert in the Temple High Priest's breastplate) and dictated them to his wife and other scribes.

The text of the plates told of an ancient Jewish prophet name Lehi, who, in about 600 BCE was called upon by G-d to lead a group of Jews from Jerusalem to the New World. The Mormons believe that some North American natives descended from these original Jewish settlers (reference my earlier chapter on the 10 Lost Tribes). They also believe that eventually, Jesus appeared to these people and taught them the Christian Gospel.

In 1830 they published <u>The Book of Mormon</u> and in that same year Smith founded the Church of Christ (of Latter-Day Saints) in Fayette, New York. The religion gained converts and established communities in Ohio, Missouri, and Illinois. They were highly criticized for their practices such as polygamy and in 1844, Smith was murdered.

Two years later, Smith's successor, Brigham Young, led an exodus of Mormons from Illinois as they traveled west in search of religious freedom. In 1847 they reached Utah's Great Salt Lake and settled there.

The key beliefs of Mormonism are contained in their 13 Articles of Faith (sound familiar?) and a belief in G-d the Father, his son, and the holy spirit. They believe in modern-day prophets and ongoing revelation. The Book of Mormon is given equal importance with the Bible. One critical deviation from Christianity is the belief that the messiah will establish his new kingdom in North America.

Mormons believe that after death, the spirit leaves the body and moves on to a spirit-world awaiting resurrection. The Plan of Salvation teaches that Heaven is divided into three kingdoms of glory: The Celestial, the Terrestrial, and the Telestial. There, all men and women will go after receiving G-d's judgement. Then, the bodies of the good will be reunited with their spirit and become immortal. The most faithful will go to G-d's Celestial Kingdom. Sinners, known as "The Sons of Perdition" will go to a place called: "Outer Darkness."

I have listed Mormonism as a separate religion from Christianity. It is true that most Mormons do consider themselves to be Christians, but their rejection of much of Christian theology (such as their belief in ongoing revelation and modern prophets) sets them apart.

The Mormon Temple is considered a point of contact, here on earth, with the forces of higher spheres. There are many rituals conducted in their temples (the largest one is in Salt Lake City, Utah) including celestial marriage, family sealings, baptism of the dead, anointing the sick, and more. The faithful do not drink anything containing caffeine, do not get tattoos, don't consume alcohol, and don't smoke, cherishing the body as a "temple." They must tithe (give 10% of their income to the Temple), dress modestly, and honor the family unit.

Most Mormons live in North America, but there is a growing presence in other countries including Israel and parts of Asia and Africa.

A time for some perspective: Now that you have taken a look at many of the world's religions representing billions of followers, it is important to take note of a few common factors that define the foundations of these faiths.

Notice that every one of these religions began with a single founder, self-proclaimed prophet, or teacher. Also, a <u>private</u> revelation or dream was experienced by these individuals. Was anyone else there to hear or witness the revelation?

The Jewish People stood as one at Mount Sinai. Everyone heard and witnessed the revelation of G-d's Ten Statements. They witnessed multiple miracles in Egypt, at the Reed Sea, in the desert, in the Temple in Jerusalem, and over many centuries. For us, it is always "we" and not "he" or "us" and not "him."

Judaism is not a religion with just a single founder or a singular prophet. Yes, Avraham was the first Jew, but he did not write any laws, declare any holidays, or claim any special status. That which we believe and follow came directly from G-d's commandments and His Torah during a span of time in the Sinai Desert when <u>every</u> Jew in the world was there as a witness.

While it is true that the actual words of the Torah went from G-d's "mouth" to Moshe's quill as he wrote-down the Torah, those words were read to the entire Jewish People and later, by the prophets, kings, and scholars, to everyone. As a naturally skeptical and stiff-necked people, wouldn't we have challenged those who transmitted our Mesorah if there was even then slightest doubt that they were not faithfully transcribing G-d's word?

What do we claim?

Tanach teaches that G-d took us out of Egypt with many miracles, took us across the sea, gave us the Torah, took us to Israel, helped us establish a nation and build the Temple.

As a matter of faith and belief I accept the words of the Torah and the traditions of my ancestors. Once I do that, I have no need to seek any other religion or doctrine to help me govern or make sense of my life. There is no place in the life of a Jew for any "successor" religion. We all stood together and heard the voice of G-d over 3,333 years ago.

It is important to expose ourselves to the basic beliefs of other religions so we can have an intelligent discussion about comparative religious subjects. If you want to meditate, there is plenty of room within Judaism for that. If you want to do yoga, be my guest. Taking things anywhere beyond that by seeking comfort or meaning in other religions or by trying to fill some kind of emotional void, can lead one down a very steep and dangerous slope.

The best thing we can do to fill any gaps is to delve into the secrets of Judaism by studying and decoding Tanach and the commentaries.

We must educate ourselves and learn the basic beliefs of Judaism as lifelong students of _our_ religion.

BIBLICAL NAMES WE ALL NEED TO KNOW

This is a glossary of some of the men and women who appear in the Torah and Nach. One needs to be familiar with them in order to have a working knowledge of Jewish history.

The names have been alphabetized using a common English version of their name, a transliteration where appropriate, the Hebrew spelling, and a short explanation of that individual's significance in Jewish history. If they are not mentioned in the Torah, I have included where they can be found in *Neviim* or *Kesuvim*.

A:

Aaron (Aharon) אהרן : older brother of Moshe, first High Priest

Abel (Hevel) הבל : 2nd son of Adam and Eve, killed by Cain

Achashverosh אחשורוש : (Book of Esther) King of Persia/Media who made Esther his queen

Adam אדם : first man, formed by G-d from the dust of the earth

Agag אגג : (Shmuel I, 15:8) King of Amalek, King Saul let him live, the prophet Shmuel killed him. Ancestor of Haman

Ahab (Ach'av) אחאב : (Book of Kings I) wicked king of Northern Kingdom of Israel

Amalek עמלק : grandson of Eisav, perpetual enemy of Israel

Amram עמרם : father of Moshe (and Aharon, Miriam)

Asenas (Osnas) אסנת : daughter of Dina (fathered by Shechem), taken to Egypt and adopted by Potifar, became wife of Yosef

Asher אשר : son of Yaakov, head of one of 12 tribes, father of Serach (woman who kept Yaakov's tradition alive throughout Egyptian bondage)

Avigayil אביגיל : (Shmuel I, perek 25) third wife of King David, known as a righteous and exceedingly beautiful woman, one of 7 female prophetesses (see Esther below)

Avimelech אבימלך : king of Gerar, tried to take Sarah from Avraham, made a pact with him

Avishai אבישי : (Book of Samuel I) general of King David's army, rescued David from Goliath's brother, Yishbi B'nov

Avram (later, Avraham) אברם – אברהם : first Jew, fought idolatry, husband of Sarah, father of Yishmael and Yitzchak, G-d made lasting covenant with Avraham (Bris Bein Habesarim).

B:

Balak בלק : King of Moav, sorcerer, sought to destroy B'nei Yisrael

Barak ברק : (Shoftim, perek 4) general of army of Israel, Midrash says he was the husband of the prophetess Devorah, led army against Sisera

Bathsheba בת שבע : (Shmuel II, perek 11) wife of King David, mother of King Solomon

Belshazzar בלשאצר : son of Nebuchadnezzar King of Bavel, calculated the 70 years of the First Temple exile incorrectly and was punished for using the Temple vessels at a banquet (story of "writing on the wall," Daniel, perek 5).

Benjamin (Binyamin) בנימין : youngest son of Yaakov (and Rachel), head of one of the 12 tribes, only son born in Eretz Yisrael

Bil'am בלעם : prophet and sorcerer, advisor to Pharaoh, hired by Balak to put a curse on Israel but ended up blessing them instead with the words we use in our daily davening: מה טבו אהליך יעקב, משכנתיך ישראל

Bilhah בלהה : maidservant of Rachel, mother to Dan and Naphtali

Besuel בתואל : father of Rivka, King of Aram Naharaim

Bezalel בצלאל : architect of the Mishkan (Tabernacle) and the holy vessels

Boaz בעז : (Ruth, perek 2) married Ruth, great-grandfather of King David.

C:

Cain קין : oldest son of Adam and Eve, killed Abel his brother

Caleb כלב : one of two spies (with Joshua) who was in favor of fighting for Eretz Yisrael, some say he was Miriam's husband, entered Eretz Yisrael with Joshua following the death of Moshe.

Canaan כנען : son of Cham, grandson of Noach, Midrash B'reishis Rabbah says that he became Eliezer, the servant of Avraham. Earliest name of Eretz Yisrael was "Eretz Canaan"

Cozbi כזבי : daughter of Tzur the King of Moav (some say Tzur was Balak), sinned immorally and publicly with Zimri and was impaled on a spear thrust by Pinchas.

D:

Dan דן : son of Yaakov, head of one of the 12 tribes

Daniel דניאל : (see Book of Daniel) prophet, survived being thrown into the den of lions in Babylon, interpreted dreams of the king, some say he was either Memuchan or Hasach in Megillas Esther.

Dathan (Dasan) דתן : wicked leader who repeatedly rebelled (along with his co-conspirator Aviram) against Moshe and Aharon. The Midrash says that Dasan and Aviram were the two men who were quarreling in Egypt when Moshe encountered them (Sh'mos 2:13) and also rebelled at the Reed Sea demanding that Moshe return the Jews to Egypt.

David (King David) דוד המלך : (Book of Shmuel 1) shepherd, killed Goliath, became first King of Israel from tribe of Yehuda, moved the Ark to Jerusalem from Givah, wrote Tehillim (Psalms), expanded Land of Israel, father of King Solomon

Deborah (Devorah) דבורה : (Book of Shoftim, Judges, perek 4) one of the 7 prophetesses, taught Torah to the public, Devorah and Barak led the war against Sisera at Mt. Tabor.

Delilah דלילה : (Book of Shoftim, Judges, perek 16) tempted Shimshon (Samson), became his wife, tricked him, cut off his hair and turned him over to the Philistines

Dina דינה : daughter of Yaakov and Leah who went out of the camp to "look at the daughters of the land..." (B'reishis 34:1) and was violated by Shechem. She bore Asenas who was sent to Egypt (Gemara Bava Basra 15b says she married Job – Iyuv).

E:

Eglon עגלון : (Book of Shoftim, perek 3) grandson of Balak King of Moav, Gemara says in Nazir 23b that his granddaughter was Ruth whom he merited having because he stood in respect for a message from G-d delivered by Ehud ben Gerah.

Elazar אלעזר : third son of Aharon, father of Pinchas, became High Priest after death of Aharon, oversaw the dividing of the Land of Israel among the tribes after the initial conquest by Yehoshua

Eldad and **Medad** מידד, אלדד : had not been chosen as elders by Moshe, but had prophecy in the camp of Israel (Bamidbar, perek 11), Midrash says they were Moshe's half-brothers (from when his mother, Yocheved, had been divorced by Amram and married Elizafan ben Parnach)

Eli עלי : (Book of Shmuel I, perek 1) High Priest (he was known as "*Eli Ha'Kohen*"), head of Sanhedrin, promised Channah she would have a son (who became Samuel the Prophet)

Eliezer אליעזר : Avraham's faithful servant, sent as messenger to bring a wife (Rivka) for Yitzchak

Elijah (Eliyahu) אליהו : (Book of Melachim, Kings, perek 17) known as *Eliyahu Ha'Navi* (Eliyahu the Prophet), challenged and defeated the prophets of Baal at Mt. Carmel, will herald the coming of the Mashiach.

Elimelech אלימלך : (Ruth, perek 1) leader of Israel, husband of Naomi, during severe famine in Israel fled with his family to Moav fearing that too many neighbors would want financial assistance, was punished with death

Elisha אלישע : (Book of Melachim, Kings, perek 19) disciple of Eliyahu Ha'Navi, prophet, performed many miracles, brought son of the Shunamis back to life (Melachim II, perek 4)

Elkanah אלקנה : (Book of Shmuel I, perek 1) father of Shmuel, righteous leader of his generation, husband of Channah

Elkanah son of Korach אלקנה בן קרח : repented as the ground opened to swallow Korach and his followers

Ephraim אפרים : head of one of the 12 tribes, younger son of Yosef

Ephron עפרון : sold the Cave of Machpelah in Hebron to Avraham as a family burial tomb

Esau (Esav) עשו : twin brother of Yaakov, sold his birthright to Yaakov, his descendants founded Rome, commentaries say that he gave tremendous honor to his father and mother

Esther אסתר : (Megillah of Esther), other name was "Hadassah," heroine of Purim story, considered one of the 4 most beautiful women ever to live (the other 3 as described in Gemara Megillah 15a, are Sarah, Rachav, and Avigail), adopted and raised by Mordechai, one of the seven prophetesses (Sarah, Miriam, Devorah, Channah, Avigayil, Chuldah, Esther), her son with Achashverosh, Darius II (Daryavesh), allowed the Jews to return to Jerusalem to rebuild the Temple.

Eve (Chavah) חוה : first woman, created from Adam, mother of Cain, Hevel, and Seth (Shais), ate the forbidden fruit in the Garden of Eden, buried in the Cave of Machpelah (which Avraham later purchased)

Ever (Ay'ver) עבר : grandson of Noach's son Shem, teacher to Avraham, Yitzchak, and Yaakov ("Yeshiva" of Shem and Ever)

Ezekiel (Yechezkel) יחזקאל : (Book of Yechezkel) prophet, mocked by the populace of Israel, prophesied destruction of the First Temple, story of resurrection of the dead – Valley of the Dry Bones.

Ezra עזרא : (Book of Nechemia, perek 8), led the first return to Jerusalem from Babylonia, known as *"Ezra Ha'Sofer"* – Ezra the Scribe, established many new customs (including reading the Torah on Monday, Thursday, and Shabbos Mincha), leader of his generation

G:

Gad גד : leader of one of the 12 tribes, son of Yaakov

Gad גד : (Book of Shmuel) prophet and advisor to King David

Gideon גדעון : (Book of Shoftim, Judges, perek 6) a judge and military leader who led 300 men of Israel to war against Midian and Amalek.

Goliath (Gol'yas) גלית : (Book of Samuel 1, perek 17) giant and warrior who fought for the Philistines, killed with slingshot by David, descended from Orpah (from the Book of Ruth) along with 4 giant brothers, Saph, Madon, Yisbi B'Nov, and Lachmi, killed the two sons of Eli Ha'Kohen; Chofni and Pinchas

H:

Habakuk (Chavakuk) חבקוק : (Book of Trei-Asar) prophet of Israel, prophesied the saving of Chananyah, Mishael, and Azariah who were thrown into the fiery furnace in Babylon, Zohar says that he was the child of the Shunami woman who was saved from death by Elisha

Hagar הגר : handmaid of matriarch Sarah, mother of Yishmael, sent away following the birth of Yitzchak, returned to Egypt (Midrash says she was a daughter of Pharaoh), following death of Sarah, Avraham married her (she had re-taken her Egyptian name; *Keturah*).

Haggai חגי : (Book of Trei Asar) prophet, according to Zohar he was one of the last 3 prophets along with Zecharyah and Malachi, Gemara Megillah says he prophesied following the reign of Esther, during the time of her son Darius II.

Ham (Cham) חם : one of Noach's three sons, sinned following the flood by violating his father and was banished.

Haman המן : (Book of Esther) descendant of Amalek king Agag, attempted to destroy the Jews, was hanged with his sons, prototypical enemy of Israel

Hananiah and **Mishael, Azariah** חנניה, מישאל, עזריה : (Book of Daniel) three Jewish servants of King Nebuchadnezzar, refused to bow to Babylonian idols, were thrown into a fiery furnace and emerged unscathed (also known by their Babylonian names Shadrach, Meshach, Avadnego)

Hannah (Channah) חנה : (Book of Samuel I, perek 1) righteous woman and one of the seven prophetesses, wife of Elkanah, could not have children, prayed at the Mishkan, was promised by Eli Ha'Kohen that she would have a child. She bore Samuel (who became Shmuel Ha'navi)

Hezekiah (Chizkiyahu) חזקיהו : (Book of Kings II) King of Israel three centuries after King Solomon. Influenced by the prophet Isaiah, became righteous king, prepared Jerusalem for war with the Assyrians and redirected the waters of the Gichon spring into the city

Hulda (Chuldah) חולדה : (Book of Kings II) one of the seven prophetesses, relative of prophet Jeremiah, merciful and gentle, the gates at the south entrance of the Temple in Jerusalem were named for her.

I:

Isaac (Yitzchak) יצחק : son of Avraham and Sarah, half-brother to Ishmael, one of the three patriarchs, brought by Avraham as an offering (the Akeidah) on Mt. Moriah, married Rivka, father of Yaakov and Esav

Isaiah (Yeshayahu) ישעיהו : (Book of Isaiah) prophet, advisor to multiple kings, was killed by King Menashe (the wicked son of Chizkiyahu) after warning of impending punishment by G-d for the worship of false gods

Isamar איתמר : youngest son of Aharon

Ish Boshess איש בשת : (Book of Samuel II) son of King Saul, following the death of Saul and three of his sons at the battle with the Philistines at Mt. Gilboa, Avner (the captain of Saul's army) declared Ish Boshess the king. The tribe of Yehuda seceded and declared David as their king. Ish Boshess was assassinated by two of his own army captains, leading to David becoming king of the entire country.

Ishmael (Yishmael) ישמעאל : son of Avraham and Hagar, exiled by Avraham following birth of Yitzchak, patriarch of the Arab nations

Issachar (Yissachar) יששכר : son of Yaakov, head of one of the twelve tribes, Midrash says that his tribe studied Torah while being supported by sea-merchants of the Tribe of Zevulun (B'reishis Rabbah 72:5)

J:

Jacob (Yaakov) יעקב : son of Yitzchak, one of the three patriarchs, purchased birthright from twin brother Esav, fled to Aram and lived with Lavan's family, married Leah and Rachel and had 12 sons and one daughter with them and with two concubines, Bilhah and Zilpah, descended to Egypt with his entire family (70 people) in his old age

Japheth (Yaphes) יפת : one of Noach's three sons, ancestor of the Greek nation

Jeremiah (Yirmiyahu) ירמיהו : (Book of Jeremiah) prophet of the First Temple period, descendant of Joshua and Rachav, prophesied destruction of Israel, rebuked the people for their sins, wrote Eicha (Lamentations).

Jeroboam (Yeravam) ירבעם : (Book of Kings I) after death of King Solomon (and Rechavam becoming king), led revolution against the

Southern Kingdom of Israel (Yehuda and Binyamin) and became king of the northern kingdom of 10 tribes. He erected two golden calves in Dan and Beit-el and declared that there was no need for the populace to pray in the Temple.

Jesse (Yishai) ישי : (Book of Samuel I) father of King David, Gemara in Shabbos 55b says that he was one of the four most righteous and sinless men in Jewish history (Binyamin, Amram, Yishai, Kilav ben David)

Jethro (Yisro) יתרו : Moshe's father-in-law, priest of Midian, advisor to Pharaoh who left Egypt after counseling Pharaoh not to kill the Jewish children, gave Moshe advice on how to manage his leadership role

Jezebel (Ezevel) איזבל : (Book of Kings I) wicked wife of King Achav who led the people of the Northern Kingdom to sin

Joab (Yoav) יואב : (Book of Samuel 1) general of King David's army, led the conquest of the city of Jerusalem (from the Jebusites)

Job (Iyov) איוב : (Book of Job) righteous and blessed man who was challenged by Satan to see if he would change if his blessings were taken away. Some say he had been an advisor to Pharaoh.

Jonah (Yonah) יונה : (Book of Trei Asar) prophet chosen by G-d to bring a message of impending destruction to the king of Nineveh in Assyria, subject of story of being thrown into the sea and swallowed by a great fish, eventually continued on his journey to Nineveh where the king and populace repented

Jonathan (Yehonasan) יהונתן : (Book of Samuel I) son of King Saul, faithful friend to David (who became king)

Joseph (Yosef) יוסף : favored son of Yaakov, sold by his brothers into slavery, became viceroy of Egypt and advisor to Pharaoh, reconciled with his brothers and arranged for them to move to Egypt, married Osnas and fathered Menashe and Ephraim who became tribal leaders in his stead

Joshua (Yehoshua) יהושע : one of the 12 spies, second in command to Moshe, received the Mesorah directly from him, became leader following Moshe's death and led the conquest of Israel

Judah (Yehuda) יהודה : son of Yaakov, head of one of the twelve tribes, Davidic Dynasty emerged from Judah and Tamar (Boaz, husband of Ruth and great-grandfather of King David, was a descendant)

K:

Koheles קהלת : (Megillah of Koheles) one of the three names of King Solomon; Koheles, Yedidyah, Shlomo

Keturah קטורה : Egyptian name of Hagar, 2nd wife of Avraham

Korach קרח : descendant of Levi who claimed that Moshe was abusing his leadership, wanted position as leader for himself, led rebellion against Moshe and Aharon, Midrash says he was exceedingly wealthy from having found Yosef's treasure (from the grain he sold during the famine in Egypt), he and his co-conspirators died when the earth split and swallowed them

L:

Laban (Lavan) לבן : father of Leah and Rachel, father-in-law of Yaakov, practitioner of black magic, idol worshiper

Leah לאה : eldest daughter of Lavan, married Yaakov by taking the place of her sister Rachel, one of the Four Matriarchs (Sarah, Rivka, Leah,

Rachel), mother of 6 of the tribal leaders (Reuven, Yehuda, Levi, Shimon, Yissachar, Zevulun) and Dina

Levi לוי : one of Yaakov's twelve sons, outlived all his brothers, the slavery in Egypt did not begin until after his death. Both the Kohanim and Leviim descended from his great-great grandsons Aharon and Moshe (they were the two sons of Amram who was the son of Yitzhar the son of Kehas the son of Levi).

Lot לוט : nephew of Avraham (his brother Haran's son), was rescued by an angel before the destruction of Sodom, fled with his daughters (his wife was turned into a pillar of salt when she turned to look at the destruction), father of Moav and Midian (after committing incest to repopulate the world, thinking the world had been destroyed). Ruth and the Davidic Dynasty eventually descended from him.

M:

Machlon (and **Chilion**) מחלון, כליון : (Book of Ruth) sons of Elimelech and Naomi, married Moavi women (Ruth and Orpah), died, as did their father Elimelech, for having left Israel during a time of famine and not staying to support their countrymen

Malachi מלאכי : (Book of Trei Asar) one of the last prophets (along with Chagai and Zechariah), Gemara in Megillah says that he was Mordechai

Medad – see **Eldad**

Menasheh מנשה : eldest son of Yosef, head of one of the 12 tribes

Menasheh מנשה : (Book of Kings II) evil king of Yehuda, son of King Chizkiyahu (Hezekiah), brought idols into the Temple, killed Yeshayahu (Isaiah) the prophet

Michal מיכל : (Book of Samuel, perek 14) daughter of King Saul, helped David escape from her father's palace, married King David after her sister Merav died

Miriam מרים : sister of Aharon and Moshe, one of the seven prophetesses, was sent by her mother Yocheved to follow Moshe when he was placed in a basket on the Nile River, struck with leprosy (*tsaraas*) for speaking *lashon harah* about Moshe. The well providing water for the Jews in the desert dried-up when she died.

Mordechai מרדכי : (Book of Esther) uncle of Esther, member of the Great Assembly (*Anshei Knessess Ha'Gedolah*), urged Esther to save the Jews (in the Purim story).

Moses (Moshe) משה : greatest of all prophets, most humble man to ever live (Bamidbar 12:3), leader of B'nei Yisrael, came to Pharaoh to demand freedom for the Jewish People (10 plagues), led Jews out of Egypt and across the Yam Suf (Reed Sea), received the Torah on Mt. Sinai, wrote-down the first Torah as directed by G-d, oversaw construction of the Mishkan, trained Yehoshua to take his place, died at the age of 120 corresponding to the 120 total days he spent on Mt. Sinai (3 trips of 40 days each)

N:

Nadav and **Avihu** נדב, אביהו : two of Aharon's sons who were consumed by fire when they brought an "alien" incense offering (Vayikra 10:1) to the Mishkan and died on the 8th day of its dedication

Naomi נעמי : (Megillas Ruth) Ruth's mother-in-law, returned from Moav to Israel after her family's death, Ruth returned with her, Ruth married Boaz and had a child, Megillas Ruth 4:17 writes that Naomi's neighbors said: "A child (Oved) is born to Naomi" (perhaps the birth of a grandchild was consolation for her loss of husband and two sons in Moav).

Naphtali נפתלי : son of Yaakov, leader of one of the twelve tribes, Midrash says that he is the one who brought word to Yaakov that Yosef was alive in Egypt.

Nathan (Nassan) נתן : (Book of Samuel II) early prophet, advisor to Kings David and Solomon

Nebuchadnezzar נבוכדנצר : (Book of Kings II) king of Babylon, destroyed 1st Temple in Jerusalem, Midrash says he was the grandson of King Solomon and the Queen of Sheba. Queen Vashti (from Megillas Esther) was his granddaughter (see Gemara Megillah 10b).

Nehemiah (Nechemiah) נחמיה : (Book of Nehemiah) returned to Israel following the exile in Babylon and helped rebuild the Temple, composed the Book of Ezra, became the governor of Persian-ruled Judea

Nimrod נמרד : Mesopotamian king who built the Tower of Babel, also known as "Cush," threw Avram into the fiery furnace

Noah (Noach) נח : most righteous man of his generation, born in the tenth generation from creation, commanded by G-d to build the ark, survived the Great Flood

O:

Obadia (Ovadiah) עובדיה : (Book of Trei Asar) prophet, predicted the downfall of the descendants of Esav for having persecuted Israel

Og עוג : king of Bashan, enemy of the Jews (some say that he was Eliezer the servant of Avraham), Moshe waged war against him (and his brother, Sichon, king of the Emori). The Midrash says that Og lived since the days of Noach and survived the flood by attaching himself to the ark (Og is associated with evil and the Midrash may be allegorically telling us that "evil" survived the flood).

Orpah ערפה : (Book of Ruth) daughter-in-law of Naomi, after her husband Chilion died she returned to her home (that of Eglon, king of Moav), Five giants descended from her (Goliath, Saph, Madon, Yishbi B'nov, and Lachmi)

P:

Peninah פנינה (Book of Samuel I, perek 4) one of the two wives of Elkanah (the other being Hannah – Channah), derided Channah who could not have children (Channah eventually became the mother of Samuel the prophet, Shmuel Ha'navi)

Pharaoh (Par'oh) פרעה : generic term for an Egyptian king, earliest mention in the Torah was Avraham descending to Egypt and Pharaoh trying to take Sarah from him. This term is used to describe all Egyptian monarchs until the late Roman period. It is postulated by many scholars that Necco I and Necco II were the Pharaohs during the time of Yosef and up to the time of the slavery in Egypt (although the Midrash says that it was Pharaoh Necco who stole the throne of King Solomon and brought it to Egypt, so that dynasty appears to have begun later).

Phineas (Pinchas) פנחס : son of Elazar ben Aharon the Kohen Gadol, took retribution against Cozbi and Zimri when they sinned openly, zealous warrior, some say he was one of the two spies (with Calev) that Moshe sent in Parshas Chukas (Va'yikra 21:32) to spy on the land of Sichon, and the same two men (Calev and Pinchas) were sent later by Joshua to spy-out the city of Jericho (Joshua 2:1)

Phineas ben Eli (Pinchas ben Elie) פנחס בן עלי : (Book of Samuel I) became the Kohen Gadol after his father Eli Ha'Kohen "retired" because he had become old and infirm. He and his brother Chafni were captured and killed by Goliath who was seeking retribution for Pinchas the son of Elazar having killed his ancestor, Kozbi. King David, when he picked up the stones for his slingshot, is said to have picked one of the stones to represent retribution for the killing of Pinchas (Midrash Shmuel).

Puah (and **Shifra**) פועה, שפרה : Gemara in Sotah (11b) says that she was Miriam, sister of Moshe, and that Shifra was Yocheved, his mother; midwives in Egypt who defied the orders of Pharaoh to kill the Jewish babies

R:

Rachel רחל : one of the Four Matriarchs, favored wife of Yaakov, mother to Yosef, stole her father's small idols (*t'raphim*), died in childbirth (of Binyamin) and was buried on the side of the road that leads from Hebron to Jerusalem in what is now Bethlehem (*Bais Lechem*).

Rahab (Rachav) רחב : (Book of Joshua, perek 2) described as a harlot who was, according to the Gemara, one of the four most beautiful woman to ever live (Gemara Megillah 15a), hid the spies in Jericho, Gemara in Megillah also says she became the wife of Joshua and that eight prophets descended from her

Rebecca (Rivka) רבקה : one of the Four Matriarchs, married Yitzchak, mother to Yaakov and Eisav, aided Yaakov in getting the blessing from Yitzchak

Rechavam רחבעם : (Book of Kings II) son of King Solomon, became first king of Yehuda (the Southern Kingdom) after the split between Yehuda and Yisrael (which had Yeravam as its first king)

Reuben (Reuven) ראובן : firstborn of Yaakov's sons, head of one of the twelve tribes, returned to the pit to save Yosef but was too late (B'reishis 37:29)

Ruth רות : (Book of Ruth) princess of Moav, married Machlon (one of the sons of Elimelech and Naomi), converted to Judaism, returned to Israel with Naomi, prototypical example of a righteous convert, gleaned for grain in the fields of Boaz, married him, gave birth to Oved, and was the great-grandmother of King David

S:

Samson (Shimshon) שמשון : (Book of Judges) one of the judges between the time of Joshua and King Saul, a Nazirite (did not cut his hair, drink wine, etc.), conducted a personal war against the Philistines, man of great strength (the Gemara in Sotah 10a refers to his strength as supernatural). His marriage to Delilah was his downfall as she got him drunk, cut his hair, and turned him over to the Philistines. After they blinded him, he took revenge by collapsing their temple, killing himself along with the temple spectators.

Samuel (Shmuel) שמואל : (Book of Shmuel) prophet during the time of King Saul, given by his mother (Channah) when he was a child to Eli Ha'Kohen as an apprentice, one of the greatest of the early prophets in Neviim, killed Agag the king of Amalek (who King Saul had allowed to live).

Sarah שרה : first of the Four Matriarchs, wife of Avraham, mother of Yitzchak, first prophetess, demanded that Avraham send away Hagar and Yishmael, died after the Akeidah (the offering of Yitzchak on Mt. Moriah), buried in the Cave of the Patriarchs (Maaras Hamachpelah) purchased by Avraham.

Saul (Shaul) שאול : (Book of Samuel I) first king of Israel, from the tribe of Binyamin (David's lineage was from Yehudah), conquered the Amalek nation but failed to kill their king, Agag, killed the priests of the city of Nov for harboring and feeding David, fought against the Philistines and was badly wounded, fell on his own sword to avoid capture and died alongside three of his sons; Jehonasan, Avinadav, and Malchishuah.

Sennacherib (Sannecheriv) סנחריב : (Book of Kings II) king of the Assyrians who fought against and exiled the seven tribes of northern Israel and the three tribes on the eastern side of the Jordan (Reuven, Gad, Menashe), established a siege against Jerusalem during the reign of Hezekiah but was foiled by a miracle in which 185,000 of his soldiers died in one night

Serach שרח : daughter of Asher, one of the most righteous women of her generation (spanning the lives of Yosef and Moshe), lived a very long time and provided the location of the burial-place of Yosef to Moshe just before the exodus from Egypt, Midrash says she was the first to recognize Moshe as the one who would deliver the Jews from Egypt (Sh'mos Rabbah 5:13)

Shem שם : son of Noah, Midrash says he taught our Patriarchs (Yeshiva of Shem and Ayver), Jews are descended from him (thus we are called "Shemites" which has been shortened to "Semites"), Zohar says that Shem was the repository of the world's history that he learned from Enosh, who had learned from Adam's third son Seth (Shais)

Shimi (known as Shimi ben Gera) שמעי בן גרא : (Book of Samuel II, perek 16) from the family of Saul, threw rocks at King David and cursed at him, reconciled and became the teacher of David's son - Solomon

Shimon שמעון : one of the twelve sons of Yaakov, leader of his tribe, massacred the clan of Shechem and Chamor (along with his brother

Levi), after the violation of Dena, threw Yosef into the pit, was the one who Yosef threw into prison in Egypt

Solomon שלמה : (Book of Kings I) son of King David (from Batsheva), considered among the wisest of all men, also known as Yedidyah and Koheles, greatly expanded the borders of Israel, is said to have had 1,000 wives, built the First Temple in Jerusalem, wrote <u>Shir Ha'Shirim</u> – Song of Songs, <u>Mishlei</u> (The Book of Proverbs), and <u>Koheles</u> (Ecclesiastes), experienced a period of banishment after being punished for having too many wives, too many horses, and for overtaxing the people to expand his treasury

T:

Tamar תמר : married Er (son of Yehuda) who died, then married Yehuda's second son (Onan) who also died. B'reishis perek 38 tells the story of her enticement of Yehuda her father-in-law and the subsequent birth of her son from him; Perez, who became the ancestor of Boaz and led to the dynasty of King David. She is considered by the commentaries to have acted righteously with Yehuda.

Terach תרח : father of Avram (Avraham), Midrash states that he was a manufacturer of idols, left Ur Casdim with Avram after the incident with the breaking of the idols and Avram's being thrown into the fiery furnace by Nimrod

U:

Uriah אוריה : (Book of Samuel II, perek 11) husband of Bathsheba, sent to his death at the front lines in battle by King David (David then married Bathsheba)

V:

Vashti ושתי : (Book of Esther, perek 1) wicked daughter of the king of Babylon, Nebuchadnezzar, wife of King Achashverosh of Shushan who killed her because she would not come to his party as he had ordered. This led to Esther being chosen as the new queen.

Y:

Yael יעל : (Book of Judges, perek 4) woman who drove a tent peg through the head of the enemy general Sisera at the battle of Mt. Tabor (led by Devorah and Barak) and killed him

Yehuda יהודה: see Judah

Yeravam ירבעם: see Jeroboam

Yiphtach יפתח : (Book of Judges, perek 11) a member of the tribe of Ephraim who agreed to lead a battle against Ammon. He made a vow to G-d that if he would win the battle, when he came home, the first thing to approach him from the door of his home would be offered as a sacrifice. When he came home, his daughter came out to greet him. Even though he did not offer her as a sacrifice she was isolated from her people as a fulfillment of the vow.

Yochebed יוכבד : mother of Moshe, Aharon, Miriam, also called "Shifra" in the first perek of Shemos, wife of Amram from the tribe of Levi

Z:

Zechariah זכריה : (Book of Zechariah) prophet during the time of Darius and the rebuilt Second Temple, one of the last three to receive prophecy

Zelophechad צלפחד : the "gatherer of sticks" as described in Bamidbar perek 26) who was killed for his sin performed on Shabbos. He had no sons to inherit him and his five righteous daughters (Machlah, Noah, Chaglah, Milkah, Tirza) asked Moshe to allot them an inheritance in Israel. He gave them what is referred-to as the חצי שבט מנשה (the portion of half the tribe of Menashe) located in the Golan Heights on the east side of the Jordan River.

Zeresh זרש : (Book of Esther) wicked wife of Haman

Zevulun זבלון : son of Yaakov, one of the leaders of the twelve tribes, tribe became seagoing traders and merchants and supported the tribe of Yissachar so they could study Torah

Zilpah זלפה : maidservant of Leah, mother of Gad and Asher

Zimri זמרי : prince of the tribe of Shimon, sinned publicly with Cozbi, killed by Pinchas

Zipporah צפרה : daughter of Yisro, wife of Moshe, mother to Gershom and Eliezer

QUOTES TO LIVE BY

The following is a collection of selected inspirational and thought-provoking quotes.

It is helpful to hear the perspective of those who came before us. That which they experienced and wrote about can provide us with affirmation and strength, helping us to deal with the many cares, fears, and frustrations of our modern world.

It is important to read the words of those who lived before us and to reflect on our common thoughts, emotions, and desires.

I have been collecting quotes in a notebook for over 40 years. Some of the reference books I use regularly are <u>Words of the Wise</u> by Reuven Alcalay, <u>Dictionary of Quotations</u> by Bergen Evans, quotes from secular newspaper columns, famous authors, politicians, Greek and Roman philosophers, and many others. The door to my office is covered with many quotes and satirical cartoons that provide me with some much-needed humor and perspective.

King Solomon wrote in Koheles (Ecclesiastes 1:9) *"What has been will be again, what has been done will be done again. There is nothing new under the sun"* (אין... חדש תחת השמש). It is comforting to know that those who preceded us had many of the same challenges that we have. Their words may be unique but they describe a human condition which has not changed.

Even though many of these quotes are from secular leaders, historical figures (including some of our enemies), writers, and musicians, they have been included because of their relevance to contemporary life and their reflections on our collective experiences.

A:

ADVICE:

שומע לעצה חכם : (Mishlei - Proverbs) "A wise man listens to advice"

קל יותר לתן עצה לאחר מלעצמו : (Reb Nachman of Breslov) "It is easier to give advice to others than to yourself"

"Advice is judged by results, not by intentions" (Cicero)

מרבה עצה מרבה תבונה : (Mishna Avos 2:7) "The more advice, the more understanding"

ANGER:

כבד אבן ונטל החול, וכעס אויל כביד משניהם : (Mishlei - Proverbs) "A rock is heavy as is sand, but the anger of a fool is heavier than both put together"

בשלשה דברים אדם ניכר: בכוסו, ובכיסו, ובכעסו : (Gemara Eruvin 65b) "A man's character is revealed through three things: his cup (how he acts when drunk), his pocket (what he does with his money), and his anger"

"Anyone can become angry – that is easy, but to be angry with the right person, to the right degree, at the right time, for the right purpose, and in the right way – that is not easy" (Aristotle)

"When angry, count to ten before you speak; if very angry, count to one hundred" (Thomas Jefferson)

ASPIRATION

"The higher I get, the higher I want to be" (translation of popular Ladino saying)

אם לא תשאף לגדולות, עד הקטנות לא תבוא : (Rabbi Dov Ber Schneur 2nd Lubavitcher Rebbe in <u>Imrei Binah</u>) "If you do not aspire to do great things, you will not even accomplish the small ones"

"The youth gets together his materials to build a bridge to the moon, or perchance to build a palace or temple on earth, and at length, the middle-aged man concludes to build a woodshed with them" (Thoreau)

B:

BEAUTY

שקר החן והבל היפי : (Mishlei - Proverbs) "Charm is deceitful and beauty is vain"

ברוך שברא בריות נאות בעולמו : (Gemara B'rachos Yerushalmi 9a) "Blessed is the One who created beautiful things in His world"

"The saying 'beauty is but skin' deep is a skin-deep saying" (Spencer)

BEGINNING

התחלת – גמור (Midrash B'reishis Rabbah) "Once you begin – finish"

"Well begun is half done" (Horace)

"The beginning is always today" (Mary Shelley)

"The beginning is the most important part of the work" (Plato)

"The difference between a beginning teacher and an experienced one is that the beginning teachers asks: 'How am I doing?' and the experienced teacher asks: 'How are the children doing?'" (anonymous)

"There is no worse failure than a beginning that stops there" (Bialik)

BELIEF & BELIEVING

"Whoever does not see G-d everywhere does not see him anywhere" (Kotzker Rebbe)

"A believer asks no questions, while no answer can satisfy an unbeliever" (anonymous)

אם לא תאמינו כי לא תאמנו : (Isaiah 7:9) "If you do not believe others you will not be believed yourselves"

A popular saying: "Those who do not believe in G-d do not believe in 'nothing.' They believe in anything!"

"Nothing is so firmly believed as that about which we know the least" (Montaigne)

"Man prefers to believe what he prefers to be true" (Francis Bacon)

"I am always at a loss to know how much to believe of my own stories" (Washington Irving)

"To wish to talk to G-d is absurd. We cannot talk to one we cannot comprehend and cannot comprehend G-d. We can only believe in Him" (Kant)

אי אפשר לבוא לאמונה אלא על ידי אמת : (Reb Nachman of Breslov) "It is impossible to come to belief unless you know the truth"

BITTER

לא ידע אנש טעמה דמתיקה עד דטעם מרירה : (Zohar) "Man does not know the taste of sweet until he knows the taste of bitter"

"Only courageous hearts can bear the bitterness of truth" (Johnson)

"When bitter, say little; when angry, say nothing; when happy, say much; when joyful, say all" (Jabulani Dhliwayo)

"Bitter people are those who are not happy with themselves and cannot possibly be happy with you" (anonymous)

"I learned a long time ago not to wrestle with a pig. You get dirty. And besides, the pig likes it!" (George Bernard Shaw)

BLESSING

כשם שמברך על הטובה כך מברך על הרעה : (Vayikra 19:14) "In the same way you bless G-d for the good, bless Him for the bad"

אין הברכה שרויה אלא במי שיושב במקום אחד : (Gemara Taanis 8b) "There is no blessing unless one stays in one place"

"What seem to us bitter trials are often blessings in disguise" (Oscar Wilde)

"Don't just count your blessings. Be the blessing other people count on" (anonymous)

"Count your blessings and you'll have little time to count anything else" (Kroll)

BLINDNESS

בשוק סמיא צוחין לעוירא סגי נהור : (Midrash B'reishis Rabbah) "In the marketplace of men with eyes shut tight, a blind man is rich of light" (also quoted by Machiavelli as: "In the land of the blind, the one-eyed man is lord"

"Who is blind? One who refuses to see the light" (Ladino saying)

"The only thing worse than being blind is having no vision" (Helen Keller)

"Living is easy with eyes closed" (John Lennon / The Beatles)

"Kindness is the language which the deaf can hear and the blind can see" (Mark Twain)

BOOKS

לב חכם לימינו ולב כסיל לשמאלו : (Koheles 10:2) "A wise man's heart inclines him to the right, the fool's to the left" (speaking of Hebrew books which are read from right to left – a wise man scans from the right to the left to review what he has already read, a fool scans from the left side, the back of the book, to see how much he still has to read)

הדברים הנכתבים נשארין לעד : (Rav Yitzchak Abarbanel) "What is written-down will last forever"

"Books without knowledge of life are useless" (Samuel Johnson)

"If you only read the books that everyone else is reading, you can only think what everyone else is thinking" (Murikami)

"When I have little money, I buy books; and if I have any left, I buy food and clothes" (Erasmus)

BROTHER

מה טוב ומה נעים שבת אחים גם יחד : (Psalms 133) "How good and how pleasant are brothers living as one"

אח לצרה יולד : (Proverbs 17:10) "A brother is born to help in times of trouble"

"It takes two men to make one brother" (Israel Zangwill)

"Help your brother's boat across and your own will reach the shore" (Hindu proverb)

"My father used to play with my brother and me in the yard. My mother would come out and say 'you're tearing up the grass!' 'We're not raising grass' my dad would reply, 'we're raising boys!'" (Harmon Killebrew)

BUSINESS

לעולם ישליש אדם את מעותיו, שליש בקרקע, ושליש בפרקמטיא, ושליש תחת ידו : (Gemara Bava Metzia 42a) "A person should divide his investments into three parts: one third in land, one third in commerce, and one third in hand"

"Success is going from failure to failure without losing your enthusiasm" (Winston Churchill)

"If your ship does not come in, swim out to meet it" (comedian Jonathan Winters)

"Far and away, the best prize that life offers, is the chance to work hard at work worth doing" (Teddy Roosevelt)

"Jews have always controlled the business. The motion picture influence of the United States and Canada is exclusively under the control, moral and financial, of the Jewish manipulators of the public mind" (Henry Ford)

"A contract is valid only for honest men" (Yiddish saying)

"It is better to eat herbs and fear no creditors than to eat meat and have to hide from them" (Gemara Pesachim 114a)

"Not everyone poor today will be poor tomorrow; nor everyone rich today be so tomorrow, for the world is a turning wheel" (Midrash Tanchuma)

"There are really three types of people: those who make it happen, those who watch it happen, and those who say 'what happened?'" (Ann Landers)

C:

CAUTION

זהירות מביאה לידי זריזות : (Gemara Avodah Zarah 20b) "Caution leads to speed"

"Slow is smooth and smooth is fast" (US Navy Seals training mantra)

"Choose your friends with caution, plan your future with purpose, and frame your life with faith" (Monson)

"Let us with caution indulge the supposition that morality can be maintained without religion. Reason and experience both forbid us to expect that national morality can prevail in exclusion of religious principle" (George Washington)

CHANGE

משנה מקום משנה מזל : (Gemara Rosh Hashanah 16b) "Change your place change your luck"

"There is nothing permanent except change" (Heraclitus)

"It is best not to swap horses while crossing a river" (Abraham Lincoln)

CHARACTER

ארבע מדות בדעות: נוח לכעוס ונוח לרצות - יצא שכרו בהפסדו, קשה לכעוס וקשה לרצות - יצא הפסדו בשכרו, קשה לכעוס ונוח לרצות – חסיד, נוח לכעוס וקשה לרצות – רשע : (Mishna Avos 5:11) "There are four kinds of character: Easy to provoke and easy to soothe – he will lose, not gain. Hard to provoke and hard to soothe – he gains, not loses. Hard to provoke and easy to soothe – a pious man. Easy to provoke and hard to soothe – a wicked man.

לעולם יהא אדם רך כקנה, ואל יהא קשה כארז : (Gemara Taanis 20b) "As a rule, man should be as flexible as a reed, not as unyielding as a cedar"

"Character is simply habit, long continued" (Plutarch)

CHARITY

צדקה תציל ממות : (Proverbs 10:2) "Charity saves one from death"

כל הרודף אחר צדקה, הקדוש ברוך הוא ממציא לו מעות : (Gemara Bava Basra 9b) "All who run to give charity, G-d blesses them with the means"

כל המעלים עינו מן הצדקה כאילו עובד עבודה זרה : (Gemara Kesuvos 65b) "All who turn their eyes from giving charity – it is as if they worship idols"

בשביל החסד העולם מתקים : (Rashi – Pirkei Avos) "Because of charitable acts the world is established"

"In charity there is no excess" (Francis Bacon)

"Tenderness and generosity are the manly forms of the female virtues of charity and love" (Camus)

"That which we give to the wretched, we lend to fortune" (Seneca)

CHILDREN

אין העולם מתקים אלא בשביל הבל תינוקות של בית רבן (Gemara Shabbos 119b) "The world exists only because of the innocent breath of schoolchildren"

אם לא תכבד הוריך, לא יכבדוך בניך : (Rambam) "If you do not honor your parents, your children will not honor you"

"Little children are still a symbol of the eternal marriage between love and duty" (George Eliot)

"Children begin by loving their parents. After a time, they judge them. Rarely, if ever, do they forgive them" (Oscar Wilde)

"One father can take care of ten children, but ten children cannot take care of one father" (anonymous)

CHOICE

מי שאין לו בחירה: אין לו יצר טוב ויצר הרע : (Rav Yosef Karo) "One who has no good urge or evil urge has no free choice"

החיים והמות נתתי לפניך, הברכה והקללה, ובחרת בחיים למען תחיה אתה וזרעך : (Devarim 30:19) "I have put in front of you life and death, blessing and curse, and you shall choose life so that you and your descendants may live"

"The strongest principle of growth lies in human choice" (George Eliot)

"I am who I am because of the choices I made yesterday" (Eleanor Roosevelt)

"Every morning we have two choices: continue to sleep with our dreams or wake up and chase our dreams" (anonymous)

"You are free to make whatever choices you want, but you are not free from their consequences" (anonymous)

COMMUNITY

אל תפרש מן הצבור : (Mishna Avos 2:4) "Do not separate yourself from the community"

CONTENTMENT

איזהו עשיר, השמח בחלקו : (Mishna Avos 4:1) "Who is rich? One who is content with his share"

"A slave is free when he is content with his share and a free man is a slave when he asks for too much" (anonymous)

"I have mental joys and mental health, mental friends and mental wealth, I've a wife that I love and she loves me, I've all but riches bodily" (William Blake)

COURAGE

"If all men were just, there would be no need of courage" (Plutarch)

"It takes a lot of courage to show your dreams to someone else" (Erma Bombeck)

"Fear is a reaction. Courage is a decision" (Winston Churchill)

"Courage is the art of being the only one who knows you're scared to death" (Earl Wilson)

"Courage is the most important of all the virtues because without courage you can't practice any other virtues consistently" (Maya Angelou)

"It is curious that physical courage should be so common in the world and moral courage so rare" (Mark Twain)

"Sometimes we are tested, not to show our weaknesses, but to discover our strengths" (anonymous)

"Courage is what it takes to stand up and speak; courage is also what it takes to sit down and listen" (Winston Churchill)

CREATION

הבריאה יש מאין הוא דבר שלמעלה משכל הנבראים : (Book of Tanya) "The creation of something from nothing is beyond the understanding of the created"

CRITICISM

"The test of democracy is the freedom to criticize" (David Ben Gurion)

"There is only one way to avoid criticism: do nothing, say nothing, be nothing" (Aristotle)

"Don't criticize what you don't understand. You never walked in that man's shoes" (Elvis Presley) – This is a take on a *passuk* from *Pirkei Avos* that says: "Don't judge your friend until you are in his place."

"Criticism is the disapproval of people, not for having faults, but having faults different from your own" (anonymous)

"Everyone is critical of the flaws of others but blind to their own" (Arab proverb)

"If people criticize you, hurt you, or shout at you, don't bother. Just remember that in every game the spectators make the noise, not the players" (anonymous)

D:

DANGER

"Avoiding danger is no safer in the long run as outright exposure. The fearful are caught as often as the bold" (Helen Keller)

"We hope all danger may be overcome; but to conclude that no danger may ever arise would itself be extremely dangerous" (Abraham Lincoln)

לעולם אל יעמד אדם במקום סכנה לומר שעושין לו נס : (Gemara Shabbos 32b) "As a general rule, man should not stand in a place of danger and expect to be saved by a miracle"

"Anger is one letter short of danger" (anonymous)

"Danger is real. Fear is a choice" (anonymous)

"Never was anything achieved without danger" (Machiavelli)

DARKNESS

אלמלא חשוכא לא אשתמודע נהורא : (Zohar) "Were it not for darkness, light could not be discerned"

"The darkest hour of night is a sign that the dawn is breaking" (Ladino saying)

DEAD – DEATH

בכו לאבלים ולא לאבדה, שהוא למנוחה ואנו לאנחה : (Gemara Moed Katan 25b) "Cry for the mourners but not for the lost (dead) one, for he is gone to his rest and we remain to lament"

"Death opens the gates of fame and shuts the gates of envy" (Sterne)

"In this world nothing is as certain as death and taxes" (Benjamin Franklin)

"Death reduced to the same condition Alexander and his muleteer" (Marcus Aurelius)

"I am ready to meet my Maker. Whether my Maker is prepared for the great ordeal of meeting me is another matter" (Winston Churchill)

ה' נתן וה' לקח, יהי שם ה' מברך מעתה ועד עולם : (Book of Job, Iyov 1:21) "G-d gave and G-d has taken, blessed be the name of G-d from now and forever."

"Nietzsche said: 'G-d is dead!' G-d said: 'Nietzsche is dead!' (anonymous)"

DEEDS

אין אדם יוכל לומר לחברו: מעשי גדולים ממעשיך : (Gemara Sotah 41a) "A man cannot say to his friend: 'My deeds are greater than yours!'"

"The great deeds are done in secret" (Bialik)

"It takes many good deeds to build a good reputation, and only one bad one to lose it" (Benjamin Franklin)

DESTINY

"Hardships often prepare ordinary people for an extraordinary destiny" (C.S. Lewis)

"It is not in the stars to hold our destiny but in ourselves" (Shakespeare)

"It is best to be as pretty as possible for destiny" (Coco Chanel)

"If a man is destined to drown, he will drown even in a spoonful of water" (Yiddish saying)

"If your time has not come, even your doctor will not succeed at killing you" (Yiddish saying)

DIFFICULTY

"The best way out of difficulty is through it" (Will Rogers)

DISCIPLINE

שמע בני מוסר אביך, ואל תטש תורת אמך : (Proverbs 1:8) "Listen my son to the discipline of your father and do not forsake the instruction of your mother"

"There is no contradiction between discipline and initiative – they are complimentary" (David Ben Gurion)

"Discipline is just choosing between what you want now and what you want most!" (Abraham Lincoln)

"Repetition, Repetition, Repetition! Have the discipline to practice a move three thousand times and it will come naturally when you need it!" (mantra of Commando Krav Maga self-defense)

DREAMS

אין מראין לו לאדם אלא מהרהורי לבו : (Gemara B'rachos 55b) "One's dreams only reveal the desires of his heart"

"Every act of man begins with a dream and ends with one" (Theodore Herzl)

"Dreams are mere productions of the brain, and fools consult interpreters in vain" (Jonathan Swift)

"Nothing happens unless first a dream" (Carl Sandburg)

"Dreams don't work unless you do!" (John Maxwell)

"All our dreams can come true if we have the courage to pursue them" (Walt Disney)

DUTY

"Theirs not to make reply. Theirs not to reason why. Theirs but to do or die." (Tennyson – Charge of the Light Brigade)

"Duty is what one expects from others" (Oscar Wilde)

"When a stupid man is doing something he is ashamed of, he always declares it to be his duty" (George Bernard Shaw)

"All the great things are simple and many can be expressed in a single word; freedom, justice, honor, duty, mercy, hope" (Winston Churchill)

"When duty calls, that is when character counts" (William Safire)

"It is not enough to be ready to go where duty calls. A man should stand around where he can hear the call" (Robert Louis Stevenson)

E:

EDUCATION

"There is nothing so stupid as the educated man if you get him off the thing he was educated in" (Will Rogers)

(Proverbs 22:6) : חנך לנער על פי דרכו, גם כי יזקין לא יסור ממנה "Educate a child in the way he should go, and when he is old he will not depart from it"

"Every man who rises above the common level has received two educations: the first from his teachers; the second, more personal and important, from himself" (Edward Gibbon)

"Education is what remains after one has forgotten what one has learned in school" (Albert Einstein)

"An investment in knowledge pays the best interest" (Benjamin Franklin)

"If you think education is expensive, try ignorance" (McIntyre)

"A well-educated mind will always have more questions than answers" (Helen Keller)

"The only thing that interferes with my learning is my education" (Albert Einstein)

ENVY

(Gemara Sanhedrin 105b) : בכל אדם מתקנא חוץ מבנו ותלמידו "A man is envious of everyone except his son and his student"

"The root cause of the antisemitic affliction is envy and the basest instincts…a barbaric hatred of education, freedom, and humanism" (historian Theodor Mommsen)

"He who is not envied is not enviable" (Aeschylus)

"Envy is ever joined with the comparing of a man's self; and where there is no comparison, no envy" (Francis Bacon)

"Envy is the counting of another's blessings instead of your own" (H. Coffin)

EVIL

(Isaiah 5:20) : הוי האומרים לרע טוב ולטוב רע "Woe unto those who call evil good and good evil"

(Gemara B'rachos 51a) : שני יצרים ברא הקדוש ברוך הוא, אחד יצר טוב ואחד יצר הרע "G-d created two desires; one for good and one for evil"

(Gemara Succah 52a) : יצר הרע מסיתו לאדם בעולם הזה, ומעיד עליו לעולם הבא "Evil tempts man in this world and then testifies against him in the World-To-Come"

"Good and evil, we know, in the field of this world, grow up together almost inseparably" (John Milton)

"There are thousands hacking at the branches of evil to one who is striking at the root" (Thoreau)

"It is a sin to believe evil of others, but it is seldom a mistake" (H.L. Mencken)

EYES

(Proverbs 17:24) : עיני כסיל בקצה ארץ "The eyes of a fool are focused on the ends of the earth"

(Gemara Taanis 8b) : אין הברכה מצויה אלא בדבר הסמוי מן העין " Blessing can only be found in places hidden from the eye"

"The eye believes itself, the ear believes others" (anonymous)

"Why has man not a microscopic eye? For this plain reason, man is not a fly" (Alexander Pope)

"Reading is dreaming with open eyes" (anonymous)

"The eyes shout what the lips fear to say" (William Henry)

"The real voyage of discovery consists not in seeking new landscapes, but in having new eyes" (Marcel Proust)

"The eyes are more exact witnesses than the ears" (Heraclitus)

"The hardest thing to see is what is in front of your eyes" (Goethe)

"Sight is what you see with your eyes. Vision is what you see with your mind" (Kiyosaki)

"Have eyes like a shutter and a mind like a lens" (anonymous)

F:

FAITH

(Gemara Tamid 28a) : איזוהי דרך ישרה שיבר לו האדם? יחזיק באמונה יתרה
"What is the straight path that a man should choose? That which helps him hold on to strong faith"

"Perfection of faith comes only when you can believe in G-d without philosophizing, with no omens, and without research" (Reb Nachman of Breslov)

"In the affairs of this world, men are saved not by faith, but by the want of it" (Benjamin Franklin)

"I believe <u>because</u> it is impossible" (Tertullian)

"Faith consists in believing when it is beyond reason to believe" (Voltaire)

"Faith is not belief without proof, but trust without reservation" (Trueblood)

"Faith is not the belief that G-d will do what you want, but that G-d will do what is right" (Lucado)

"Someday, everything will make perfect sense. So, for now, laugh at the confusion, smile through the tears, and keep reminding yourself that everything happens for a reason" (anonymous)

FAMILY

אין לאדם שמחה שלמה כי אם עם אשתו ובניו : (Abarbanel) "Man can only experience full happiness with his wife and children"

"A happy family is but an earlier heaven" (George Bernard Shaw)

"In family life, love is the oil that eases friction, the cement that binds closer together, and the music that brings harmony" (Nietzsche)

FAULT

מום שבך אל תאמר לחברך : (Gemara Bava Metziah 59b) "Do not reproach your neighbor with a fault that is yours also"

אין אדם רואה מומין לעצמו : (Gemara B'rachos 38b) "A person is blind to their own faults" (popularly requoted by Shakespeare)

"Except for being faultless, he has no faults" (Pliny the Elder)

"We endeavor to take pride in faults that we do not wish to correct" (La Rochefoucauld)

FEAR

ראשית חכמה יראת ה' : (Psalms 111:10) "The first step to wisdom is the fear of G-d"

הכל בידי שמים חוץ מיראת שמים : (Gemara B'rachos 33b) "Everything is in the hands of G-d except for the fear of G-d!"

"There is no passion so contagious as fear" (Montaigne)

"The only thing we have to fear is fear itself" (President Franklin D. Roosevelt)

FIRE

אש אוכלת אש : (Gemara Yuma 21b) "Fire consumes fire"

"Trust yourself. Create the kind of self that you will be happy to live with all your life. Make the most of yourself by fanning the tiny, inner sparks of possibility into flames of achievement" (Israel Prime Minister Golda Meir)

"I survived because the fire inside me burned brighter than the fire around me" (Joshua Graham)

FLATTERY

ארבע כתות אין מקבלין פני שכינה: כת לצים, כת חנפים, כת שקרים, וכת מספרי לשון הרע : (Gemara Sotah 42a) "There are four types of men upon whom the Shechinah will not rest: jokers, flatterers, liars, and slanderers"

"Flatterers are the worst kind of enemies" (Tacitus)

"We can be stabbed without being flattered, but we are rarely flattered without being stabbed" (Quevado)

"Consider what your flattery is worth before you bestow it so freely" (Samuel Johnson)

"It is simpler and easier to flatter a man than to praise him" (Richter)

FORBIDDEN

(Midrash Rabbah, Sh'mos 25) : לא תהא אוסר לאחרים ומתיר לעצמך "Do not forbid for others that which you allow for yourself"

"To forbid anything is to make us have a mind for it" (Montaigne)

FREEDOM

"I disapprove of what you say, but I will defend to the death your right to say it" (Voltaire)

"This will remain the land of the free only so long as it is the home of the brave" (Elmer Davis)

"It is by the goodness of G-d that in our country we have three unspeakably precious things: freedom of speech, freedom of conscience, and the prudence never to practice either" (Mark Twain)

"Freedom is the freedom to say that two plus two make four. If that is granted, all else follows" (George Orwell in <u>1984</u>)

FRIENDS

"Be careful of two men and guard yourself against them: the friend of your enemy and the enemy of your friend" (anonymous)

"Better one old friend than ten new ones" (Bialik)

"Friendship makes prosperity brighter, while it lightens adversity by sharing its griefs and anxieties" (Cicero)

"A friend to all is a friend to none" (Aristotle – also quoted by Taylor Swift in her song "Cardigan")

FUNNY

"Everything is funny as long as it is happening to someone else" (Will Rogers)

G:

GENEROSITY

"We make a living by what we get, but we make a life by what we give" (Winston Churchill)

"If you always give you will always have" (Chinese proverb)

"No woman can control her destiny if she does not give <u>to</u> herself as much as she gives <u>of</u> herself" (Suze Orman)

"No one has ever become poor by giving" (Anne Frank)

"Gentleness, self-sacrifice, and generosity, are the exclusive possession of no one race or religion" (M. Gandhi)

"Make generosity part of your growth strategy" (LaPorte)

"What we have done for ourselves alone dies with us; what we have done for others and the world remains and is immortal" (Albert Pike)

GOOD and GOOD DEEDS

גם את הטוב נקבל...ואת הרע לא נקבל : (Job 2:10) "Should we receive only good (from G-d) and not bad as well?"

מגלגלין זכות על ידי זכאי : (Gemara Shabbos 32a) "Good deeds are performed by good (worthy) people"

"Good is not good where better is expected" (Thomas Fuller)

"Do all the good you can, by all the means you can, in all the ways you can, in all the places you can, at all the times you can, to all the people you can, as long as ever you can" (John Wesley)

"Whatever you are, be a good one" (Abraham Lincoln)

"Don't try to be original – just try to be good" (Paul Rand)

"The good must merit G-d's peculiar care: But who but G-d can tell us who they are?" (Alexander Pope)

GREAT and GREATNESS

לא רבים יחכמו : (Job 32:9) "Not many great men acquire wisdom"

"Great and good are seldom the same man" (Thomas Fuller)

"But be not afraid of greatness. Some are born great, some achieve greatness, and some have greatness thrust upon them" (Shakespeare)

GUILT

"Guilt is regret for what we have done. Regret is guilt for what we did not do" (Mark Amend)

"No amount of guilt can change the past and no amount of worrying will change the future" (Al-Khattab)

"Every man is guilty of the good he did not do" (Voltaire)

"Guilt says: 'I made a mistake.' Shame says: 'I am a mistake.'" (Brene Brown)

"One thing I have learned in life is that the guilty dog barks first" (anonymous)

H:

HAPPINESS

"The best way to gain happiness is not to look for it" (Sir Moses Montefiore)

"Happiness is no laughing matter" (Whatley)

"We have no more right to consume happiness without producing it than consume wealth without producing it" (George Bernard Shaw)

"For every minute of anger, you lose 60 seconds of happiness" (Ralph Waldo Emerson)

"Happiness is when what you say, what you think, and what you do, are in harmony" (M. Gandhi)

"Being happy doesn't mean that everything is perfect. It means that you have decided to look beyond the imperfections" (anonymous)

HASTE

עמא פזיזה, דקדמיתו פומיכי לאודניכו : (Gemara Shabbos 88a) "A nation that is rash answers in haste before they hear"

"A lazy man does a job twice" (my father, Joseph Russak)

"One step forward, seven steps back, that's what you get for hurrying" (Yemenite folk-saying)

"Good and quick seldom meet" (George Herbert)

"Make haste slowly" (Augustus Caesar)

"Falsehood avails itself of haste and uncertainty" (Tacitus)

"Haste is bad because it is very time consuming" (Chesterson)

"Calm is from G-d, haste is from Satan" (Arabic saying)

HATE

שקולה שנאת חנם כנגד ג' עברות: עבודה זרה, גלוי עריות, ושפיכות דמים : (Gemara Yuma 9b) "Baseless hatred is as bad as three sins: idol worship, illicit relationships, and bloodshed"

"It is human nature to hate those we have injured" (Tacitus)

"Now hatred is by far the longest pleasure; men love in haste, but they detest at leisure" (Byron)

"Love, friendship, respect, do not unite people as much as a common hatred for something" (Chekhov)

"I don't like Jews, but if I did, I would like you" (as said to me by a neo-Nazi I invited to lunch and with whom I shared a long discussion)

HEART

האדם יראה לעינים, וה' יראה ללבב : (Samuel I, 16:7) "Man looks outward, but G-d looks into the heart"

אין אדם יודע מה בלבו של חברו : (Gemara Pesachim 54b) "No man knows what is in the heart of his friend"

דברים היוצאים מן הלב נכנסים אל הלב : (Gemara B'rachos 6) "Words that come from the heart enter the heart"

"If a good face is a letter of recommendation, a good heart is a letter of credit" (E.G. Bulwer Lytton)

"A faint heart makes feeble hands" (Euripides)

"Among the things you can give and still keep are your word, a smile, and a grateful heart" (Zig Ziglar)

"A tongue has no bones, but it can break a heart" (anonymous)

"Sometimes your heart needs more time to accept what your mind already knows" (anonymous)

"I am proud of my heart. It has been played, stabbed, cheated, burned, and broken, but somehow still works" (anonymous)

"Having a soft heart in a cruel world is courage, not weakness" (anonymous)

HEAVEN

דאיכא בארעא לא ידעת דאיכא בשמיא ידעת : (Gemara Sanhedrin 39b) "If you don't know what is on this earth, how can you hope to know what heaven holds?"

HERO

איזהו גבור? הכובש את יצרו : (Mishna Avos 4:1) "Who is a hero? One who can conquer his desires!"

"In the world's broad field of battle, in the bivouac of life, be not like dumb driven cattle, be a hero in the strife!" (Longfellow)

"We can't all be heroes because somebody has to sit on the curb and applaud them as they go by" (Will Rogers)

HISTORY

גלגל הוא שחוזר בעולם : (Gemara Shabbos 151b) "The wheel always comes full circle" (same as – "History repeats itself")

"Those who cannot remember the past are condemned to repeat it" (George Santayana) (often quoted as: "Those who do not learn from the past are condemned to repeat it")

"To be ignorant of what occurred before you were born is to remain always a child" (Cicero)

HOME

יהי ביתך בית ועד לחכמים : (Mishna Avos 1:4) "Let your home be a meeting-place for wise men"

"Home is where the heart is" (Pliny the Elder)

"A man travels the world over in search of what he needs, and returns home to find it" (George Moore)

"It's not how big the home is, it's how happy the home is" (anonymous)

"Your home should tell the story of who you are and be a collection of what you love brought together under one roof" (Nate Berkus)

"There is nothing like staying at home for real comfort" (Jane Austen)

HONOR

לפני כבוד ענוה : (Proverbs 15:33) "Before honor comes humility"

יהי כבוד חברך חביב עליך כשלך : (Mishna Avos 2:12) "Let the honor of your friend by as dear to you as your own"

לא מקומו של אדם מכבדו, אלא אדם מכבד את מקומו : (Gemara Taanis 21b) "It is not the place that brings honor to the man, but the man that brings honor to his place"

"Those who pursue honor will have it flee from before them" (Midrash Tanchuma)

"Whoever seeks honor is a fool" (Reb Nachman of Breslov)

"Honor is simply the morality of superior men" (H.L. Mencken)

HOSPITALITY

יהי ביתך פתוח לרוחה : (Mishna Avos 1:5) "Let your home be open to those in need"

גדולה הכנסת אורחין מקבלת פני השכינה : (Gemara Shabbos 127a) "Hospitality is greater than greeting the Divine Presence"

"True hospitality consists of giving the best of yourself to your guests" (Eleanor Roosevelt)

"The best way to find yourself is to lose yourself in the service of others" (M. Ghandi)

I:

IGNORANT

"Everyone is ignorant, only on different subjects" (Will Rogers)

INSULT

טוביה דשמע ואדיש חלפוה בישתא מאה : (Gemara Sanhedrin 7a) "One who hears himself insulted and keeps quiet, saves himself a great deal of trouble"

"An injury is much sooner forgotten than an insult" (Lord Chesterfield)

"Insults are the last resort of insecure people with a crumbling position, trying to appear confident" (anonymous)

"Insults are the arguments employed by those in the wrong" (Rousseau)

"Never insult an alligator until you have crossed the river" (Cordell Hull)

"How beautiful is it to stay silent when someone expects you to be enraged" (anonymous)

"Strong people don't put others down…They lift them up" (M.P.Watson)

"Be sure to taste your words before spitting them out" (anonymous)

J:

JEALOUSY

אכזריות חמה ושטף אף ומי יעמד לפני קנאה : (Proverbs 27:4) "Anger is cruel and fury is overwhelming, but who can stand before jealousy?"

הקנאה והתאוה והכבוד מוציאים את האדם מן העולם : (Mishna Avos 4:21) "Jealousy, lust, and honor, drive a man out of this world"

"Jealousy is a hatred no man can heal" (R. Bachya)

"Yet he was jealous, though he did not show it, for jealousy dislikes the world to know it" (Byron)

JEW

כל ישראל ערבים זה בזה : (Gemara Sh'vuos 39a) "All Jews are responsible for one another"

"We accept this word 'Jew,' ostensibly a term of abuse, and turn it into a title" (Theodore Herzl)

"The highest test for the Jewish State will be in its spirit and in its loyalty to the great purpose of the Prophets as envisioned for the end of days" (David Ben Gurion)

"A Jew in exile, even if his desire is to remain a Jew, will be, against his designs, a goy. A Jew in the Land of Israel, even if he wants to be a goy, is, against his designs, a Jew!" (Ussishkin)

JUDGEMENT

אל תהי דן יחידי, (שאין דן יחידי אלא אחד) : (Mishna Avos 2:8) "Do not judge alone, for none may judge alone but The One!"

אשרי דין שמחמץ את דינו : (Gemara Sanhedrin 35a) "Praise the judge who reserves his judgement overnight"

לא תעשו עול במשפט, לא תשא פני דל ולא תהדר פני גדול, בצדק תשפט עמיתך : (Va'yikra 19:15) "You shall not render a partial verdict, and do not favor the poor or show deference to the rich, judge your neighbor fairly!"

"Never look down on anyone in judgement. Only G-d sits that high!" (anonymous)

"When you point a finger at someone else you also have three fingers pointing back at yourself. That means that you must look at yourself three times before judging others." (anonymous)

"Good judgement comes from experience, and a lot of that comes from bad judgement" (Will Rogers)

JUSTICE (and INJUSTICE)

צדק צדק תרדף : (Devarim 16:20) "Justice (and only) justice shall you follow!"

על שלושה דברים העולם קים: על הדין ועל האמת ועל השלום : (Mishna Avos 1:17) "The world is established on three things: justice, truth, and peace"

"The worst form of injustice is pretended justice" (Plato)

"Let us be enraged about injustice, but let us not be destroyed by it!" (B. Rustin)

"The world is a dangerous place to live; not because of the people who are evil, but because of the people who don't do anything about it" (Albert Einstein)

"It is better to suffer an injustice than commit one" (Yiddish saying)

"There is a point beyond which even justice becomes unjust" (Sophocles)

"The love of justice in most men is only the fear of suffering injustice" (La Rochefoucauld)

"Justice is always violent to the party offending, for every man is innocent in his own eyes" (Daniel Defoe)

K:

KINDNESS

על שלושה דברים העולם עומד: על התורה ועל העבודה ועל גמילות חסדים (Mishna Avos 1:2) "The world stands on three things: Torah, service, and loving-kindness"

"You cannot do kindness too soon, for you never know how soon will be too late" (Ralph Waldo Emerson)

"If you're helping someone and expecting something in return, you're doing business, not kindness!" (Shirayuki)

KNOWLEDGE

אין עני אלא בדעה : (Gemara Nedarim 41a) "No one is poor except he who lacks knowledge"

יראת ה' ראשית דעת : (Proverbs 1:7) "The fear of G-d is the beginning of knowledge"

"It is better to know well than to know much" (Mishlei Yehoshua)

"Any fool can know. The point is to understand" (Albert Einstein)

"Knowledge is of no value unless you put it into practice" (Anton Chekhov)

"Knowledge is knowing a tomato is a fruit. Wisdom is not putting it into a fruit salad" (anonymous)

"What we want is to see the child in pursuit of knowledge, not knowledge in pursuit of the child" (George Bernard Shaw)

"You can lead a human to knowledge but you can't make him think" (Mister Ed)

L:

LAND OF ISRAEL

אין מקום פנוי בארץ מן השכינה : (Midrash Bamidbar Rabbah 12) "There is no place in Israel empty of G-d's presence"

"This land made us a people" (David Ben Gurion)

(Devarim perek 8) : ארץ חטה, ושעורה, וגפן, ותאנה, ורמון, ארץ זית שמן ודבש "A land of wheat, barley, grape vines, figs, pomegranates, a land of olive oil and honey" (the *Shiva Minim* – 7 species of Israel)

(Kings I, 9:7) : ...והיה ישראל למשל ולשנינה בכל העמים "...and Israel will be a proverb and a byword among all peoples"

"Israel was not created in order to disappear – Israel will endure and flourish. It is the child of hope and the home of the brave. It can neither be broken by adversity nor demoralized by success. It carries the shield of democracy and it honors the sword of freedom" (John F. Kennedy)

"We Jews have a secret weapon in our fight with the Arabs; we have nowhere to go...we have to fight" (Golda Meir)

"The very existence of Israel is as near to a miracle as we will find in the sober pages of empirical history" (R.L. Jonathan Sacks)

"There's just one country in the world (Israel) that would allow missiles to be rained down on them without fighting back. What I find ironic is that after World War II, everybody said: 'I don't understand the Jews. How could they have just gone to their slaughter like that?' Ok, and then, when they fight back: 'I don't understand the Jews. Why can't they just go to their slaughter?'" (Bill Maher)

"The Land of Israel is called 'life'" (Avos d'Rebbi Nassan 12)

LEADERSHIP

"The leader is one who, out of the clutter, brings simplicity...out of discord, harmony...and out of difficulty, opportunity" (Albert Einstein)

"Leadership is an action, not a position" (McCarron)

"If you want to make everyone happy, don't be a leader! Make ice-cream instead!" (Steve Jobs)

"A person always doing his or her best becomes a natural leader just by example" (Joe Demaggio)

"Great leaders do not set out to be a leader. They set out to make a difference. It's never about the role, it's about the goal!" (Haisha)

LIE

ויפיח כזבים לא ימלט : (Proverbs 19:5) "He who utters lies will not escape"

מדבר שקר תרחק : (Sh'mos 23:7) "Stay far away from a lie!"

כך ענשו של בדאי, שאפילו אמר אמת אין שומעין לו : (Gemara Sanhedrin 89b) "So is the punishment of a liar, that even when he tells the truth, people do not listen to him"

"The difference between you and me is that you like the truth and I hate the lie!" (anonymous)

"A lie travels around the world while the truth is still putting its pants on" (anonymous)

"He who tells a lie is not sensible of how great a task he undertakes; for he must be forced to invent twenty more to maintain that one" (Alexander Pope)

"One of the most startling differences between a cat and a lie is that a cat has only nine lives" (Mark Twain)

"The great masses of the people…will more easily fall victim to a great lie than to a small one" (Adolf Hitler – also attributed to Joseph Goebbels, Nazi Minister of Propaganda)

LIFE

המאבד נפש אחת מישראל...כאלו איבד עולם מלא, וכל המקיים נפש אחת מישראל...כאילו קים עולם מלא : (Gemara Sanhedrin 37a) "Whoever causes the loss of one soul of Yisrael...it is as if he caused the loss of the entire world, and whoever saves a single soul of Yisrael...it is as if he saved the entire world!"

"A long life, a short life – what does it matter? The essence is that it be a life of beauty" (Nordau)

"Life is the art of drawing sufficient conclusions from insufficient premises" (Samuel Butler)

"The hour which gives us life begins to take it away" (Seneca)

"To be what we are, and to become what we are capable of becoming, is the only end of life" (Robert Louis Stevenson)

ובחרת בחיים : (Devarim 30:19) "And you shall choose life!"

"Never regret a day in your life. Good days give you happiness and bad days give you experience" (Dhillon)

"Life is not measured by the number of breaths you take but by the moments that take your breath away!" (Maya Angelou)

"The more you praise and celebrate your life, the more there is of life to celebrate" (Oprah Winfrey)

LUCK

Note: In Hebrew, "luck" is מזל (*mazal*) and actually means "constellation" or "star." Much of fate, destiny, luck, or whatever you want to call it, has been viewed for centuries as "written in the stars."

משנה מקום משנה מזל : (Gemara Rosh Hashanah 16b) "Whoever changes his place changes his luck"

"Better an ounce of luck than a pound of gold" (Yiddish saying)

"Diligence is the mother of good luck" (Benjamin Franklin)

"Those who mistake good luck for merit are inevitably bound for disaster" (J.C. Herold)

"Remember that sometimes, not getting what you want is a wonderful stroke of luck" (Dalai Lama 14)

"I am a great believer in luck and I find that the harder I work, the more I get of it" (Thomas Jefferson)

"Luck is a matter of preparation meeting opportunity" (Seneca)

M.

MIRACLES

אין סומכין על הנס : (Gemara Pesachim 64a) "We do not rely on miracles"

בעל הנס אינו מכיר בנסו : (Gemara Niddah 31a) "The person to whom a miracle happens is not aware of it"

"He who depends on miracles will experience none" (Sefer HaChinuch)

"There are two ways to live. You can live as if nothing is a miracle. You can live as if everything is a miracle" (Albert Einstein)

"To me every hour of the light and dark is a miracle. Every cubic inch of space is a miracle" (Walt Whitman)

"Miracles start to happen when you give as much energy to your dreams as you do to your fears" (R. Wilkins)

MODESTY

כל טובה מעוררת קנאה חוץ מהענוה : (Reb Sholom Ibn Gabirol) "With the exception of modesty, every quality arouses jealousy"

"The modesty of the great is the greatest modesty" (Reb Sa'adia Gaon)

"Modesty is the highest elegance" (Coco Chanel)

"The decoration of woman is modesty and decency" (Plutarch)

"Modesty should be typical of the success of a champion" (Major Taylor)

"Have more than you show and speak less than you know!" (anonymous)

MONEY

אוהב כסף לא ישבע כסף : (Koheles 5:9) "One who loves money will never be content with it"

כל שהכסף בידו, ידו על העליונה : (Gemara Bava Metziah 44a) "He who has the money in hand, he has the upper hand"

"If your riches are yours, why don't you take them with you to the other world?" (Benjamin Franklin)

"There are no pockets in a shroud" (John Joyce)

"Put not your trust in money, but put your money in trust" (Oliver W. Holmes)

N:

NAME

נבחר שם מעשר רב : (Proverbs 22:1) "A good name is better to be chosen over great riches"

נגד שמיה אבד שמיה : (Mishna Avos 1:13) "He who glorifies his own name loses it"

השם הוא עצם הנפש של האדם : "One's name is the very essence of the soul of a man" (Reb Chaim of Volozhin)

אשרי מי שגדל בשם טוב ויצא בשם טוב מן העולם : (Gemara B'rachos 17a) "Praiseworthy is the one who grows up with a good name and departs the world with a good name"

"Honest debate stops when name-calling begins" (Jeffrey Benjamin)

"Young man, make your name worth something!" (Andrew Carnegie)

NATURE

"Nature is the art of G-d" (Dante)

"The chess board is the world, the pieces are the phenomena of the universe, the rules of the game we call the Laws of Nature. The player on the other side is hidden from us. We know that His play is always fair, just, and patient. But also, we know, to our cost, that He never overlooks a mistake or makes the smallest allowance for ignorance" (T.H. Huxley on Nature and G-d)

"Never does nature say one thing and wisdom another" (Juvenal)

O:

OLD AGE

מפני שיבה תקום והדרת פני זקן : (Va'Yikra 19:32) "You shall rise before the aged and show deference to the elderly"

(Proverbs 71:9) אל תשליכני לעת זקנה, ככלות כחי אל תעזבני: "Do not cast me aside to the time of old age, as my strength ebbs, do not abandon me"

"If you can overcome your troubles in a hundred years, you'll live a long time" (Yiddish saying)

"At age 20 we worry about what others think of us. At age 40 we don't care what they think of us. At age 60 we discover they haven't been thinking about us at all" (Ann Landers)

"One advantage of being 96 is that there's no more peer pressure" (my mother-in-law, Dorothy Korchak)

"Age is a matter of mind over matter. If you don't mind, it doesn't matter!" (Mark Twain)

"Listen to your elder's advice; not because they are always right but because they have more experience at being wrong" (anonymous)

"Wrinkles mean you laughed. Grey hair means you cared. Scars mean you have lived" (anonymous)

OPTIMISM

גם זו לטובה : (Gemara Taanis 21a) "This too, is for the best"

לעולם יהא אדם רגיל לומר: כל דעבד רחמנא לטב עבד : (Gemara B'rachos 9b) "As a rule, a man should make a habit of saying that everything G-d does is for the best"

"The optimist proclaims that we live in the best of all possible worlds. The pessimist fears that this is true!" (James B. Cabell)

"All is for the best in the best of all possible worlds" (Voltaire)

P:

PARENTS

אם לא תכבד הוריך לא יכבדוך בניך : (Moreh Nevuchim – <u>Guide To The Perplexed</u>) "If you do not respect your parents, your children will not respect you"

אלו דברים שאדם אוכל פרותיהן בעולם הזה והקרן קימת לו לעולם הבא: כבוד אב ואם... : (Gemara Peah 1a) "These are the things whose fruits man enjoys in this world and capital is put aside for him in the World-To-Come: honoring your mother and father..."

"Let parents bequeath to their children not riches, but a spirit of reverence" (Plato)

"Parents...treat them with loving care. For you will only know their true value when you see their empty chair" (anonymous)

"Every home is a university and the parents are the teachers" (M. Gandhi)

"Children learn more from what their parents are, than what they teach" (Dubois)

PATIENCE

טוב ארך רוח מגבה רוח : (Koheles 7:8) "One who is patient in spirit is better-off than one who is proud of spirit"

"How poor are they who have not patience!" (Shakespeare)

"Beware the fury of a patient man" (Dryden)

PEACE

תלמידי חכמים מרבים שלום בעולם : (Gemara B'rachos 64a) "Scholars multiply peace in the world"

"Peace is not the absence of conflict. It is the ability to handle conflict by peaceful means" (President Ronald Reagan)

"Those who are at war with others are not at peace with themselves" (W. Hazlitt)

"Be selective with your battles. Sometimes peace is better than being right" (anonymous)

"Peace – It does not mean to be in a place where there is not noise, trouble, or hard work. It means to be in the midst of all of these things and still be calm in your heart" (anonymous)

(Midrash Bamidbar Rabbah 11) : אין הברכות מועילות כלום אלא אם כן שלום עמהם "Benedictions are of no use if peace does not accompany them"

PERSEVERENCE and PERSISTENCE

אבנים שחקו מים : (Job 14:19) "Water wears-away stones" (source of: "A river cuts through rock not because of its power but because of its persistence")

"Great works are performed not by strength but by perseverance (Samuel Johnson)

שבע יפל צדיק וקם : (Proverbs 24:16) "A righteous man stumbles seven times and rises-up again"

"Many of life's failures are people who did not realize how close they were to success when they gave up" (Thomas Edison)

"The greatest oak was once a little nut who held his ground" (anonymous)

"The difference between a successful person and others is not lack of strength, not a lack of knowledge, but rather a lack of will" (Vince Lombardi)

"Age wrinkles the body. Quitting wrinkles the soul" (Douglas MacArthur)

"I never dreamed of success. I worked for it!" (Estee Lauder)

"If you are going through hell, keep going" (Winston Churchill)

"I'm convinced that about half of what separates successful entrepreneurs from the non-successful ones is pure perseverance" (Steve Jobs)

POVERTY

(Proverbs 21:13) : אוטם אזנו מזעקת דל, גם הוא יקרא ולא יענה "One who closes his ears from hearing the cries of the poor, will himself cry out and not be heard"

(Gemara Bava Metzia 71a) : עניי עירך קודמים "The poor of your town come first"

"There's enough on this planet for everyone's needs but not for everyone's greed" (M. Gandhi)

"Poverty is the parent of revolution and crime" (Aristotle)

"Poverty often deprives man of all spirit and virtue. It is hard for an empty bag to stand upright" (Benjamin Franklin)

"Poverty is not just a lack of money; it is not having the capability to realize one's full potential as a human being" (Amartya Sen)

PRAYER

(Gemara B'rachos 61a) : לעולם יהיו דבריו של אדם מעטים לפני הקדוש ברוך הוא "When you address G-d, let your words be few"

איזהו עבודה שהיא שבלב? הוי אומר זו תפילה : (Gemara Taanis 2a) "What is service of the heart? Let him recite prayer"

אין תפילה של אדם נשמעת אלא אם כן משים נפשו בכפו : (Gemara Taanis 8a) "A man's prayers are not heard unless his soul is offered-up with it"

שפכו לפניו לבבכם : (Psalms 62:9) "Pour out your heart before Him"

שערי תפילה אינם ננעלים לעולם : (Midrash Devarim Rabbah 2) "The gates of prayer are never closed"

"You can't pray a lie. I found that out" (Mark Twain)

"Common people do not pray – they only beg" (George Bernard Shaw)

"Prayer does not change G-d, but it changes him who prays" (Kierkegaard)

"Prayer does not change things – G-d changes things in answer to prayer" (John Calvin)

Q:

QUARREL

בת דינא בטל דינא : (Gemara Sanhedrin 75a) "If you sleep on a quarrel it will become less contentious"

האי תגרא דמיא לצנורא דבדקא דמיא, כיון דרוח רוח : (Gemara Sanhedrin 7a) "A quarrel is like a hole in a water pipe, once a hole is made it expands quickly"

"If two quarrel, the only one who makes money is a third party" (anonymous)

"In quarreling, the truth is always lost" (Syrus)

"A quarrel is quickly settled when deserted by one party; there is not a battle unless there be two" (Seneca)

"If we can open a quarrel between past and present, we shall find that we have lost the future" (Winston Churchill)

"Say what you mean but don't say it mean!" (A. Wachter)

"There may come a time when you have to give up on some people – not because you don't care but because they don't" (anonymous)

R:

REDEMPTION

(Midrash B'reishis Rabbah 20:9) : מה פרנסה בכל יום, אף גאלה בכל יום "Just as a living must be earned every day, so too redemption must be earned every day"

(Midrash Tanchuma on Parshas Nitzavim) : אין ישראל נגאלין עד שיהיו כלן כאגדה אחת "Israel will not be redeemed until all are united as one single group"

"Do not say: 'Tomorrow we shall be redeemed,' less you miss the moment now!" (Ussishkin)

REPENTANCE

: האומר: אחטא ואשוב, אחטא ואשוב, אין מספיקין בידו לעשות תשובה (Gemara Yoma 85b) "Whoever says: 'I will sin and repent, I will sin and repent,' he will not have the opportunity to repent"

"It is bad when you fail morally. It is worse when you don't repent!" (Palau)

(Mishna Avos 2:10) : רבי אליעזר אומר: שוב יום אחד לפני מיתתך "Rabbi Eliezer said: 'Return to G-d (repent) one day before you die'" (note: he appears to be advising that since we never know when we will die, we should repent immediately)

"To know that a thing is bad is halfway to repentance" (Meiri on Mishlei)

"Our repentance is not so much sorrow for the ill we have done, as fear of the ill that may happen to us in consequence" (La Rochefoucauld)

RESPONSIBILITY

(Gemara Bava Kamma 26a) : אדם מועד לעולם, בין שוגג, בין מזיד, בין ער, בין ישן "Man is always responsible, whether he performed an act inadvertently, intentionally, awake, or asleep"

"You cannot escape the responsibility of tomorrow by avoiding it today" (Abraham Lincoln)

"'I'm sorry' is a statement. 'I won't do it again' is a promise. 'How do I make it up to you?' is taking responsibility" (anonymous)

S:

SABBATH

(Gemara B'rachos 57a) : שבת היא אחת מששים לעולם הבא "Shabbos is one sixtieth of the World-To-Come"

(Gemara Shabbos 113b) : לא יהא דבורך של שבת כדבורך של חול "Your conversation on Shabbos should not be the same as your conversation during weekdays"

"More than Israel has preserved Shabbos, Shabbos has preserved Israel!" (Achad Ha'Am)

"Shabbos is a day of rest, a day of mental scrutiny, a day of bringing things into balance. Without Shabbos the rest of the week would be without flavor, insufferable" (Bialik)

"I don't roll on Shabbos!" (Walter, in The Big Lebowski)

SAVING

"The time to save is now. When a dog finds a bone, he doesn't go out and make a down-payment on a bigger bone. He buries it" (Will Rogers)

SHAME

(Gemara Bava Metzia 58a) : המלבין פני חברו ברבים כאלו שופך דמים "One who shames his friend in public is as one who sheds blood"

(Mishna Avos 3:11) : המלבין פני חברו ברבים אין לו חלק לעולם הבא "One who shames his friend in public has no share in the World-To-Come"

(Gemara B'rachos 12b) : כל העושה דבר עברה ומתביש בו, מוחלין לו על כל עוונותיו "Those who commit a sin and are shamed by it, are pardoned of all their sins"

"Shame should be reserved for the things we choose to do, not the circumstances that life puts on us" (Ann Patchett)

"Unlike guilt, which is the feeling of <u>doing</u> something wrong, shame is the feeling of <u>being</u> something wrong" (Marilyn Sorensen)

"Deceive me once, shame on you! Deceive me twice, shame on me!" (Edgar Allan Poe)

"All violence is an attempt to replace shame with self-esteem" (James Gilligan)

"There is no shame in making an honest effort" (Epictetus)

"Shame occurs when you haven't been able to get away with the 'who' you want people to think you are" (Carl Whitaker)

SILENCE

עת לחשות ועת לדבר : (Koheles 3:7) "There is a time to keep silent and a time to speak"

כל ימי גדלתי בין החכמים, ולא מצאתי לגוף טוב אלא שתיקה : (Mishna Avos 1:17) "All my days I have grown-up among the wise men and have found nothing better for the body than silence"

שתיקה כהודאה דמיא : (Gemara Yevamos 109a) "Silence (in the face of accusation) is like an admission of guilt"

"Keep silent if you have nothing to say and keep silent if you have too much to say!" (popular saying)

"I'll speak to thee in silence" (Shakespeare)

"There is no reply so sharp as silent contempt" (Montaigne)

"Blessed is the man who, having nothing to say, abstains from giving us wordy evidence of the fact" (George Eliot)

"The world would be happier if men had the same capacity to be silent that they have to speak" (Spinoza)

"Lau Kan El-Kalam min fida, as-skoot min dahab" – Arabic for: "If words are of silver, silence is of gold" (old saying of the Jews of Aleppo, Syria)

SPEECH

כל המרבה בדברים מביא חטא : (Mishna Avos 1:17) "All who use too many words bring-about sin"

השמע לאזניך מה שאתה מוציא מפיך : (Gemara B'rachos 13a) "Let you ears hear (heed) what comes out of your mouth"

"There are two kinds of speakers: one that we know in advance all that he is going to say and the other that even when he finishes his speech one does not know what he said" (Agnon)

"Discretion of speech is more than eloquence" (Francis Bacon)

"It is easier said than done!" (popular saying)

"When the heart is afire, some sparks will fly out of the mouth" (Thomas Fuller)

STUDY

יפה תלמוד תורה עם דרך ארץ : (Mishna Avos 2:2) "Beautiful is the study of Torah along with worldly pursuits"

אם יום תעזבה, יומים תעזבך : (Talmud Yerushalmi, B'rachos) "If you forsake (your studies) for a day, they will forsake you for two days!"

למוד מביא לידי מעשה : (Gemara Kiddushin 40a) "Study brings one to action"

Note: The dedicated teacher of children in the Warsaw Ghetto during World War II, Janus Korczak (the pen name of Henry Goldszmit – an author of children's books), is said to have told the following to his older students: "A university student was recruited into the army. The corporal said to him: 'My dear student, this is not a university, it is the army. Here you must think!'"

אל תאמר לכשאפנה אשנה, שמא לא תפנה : (Mishna Avos 2:4) "Do not say: 'When I have the time (when I retire) I will study,' lest you not have the time!"

T:

TIME

אֵין לְךָ אָדָם שֶׁאֵין לוֹ שָׁעָה, וְאֵין לְךָ דָּבָר שֶׁאֵין לוֹ מָקוֹם : (Mishna Avos 4:3) "There is no such thing as a man who doesn't have his hour, nor a thing without a place"

"Man plans and G-d laughs" also quoted as: "Man joins and time disjoins" (Yiddish saying)

Note: Koheles; Ecclesiastes, chapter 3, pessukim 1-8 lists all the "seasons and times under Heaven," e.g.: "A time to be born, a time to die, a time to plant a time to reap...a time to mourn a time to dance, a time to be silent a time to speak...a time of war and a time of peace.

"Draw from the past, live in the present, work for the future" (A. Geiger)

"If time is money, no man lives within his means" (anonymous)

"The two most famous warriors are patience and time" (Tolstoy)

"Time is what we want most and use worst" (William Penn)

"An inch of time is an inch of gold, but you can't buy that inch of time with an inch of gold" (Chinese proverb)

"The bad news is: Time flies. The good news is: You're the pilot!" (M. Altshuler)

TRADITION

מסרת סיג לתורה : (Avos 3:13) "Our tradition is a fence around the Torah"

אל תסג גבול עולם : (Proverbs 22:28) "You shall not remove the borders which were set by your fathers"

"Tradition – how the vitality of the past enriches the life of the present" (T.S. Eliot)

"Tradition is tending the flames, not worshiping the ashes" (Gustav Mahler)

"A love of tradition has never weakened a nation. Indeed, it has strengthened nations in their hour of peril" (Winston Churchill)

TRUTH

האמת כבדה, על כן נושאיה מעטים : (Meiri on Mishlei) "The truth is a heavy burden, therefore, those who carry it are few"

"You can't handle the truth!" (Colonel Jessup/Jack Nicholson, in <u>A Few Good Men</u>)

"There is no hammer more powerful to beat on the hearts of men than the hard and bitter truth" (Gordon)

"He who tells the truth loses his friends" (Ladino saying)

"Sometimes people don't want to hear the truth because they don't want their illusions destroyed" (Nietzsche)

"The truth is still the truth, even if no one believes it. A lie is still a lie, even if everyone believes it" (anonymous)

"People are angry when the truth you speak contradicts the life they live" (anonymous)

"Truth is, it only sounds like hate to those that hate the truth!" (anonymous)

"A truth that's told with bad intent beats all the lies you can invent" (William Blake)

"It takes two to speak the truth – one to speak and another to hear" (Thoreau)

"The best lie is the truth" (a maxim held by my father)

"When you have eliminated the impossible, whatever remains, however improbable, must be the truth" (Sir Arthur Conan Doyle)

"I never give them hell. I just tell them the truth and they think it's hell!" (President Harry Truman commenting on his nickname: "Give 'em Hell Harry")

U:

UNDERSTANDING

קנה חכמה קנה בינה : (Proverbs 13:15) "Acquire wisdom, acquire understanding"

אם אין בינה אין דעת, ואם אין דעת אין בינה : (Mishna Avos 3:17) "Without understanding there is no knowledge, and without knowledge there is no understanding"

"I have made it my earnest concern not to laugh at, nor to deplore, nor to detest, but to understand the actions of human beings" (Spinoza)

"What a man does not understand he does not have" (Goethe)

"...the end of understanding is not to prove and find reasons, but to know and believe" (Thomas Carlyle)

UNITY

והחוט המשלש, לא במהרה ינתק : (Koheles 4:12) "And a three-strand cord is not readily broken"

"A child can break a single reed but a bundle of reeds cannot be broken by a man" (Midrash Tanchuma on Parshas Nitzavim)

בנערינו ובזקנינו נלך : (Sh'mos 10:9) "We will go forth with our young and with our old"

"Remember, upon the conduct of each depends the fate of all" (Alexander the Great)

"If you want to go quickly, go alone. If you want to go far, go together" (African proverb)

"No doubt, unity is something to be desired, to be striven for, but it cannot be willed by mere declarations" (Theodore Bikel)

V:

VANITY

הבל הבלים הכל הבל : (Koheles 1:1) "Vanity of vanities, all is vanity!"

"Pride that dines on vanity, sups on contempt" (Benjamin Franklin)

"What makes the vanity of other people insupportable is that it wounds our own" (La Rochefoucald)

"Any fear of aging, I think, is simply vanity" (Leighton Meester)

"Vanity can easily overtake wisdom. It usually overtakes common sense" (J. Casablancas)

"None are so empty but those who are full of themselves" (B. Whichcote)

VENGEANCE

"Vengeance is little more than an adolescent concession to personal vanity" (anonymous)

לא תקם : (Vayikra 19:18) "You shall not take vengeance!"

פרע קינא מחריב ביתיה : (Gemara Sanhedrin 102b) "He who seeks vengeance upon his fellow will ruin his own home"

"An eye for an eye leads to more blindness" (Margaret Atwood)

"If an injury has to be done to a man it should be so severe that his vengeance need not be feared" (Machiavelli)

"Vengeance has no foresight" (Napoleon Bonaparte)

"Hatred is blind, rage carries you away, and he who pours out his vengeance runs the risk of tasting a bitter draught" (Alexander Dumas)

W:

WAR

"You can't say civilization doesn't advance...in every war they kill you in a new way" (Will Rogers)

WICKED

אשרי האיש אשר לא הלך בעצת רשעים : (Psalms 1:1) "Blessed is the man who does not walk in the counsel of the wicked"

פי רשעים תהפוכות : (Proverbs 10:32) "The mouth of the wicked utters perversity"

אין בידינו לא משלות הרשעים ואף לא מיסורי הצדיקים : (Mishna Avos 4:14) "It is beyond explanation how the wicked are well-off and the righteous suffer"

WISDOM

איזהו חכם? הרואה את הנולד : (Gemara Tamid 32a) "Who is wise? He who foresees what has not yet happened"

איזהו חכם? הלומד מכל אדם : (Mishna Avos 4:1) "Who is wise? He who learns from everyone"

חכם לב יקח מצות : (Proverbs 10:8) "He who is wise of heart will heed the commandments"

"It is a high advantage for a wise man not to seem wise" (Aeschylus)

WISHING

"Why wish upon a star when you can speak to the One who created it?" (anonymous)

"If a man could have half his wishes, he would double his troubles" (Benjamin Franklin)

"Great minds have purposes; others have wishes" (Washington Irving)

"You must be the change you wish to see in the world" (M. Gandhi)

Y:

YOUTH

"A young man has to live and an old man wants to" (Yiddish saying)

"I shall go out with the chariots to the counsel and command, for that is the privilege of the old; the young must fight in the ranks" (Homer)

"If we could be twice young and twice old, we would correct all our mistakes" (Euripides)

"The young think they know everything and are confident in their assertions" (Aristotle)

"Young men are apt to think themselves wise enough, as drunken men are apt think themselves sober enough" (Lord Chesterfield)

"Rashness attends youth, as prudence does old age" (Cicero)

"Almost everything that is great has been done by youth" (Benjamin Disraeli)

"My old age judges more charitably and thinks better of mankind than my youth ever did" (Santayana)

Z:

<u>ZIONISM</u>

"The Jews have one way of saving themselves – a return to their own people and an emigration to their own land" (Theodor Herzl)

"We will never surrender to the messages of hate; we will not surrender to anti-Zionism because it is a reinvention of antisemitism (Emmanuel Macron)

"I said: 'Mr. Balfour, if you were offered Paris instead of London would you take it?' He looked surprised. He said: 'But London is our own!' I said: 'Jerusalem was our own when London was just a marsh.' He said: 'That's true.'" (Chaim Weizman)

THE 613 MITZVOS

The focus of this chapter is on the 613 commandments which were transmitted to Moshe and written in the Torah. They have been an integral element of our Mesorah for over 3,300 years.

The Gemara says in Makkos 23b that there are 613 mitzvos, of which 365 are prohibitive commandments and 248 are positive (there are multiple opinions about exactly how many mitzvos there are). Our sages have different opinions about which mitzvos comprise these 613, and for the purposes of this chapter, I will be focusing on the list compiled by Maimonides, the Rambam. His initial compilation was in Arabic (since he lived in Moorish-controlled Spain in the 1100's) and was called: Kitab al-Farai'd, or *Sefer Hamitzvos* (ספר המצות) in Hebrew.

The most broadly-accepted compilation of these mitzvos is the book of *Sefer Hachinuch* (1200's), where Rabbi Aharon Ha'Levi not only lists the commandments but efforts to postulate the reasons for them. He catalogued the 613 mitzvos in the same order as the weekly Torah portion and I will follow that same formula in this abridged listing and description of the mitzvos.

We commonly refer-to the 613 commandments as תריג מצות (*Taryag Mitzvos*) since the Hebrew letters ת-ר-י-ג have the numerical values of 400-200-10-3 for a total of 613.

It is critical as a student of Judaism to have a basic understanding of these 613 laws. Rarely, if ever, do most Yeshiva or Seminary students actually study them as a group and I am providing this relatively concise listing so one can understand the scope and content of the 613 mitzvos. This will also give one the ability to look at the weekly Torah portion and then, using this listing, study the mitzvos that are in that *parsha*, in order.

Only 126 of the positive commandments can be observed today and 243 of the prohibitive ones. That is because we no longer have a Temple in Jerusalem. Effectively, our responsibility today is to perform 369 of the 613. When you stop to consider the fact that 122 of the positive and 122 of the prohibitive (mitzvos) cannot be performed, the resulting number is 244 that we cannot perform today.

I saw a beautiful commentary attributed to Rabbi Eliezer Danzinger that equates the number 244 to the *gematria* (the numeric value) of the Hebrew word מרד *(mered)*, which translates as: "**rebellion**." The fact that our people rebelled against one-another and hurt G-d, led to the destruction of the 2nd Temple in Jerusalem. That resulted in our losing an equivalent 244 opportunities to do mitzvos that will not be restored until Mashiach comes!

The following listing begins with the first mitzvah in the Torah ("Be fruitful and multiply" – the obligation to have children), and ends with the last ("Write this song for yourselves" - the obligation to take-part in the writing of a Torah).

The following will be catalogued from each of the 5 Books of the Torah:

B'REISHIS:	3 commandments
SHMOS:	111 commandments
VA'YIKRA:	247 commandments
BAMIDBAR:	52 commandments
DEVARIM:	200 commandments

613

Each listing will begin with the location of the mitzvah in the associated parsha in the Torah, an English translation of the Torah's command, a statement of whether it is a positive commandment or a prohibitive one, and a short description of the law.

Some of the laws may be followed by a section called: **"Finer Points"** that will provide more detail based on the commentary of the Mishna and Gemara. This listing is based on the order of appearance of each mitzvah in the Torah in ascending order.

Mitzvos in the Book of B'reishis:

B'reishis:

1. Parshas B'reishis 1:28 "Be fruitful and multiply" (Positive) Marry and have children.

Finer Points: One is obligated to (try to) have at least one boy and one girl.

Lech Lecha:

2. Parshas Lech Lecha 17:10 "Every male among you shall be circumcised" (Positive) All Jewish boys must have a circumcision on the eighth day after birth (except if there are health issues).

Vayishlach:

3. Parshas Vayishlach 32:33 "the sinew of the thigh-vein, (*gid hanasheh*) shall not be eaten by the children of Israel" (Prohibitive).

Finer Points: This is the reason we do not use the hind-quarter of an animal unless the sciatic nerve is removed through a process called *nikkur*.

Mitzvos in the Book of Shmos:
Bo:

4. Parshas Bo 12:2 "This month shall be for you the first of the months" (Positive) Sanctify the new month by announcing it based on the testimony of witnesses who saw the new moon.

Finer Points: This was the first mitzvah given to the Jewish People as a nation.

5. Parshas Bo 12:6 "and the entire congregation of Israel shall slaughter it in the afternoon" (Positive) The obligation to slaughter the *Korban Pesach* – a young lamb or goat.

6. Parshas Bo 12:8 "and they shall eat of its meat during that night" (Positive) The obligation to eat the *Korban Pesach* (which was eaten with matzoh and bitter herbs (*marror*) on the night of the 15th of Nissan.

Finer Points: Today's *afikomen* eaten at the end of the Passover seder is our way of remembering the *Korban Pesach*.

7. Parshas Bo 12:9 "do not eat of it raw or boiled, but roasted in fire" (Prohibitive) The *Korban Pesach* had to be roasted over an open fire.

8. Parshas Bo 12:10 "and you shall not leave any of it over until morning" (Prohibitive) The *Korban Pesach* had to be entirely eaten - any leftovers had to be burned.

9. Parshas Bo 12:15 "But on the first day you must remove all leaven from your homes" (Positive) All *chometz* must be removed from one's possession on the 14th of Nissan.

10. Parshas Bo 12:18 "In the evening you shall eat unleavened bread" (Positive) All are commanded to eat matzoh on the evening of the 15th of Nissan.

11. Parshas Bo 12:19 "For seven days no leaven shall be found in your houses" (Prohibitive) During the seven days of Passover, no *chometz* is allowed in our possession.

12. Parshas Bo 12:20 "You shall eat nothing leavened" (Prohibitive) Anything which contains *chometz* as an ingredient cannot be eaten on Passover.

13. Parshas Bo 12:43 "no stranger shall eat from it" (Prohibitive) Those who deny their Judaism cannot be given to eat from the *Korban Pesach*.

14. Parshas Bo 12:45 "a resident or hired servant shall not eat from it" (Prohibitive) Someone non-Jewish or a convert who has not completed the conversion process may not eat from the *Korban Pesach*.

15. Parshas Bo 12:46 "you shall not take any of the flesh outside of the house" (Prohibitive) Wherever you gather (inside) to fulfill the mitzvah of *Korban Pesach*, you have to eat it – you can't take it outside.

16. Parshas Bo 12:46 "you shall not break its bones" (Prohibitive) One is not allowed to break any of the bones of the *Korban Pesach* while eating it.

Finer Points: The experience of eating the *Korban Pesach* is supposed to be "royal" and marks our redemption from slavery. It would not be proper to break the bones and suck on the marrow like poor and hungry people. Instead, the bones are thrown outside for dogs to eat.

17. Parshas Bo 12:48 "an uncircumcised person shall not eat from it" (Prohibitive) Any male who has not had a circumcision cannot eat the *Korban Pesach*.

18. Parshas Bo 13:2 "Sanctify to me every firstborn, whoever is the first from the womb among the children of Israel, of both man and animal they are mine" (Positive) Firstborn males must be redeemed before a *Kohen* and the firstborn of domesticated animals must be given to a *Kohen*.

19. Parshas Bo 13:3 "and no unleavened bread may be eaten" (Prohibitive) During Passover you cannot eat unleavened bread or associated products made from wheat, rye, oats, barley, or spelt. The previously listed prohibitions are against owning or eating something that contains *chometz* as an ingredient. This law prohibits the eating of unleavened bread on the *Yom Tov* of *Pesach*.

20. Parshas Bo 13:7 "and no *chometz* shall be seen with you, nor shall leaven be seen with you, within all your borders" (Prohibitive) This law prohibits even having *chometz* on your property on *Pesach*.

21. Parshas Bo 13:8 "And you shall tell your son on that day saying..." (Positive) We are commanded that we should tell the story of the Exodus from Egypt on the 15th of Nissan at our Passover Seder.

22. "Parshas Bo 13:13 "and every firstborn of a donkey shall be redeemed with a lamb" (Positive) A firstborn male donkey must be redeemed by exchanging it for a lamb and bringing that lamb as a gift to a *Kohen*.

23. Parshas Bo 13:13 "and if you do not redeem it you shall break its neck" (Positive) If you are not willing to redeem the donkey you can't derive any benefit from it working as a pack or farm animal. It must be killed and buried.

Beshalach:

24. Parshas Beshalach 16:29 "No man shall go out of his place on the seventh day" (Prohibitive) It is prohibited to leave your town (the Torah places restrictions on how far outside your city you may walk) on Shabbos.

Yisro:

25. Parshas Yisro 20:2 "I am the Lord your G-d who brought you out of Egypt" (Positive) This mitzvah, from the first of the Ten Commandments ("Statements") is to believe in G-d's all-powerful being.

Finer Points: This commandment is the basis of our monotheistic faith and our belief in an omnipotent G-d who created our world, controls nature, and sustains everything and everyone.

26. Parshas Yisro 20:3 "You shall have no other gods before Me" (Prohibitive) It is forbidden to believe in any other deities.

27. Parshas Yisro 20:4 "You shall not make for yourselves any graven image or likeness" (Prohibitive) We are not allowed to make idols or multi-dimensional representations of those things or people other nations consider deities.

28. Parshas Yisro 20:5 "You shall not bow to them" (Prohibitive) We cannot bow down or prostrate ourselves on the ground, taking part in idol worship.

29. Parshas Yisro 20:5 "and you shall not serve them" (Prohibitive) We are not allowed to utilize practices that others use in worshiping idols and false gods.

30. Parshas Yisro 20:7 "You shall not take the name of G-d in vain" (Prohibitive) We may not swear, taking a false oath in G-d's name.

Finer Points: Some say that this commandment also prohibits people from using G-d and religion as justification for their own false or evil actions.

31. Parsha Yisro 20:8 "Remember the Shabbos day to keep it holy" (Positive) This is why we sanctify Shabbos and proclaim its holiness by making *kiddush* on Friday evening.

32. Parshas Yisro 20:10 "You shall not do any work" (on Shabbos) (Prohibitive) This refers to the 39 major categories of creative work which were originally used in the construction of the Tabernacle, the *Mishkan*.

33. Parshas Yisro 20:12 "Honor your father and your mother" (Positive) This enjoins us to respect our parents.

34. Parshas Yisro 20:13 "You shall not murder" (Prohibitive) This refers to the premeditated killing of an innocent person.

Finer Points: This mitzvah is often mis-translated as "Thou shall not kill." That is an incorrect use of the word תרצח which means "murder." Killing is permitted when necessary such as in war or in self-defense.

35. Parshas Yisro 20:13 "You shall not commit adultery" (Prohibitive) This is a prohibition against physical relations with a woman married to another man.

36. Parshas Yisro 20:13 "You shall not steal" (Prohibitive) Our sages say that this refers to kidnapping. It is also used as a source for not stealing from someone by misleading them with bad advice and false words (see law #224 for clarification).

37. Parshas Yisro 20:13 "You shall not bear false witness against your neighbor" (Prohibitive) Giving false testimony is a violation of this commandment.

38. Parshas Yisro 20:14 "You shall not covet your neighbor's home, his property, and his possessions" (Prohibitive) Don't covet to the degree that you would physically take what belongs to others.

39. Parshas Yisro 20:20 "You shall not make with Me gods of silver or gold…" (Prohibitive) This law refers to making ornamental depictions such as sculptures of humans, even if not for worship.

40. Parshas Yisro 20:22 "You shall not build it of carved stone" (Prohibitive) The act of building the altar using metal instruments to chisel it or to carve-out the stone is not allowed.

41. Parshas Yisro 20:23 "And you shall not go up to my altar by stairs" (Prohibitive) The priests who ascended the altar in the Tabernacle or the Temple walked up a ramp which prevented exposure of the lower body to those below. This maintained their modesty.

Mishpatim:

42. Parshas Mishpatim 21:2 "When you purchase a Jewish servant…" (Positive) This commandment refers to one whom you purchase from the Jewish court, sold as a servant in order to pay back a debt resulting from theft. The mitzvah is to follow the Torah's dictates relating to treatment of a servant.

43. Parshas Mishpatim 21:8 "If she is not pleasing in the eyes of her master…" (Positive) A Jewish girl who had been sold as a servant (because of extreme poverty); her master has a responsibility to marry her or marry her to one of his sons.

44. Parshas Mishpatim 21:8 "…he shall let her be redeemed" (Positive) In the case of the female Jewish servant above, if her master does not want to marry her, he must aid in her redemption and return her to her family home.

45. Parshas Mishpatim 21:8 "he shall not sell her to foreign people" (Prohibitive) A female Jewish servant cannot be sold to another man. The Gemara in Kiddushin says that once she is returned to her family home, her father can never again sell her.

46. Parshas Mishpatim 21:10 "her food, clothing, and conjugal rights shall not be diminished" (Prohibitive) If the master marries the maidservant, he cannot withhold any of her rights.

47. Parshas Mishpatim 21:12 "If one strikes another man, who then dies, he shall surely be put to death" (Positive) This mitzvah is to be fulfilled by the Jewish court, the Beis Din, to hold a trial, bring witnesses, and ultimately execute the perpetrator by strangulation (*chenek*) if guilty.

48. Parshas Mishpatim 21:15 "And whoever strikes his father or mother shall surely be put to death" (Prohibitive) It is considered a capital offense to hit a parent and draw blood.

49. Parshas Mishpatim 21:18 "And if two men have a confrontation and one man damages the other..." (Positive) If one hurts his fellow man in a fight (causing ==disability, pain, medical expenses, loss of income==, or ==embarrassment==) the court is to impose financial punishment.

Finer Points: The five categories of injury: נזק, צער, רפוי, שבת, בשת (*nezek, tza'ar, riphui, sheves, boshes*)

50. Parshas Mishpatim 21:20 "If one struck his slave or maidservant...and they died under his hand, they shall surely be avenged" (Positive) The Beis Din is commanded to execute such a person (by beheading with a sword - *hereg*).

51. Parshas Mishpatim 21:28 "If an ox gores a man or woman and they shall die..." (Positive) The owner of a wild or domestic animal is financially liable for any damage the animal does. The mitzvah is for the court to impose this ruling.

52. Parshas Mishpatim 21:28 "...and its flesh shall not be eaten" (Prohibitive) The animal that does damage, if killed, cannot be eaten and the carcass must be buried.

53. Parshas Mishpatim 21:33 "And if a man shall uncover (open) a pit" (Positive) This mitzvah is directed to the Beis Din that is commanded to handle cases of damages and injuries caused by an impediment that one created or allowed to remain in a place where it could cause injury.

54. Parshas Mishpatim 21:37 "If a man shall steal" (Positive) It falls upon the Beis Din to judge cases of theft.

Finer Points: Jewish law separates thieves and robbers. A thief is identified as one who tries to hide from people (a thief in the night), showing that he is more afraid of people than G-d's commandment not to steal. A robber is one who takes what he wants openly and brazenly without any regard or fear of G-d or man.

55. Parshas Mishpatim 22:4 "If a man permits livestock to eat a field or a vineyard" (Positive) This mitzvah calls upon the Beis Din to judge cases of domesticated animals causing damage through their normal course of walking and grazing.

56. Parshas Mishpatim 22:5 "If a fire will break out" (Positive) The Beis Din also must judge cases of damage by fire and any resulting injuries.

57. Parshas Mishpatim 22:6 "If a man gives to his neighbor money or vessels to safeguard" (Positive) The Beis Din has the responsibility to judge cases of loss when someone acts as a guardian (unpaid) of someone else's property which is subsequently lost or stolen because of negligence.

58. Parshas Mishpatim 22:8 "For every item of liability...for which one says: 'This is it,' the matter shall come before the court..." (Positive)

The court must judge cases of monetary dispute to decide between the plaintiff and the defendant.

59. Parshas Mishpatim 22:9 "If a man gives to his friend...to safeguard" (Positive) The Beis Din must judge cases of loss when one is watching (for a fee) the property of another.

60. Parshas Mishpatim 22:13 "And if a man borrows something from his neighbor and it breaks or dies..." (Positive) The Beis Din is also to judge disputes arising from cases where one borrows something from a neighbor.

Finer Points: There are three main categories of borrowing or guarding: The first is one who safeguards something for his friend and does not charge a fee. He is a *shomer chinam*. The next is the one who watches something and charges a fee. He is a *shomer sachar*. The one who borrows something (for instance, borrows your power drill) is called a *sho'el*, and is responsible for the item whether he loses it, breaks it, or if it is stolen.

61. Parshas Mishpatim 22:15 "And if a man seduces..." (Positive) It is a mitzvah for the Beis Din to judge cases of seduction (of under-age girls).

62. Parshas Mishpatim 22:17 "You shall not permit a sorceress to live" (Prohibitive) Those who practice witchcraft are to be put to death.

63. Parshas Mishpatim 22:20 "You shall not agitate a stranger (proselyte)" (Prohibitive) A gentile who converts to Judaism is called a "*ger*" (proselyte) and it is against the law to shame him.

64. Parshas Mishpatim 22:20 "...and you shall not oppress him" (Prohibitive) We are not allowed to take financial advantage of a proselyte.

65. Parshas Mishpatim 22:21 "You shall not cause pain to any widow or orphan" (Prohibitive) Widows and orphans are placed in a special category of those who need special protection and care. One is not allowed to use words or actions to hurt them.

66. Parshas Mishpatim 22:24 "If you shall lend money to My people, the poor among you..." (Positive) It is a mitzvah to lend money to the needy.

67. Parshas Mishpatim 22:24 "...you shall not treat him as a creditor..." (Prohibitive) We are not allowed to demand payment from one to whom we have made a loan if we know they do not have the means to make the payment.

68. Parshas Mishpatim 22:24 "...you shall not set interest upon him" (Prohibitive). One is not allowed to assist a borrower or lender in transacting a loan bearing interest.

Finer Points: Within the confines of business contracts there is a way to earn interest, but it involves the writing of a special document called a *shtar heter iskah* signed by both the lender and borrower.

69. Parshas Mishpatim 22:27 "You shall not curse judges" (Prohibitive) Technically, this is translated as: "You shall not revile G-d," but is interpreted as the cursing of judges using G-d's name.

70. Parshas Mishpatim 22:27 "You shall not curse G-d" (Prohibitive)

71. Parshas Mishpatim 22:27 "and you shall not curse the leader of your people" (Prohibitive) One is not allowed to curse the king or a communal leader.

72. Parshas Mishpatim 22:28 "You shall not delay your 'fullness offering.'" (Prohibitive) One is not allowed to separate their *t'rumah* and *maaser* in the wrong order.

73. Parshas Mishpatim 22:30 "...and you shall not eat the flesh of any animal torn in the field" (Prohibitive) The meat of any animal that is defective (*treifah*) may not be eaten.

74. Parshas Mishpatim 23:1 "Do not accept a false report..." (Prohibitive) A judge is prohibited from listening to a litigant if the other party is not present. If he suspects that one is lying, he is obligated to withdraw. If he does remain, he could be liable for the sin of *lashon harah* as well.

75. Parshas Mishpatim 23:1 "...do not extend your hand with the wicked to be a false witness" (Prohibitive) The testimony of a person who is recognized as wicked is not allowable. In this case, a wicked person is identified as one who openly violates the Torah. A few examples are: one who has been unjustifiably violent against another (or purposely caused property damage), has sworn falsely in the name of G-d, has been proven to be an informer, or has charged interest.

76. Parshas Mishpatim 23:2 "You shall not be a follower of the majority to do evil" (Prohibitive) In cases where death could be the penalty, a deciding majority of at least two judges is required.

Finer Points: In capital cases, the Gemara in Sanhedrin (17a) says that if every single member of the Sanhedrin declares that a defendant is guilty (a unanimous verdict), he is acquitted. This is called a "conspiracy" court. Perhaps the point is that if you can get 70 people to agree with you, something must be wrong!

77. Parshas Mishpatim 23:2 "...and do not respond to a controversy by yielding" (Prohibitive) A judge is not allowed to yield to the other judges even if outnumbered, and should not allow himself to be unduly influenced by them. That is why the lead judge and the elder judges do not speak first in a capital trial in the Sanhedrin. They must allow the younger and more inexperienced judges to speak first and reach their own conclusions.

78. Parshas Mishpatim 23:2 "...after a majority, to follow (lean on) the law" (Positive) We follow the majority decision in Torah law.

Finer Points: This law presents us with an example of Talmudic exegesis in the same *passuk* that commands us **not** to follow the majority blindly.

It also teaches us a finer point - that we follow the majority to help us keep the law and should not pervert law by "leaning" on the scales of justice. This is a very complicated mitzvah and applies only where two competing groups of judges are arguing a case and one of the groups, although superior in number, has less Torah knowledge. The minority group of wiser men is then deemed the "majority."

79. Parshas Mishpatim 23:3 "And you shall not favor a poor man in his grievance" (Prohibitive) A judge is not allowed to favor a poor person either because of pity or a sense of social justice. He must judge on the evidence alone.

80. Parshas Mishpatim 23:5 "…and you shall surely help him" (Positive) In the case of one who is unloading his pack-animal, even if it is a person you dislike, it is a mitzvah to help him.

81. Parshas Mishpatim 23:6 "Do not pervert the judgement of your destitute person in his grievance" (Prohibitive) A judge is forbidden to commit a miscarriage of justice in a case where one of the litigants is destitute (which is interpreted by the Rambam as his being a *rasha* -a wicked person who does not follow the commandments).

82. Parshas Mishpatim 23:7 "and the innocent and the righteous do not execute" (Prohibitive) The Beis Din can only decide on a guilty verdict in a capital trial if there are two valid eyewitnesses. Circumstantial evidence is not admissible.

83. Parshas Mishpatim 23:8 "And you shall not take a bribe" (Prohibitive)

84. Parshas Mishpatim 23:11 "And in the seventh year you shall leave it unworked and unharvested…" (Positive) The mitzvah of *shmittah* demands that we not work our fields once every seven years and instead, leave them "ownerless."

85. Parshas Mishpatim 23:12 "…and on the seventh day you shall rest" (Positive) It is a mitzvah to refrain from work on Shabbos.

86. Parshas Mishpatim 23:13 "...the name of strange gods you shall not mention" (Prohibitive) This is the commandment not to swear, invoking the names of idols or false gods.

87. Parshas Mishpatim 23:13 "...it shall not be heard from your mouth" (Prohibitive) A Jew is not allowed to speak to fellow Jews about idolatry in an effort to convince them to worship. Such a person is called a *maydiach*. See Devarim 13:9 for the law concerning a *maysis*, one who tries to lure-away a single Jew.

88. Parshas Mishpatim 23:14 "Three times in the year you shall celebrate to Me" (Positive) It is a mitzvah to make a pilgrimage to the Temple in Jerusalem for Pesach, Shavuos, and Succos and to bring a *korban shlamim* to honor the holiday.

89. Parshas Mishpatim 23:18 "You shall not offer with leavened bread the blood of My sacrifice" (Prohibitive) One cannot offer the *Korban Pesach* while still in possession of *chametz*.

90. Parshas Mishpatim 23:18 "...and the fat of my festive offering shall not remain until the morning" (Prohibitive) The priests who offer the *Korban Pesach* are not allowed to leave its fats remaining overnight. They must be burned on the altar immediately after being sacrificed.

91. Parshas Mishpatim 23:19 "The first of the first-fruits of your land you shall offer..." (Positive) This is the mitzvah of *bikkurim*, bringing your first-fruits to the Temple as a gift to the priests. This law applies only to the *shiva minim* – the 7 species; wheat, barley, grapes, figs, pomegranates, olives (olive oil), and dates (date honey).

92. Parshas Mishpatim 23:19 "...you shall not boil a kid in its mother's milk" (Prohibitive) Meat and milk may not be cooked together. We are not allowed to cook it, eat it, or derive benefit from it. This is the pre-eminent law of Kashrus and is stated three times in the Torah; Sh'mos 23:19, Sh'mos 34:26, and Devarim 14:21.

93. Parshas Mishpatim 23:32 "You shall not make a covenant with them nor with their gods" (Prohibitive) We are not allowed to make treaties with the seven nations of idol worshipers who inhabited the Land of Israel prior to our conquest and may not allow them to continue their idol worship. The seven nations are: **Chitti, Emori, Canaani, Chivi, Yevusi, Girgashi, Prizi** – the Hittites, Amorites, Canaanites, Hivites, Jebusites, Girgashites, and Perizzites.

Note: The **Plishtim** – the Philistines, are not listed in this prohibition since they were not indigenous to the Land of Israel. Originally, they were Aegean pirates who pillaged the eastern Mediterranean.

94. Parshas Mishpatim 23:33 "They shall not dwell in your land, lest they make you sin against Me" (Prohibitive) We are not allowed to let idol worshipers dwell in the Land of Israel.

Trumah:

95. Parshas Trumah 25:8 "And they shall make for me a sanctuary and I shall dwell in it" (Positive) This is the mitzvah of building the *Mishkan* (Tabernacle) and later, the *Beis Ha'mikdash* (the Temple).

96. Parshas Trumah 25:15 "In the rings of the ark shall the poles be, they shall not be removed from it" (Prohibitive) Once the horizontal carry poles of the Ark were placed through the rings on its sides, they were to remain in that position and could not be removed.

Finer Points: The permanence of the carry-poles, the *badim* (as attached to the Ark so it could be carried with the Jewish People) is symbolic of G-d's promise never to leave us, even when we are forced to travel from place-to-place. The poles were longer than the depth of the Holy-of-Holies (the *Kodesh Ha'Kedashim*) and actually pushed against the curtain (*paroches*) that closed-off that area. From the outside, the area against which the poles were pressing was visible, reminding those serving in the

Tabernacle (and the 1st Temple) that the Ark was always there, even though they could not enter and see it.

97. Parshas Trumah 25:30 "And on the table you shall place showbread before me, always" (Positive) The gold multi-tiered table that held the bread in the Tabernacle and Temple was refilled every Shabbos with fresh bread; 12 loaves.

Tetzaveh:

98. Parshas Tetzaveh 27:20 "...to cause the lamp to continually burn" (Positive) This is the mitzvah that commands the priests to re-light the Menorah in the Tabernacle every evening.

99. Parshas Tetzaveh 28:4 "...and they shall make holy garments for Aharon...and his sons" (Positive) This relates to the special clothing made for the *Kohanim*.

100. Parshas Tetzaveh 28:28 "...and the breastplate shall not be loosened from the apron" (Prohibitive) While the High Priest was performing his service it was prohibited to allow the apron (*ephod*) and the breastplate (*choshen*) to separate. They were tied-together with a string of blue wool.

101. Parshas Tetzaveh 28:32 "...it is not to be torn" (Prohibitive) The *me'il*, the High Priest's robe, could not be worn if cut or torn.

102. Parshas Tetzaveh 29:33 "They shall eat those things through which atonement is made..." (Positive) The priests ate the meat of the *Chattas* (sin) and *Asham* (guilt) offerings.

103. Parshas Tetzaveh 30:7 "And Aharon shall burn on it incense of spices every single morning" (Positive) This is the mitzvah of burning the *Ketoress* spice mixture on the golden altar every day, morning and evening.

104. Parshas Tetzaveh 30:9 "You shall not offer any 'strange' spice on it, nor burnt offering, nor meal offering, nor may you pour any libation on it" (Prohibitive) The only thing that could be burned on the golden altar was the *Ketoress*. Once a year, on Yom Kippur, the High Priest performed a special service where he sprinkled blood on that altar.

Ki-Seesah:

105. Parshas Ki Seesah 30:13 "This shall they give, everyone who passes through the census" (Positive) Every Jewish male over the age of 20 is commanded to give a half-shekel coin to the priests every year (during *Adar*)

106. Parshas Ki Seesah 30:19-20 "And Aharon and his sons shall wash from it their hands and their feet when they go into the Tent of Meeting…or when they approach the Altar" (Positive) It is a mitzvah for the priests to wash when they perform their service. The copper laver (the *Kiyor*) was used for this.

107. Parshas Ki Seesah 30:25 "…of it you shall make it a holy oil for anointing" (Positive) The Tabernacle and the Temple vessels had to be anointed (as well as the High-Priest) with special oil. This mitzvah commands the preparation of such oil.

108. Parshas Ki Seesah 30:32 "On the flesh of a man it shall not be poured" (Prohibitive) The anointing oil may not be poured onto any other persons than kings or priests.

109. Parshas Ki Seesah 30:32 "…it's formulation you shall not duplicate" (Prohibitive) This oil could not be reproduced.

110. Parshas Ki Seesah 30:37 "…according to its formula you shall not make it for yourselves" (Prohibitive) The *Ketoress* recipe could not be duplicated unless it was prepared specifically for the Temple. Even then, according to the Talmud, the recipe of how to mix the eleven ingredients was entrusted to only one family in Jerusalem and their descendants.

111. Parshas Ki Seesah 34:12-15 "Guard yourself, lest you make a covenant with the dwellers of the land...and eat from their sacrifices" (Prohibitive) Food or drink used in idol-worship is not permitted. Pagan wine used for worship is called *Yayin Nesech*.

112. Parsha Ki Seesah 34:21 "...from plowing time and harvest time you shall rest" (Positive) It is a mitzvah to stop working the land during the *shmittah* year (once every 7 years). We perform a positive commandment by letting our fields lay fallow for that year.

113. Parshas Ki Seesah 34:26 "...you shall not cook a kid in its mother's milk" (Prohibitive) This is the second instance of the use of this statement in the Torah. The first case taught the law of not cooking such a mixture. This case teaches us not to eat such a mixture.

Vayakhel:

114. Parshas Vayakhel 35:3 "You shall not kindle a fire in any of your habitations on the Shabbos day" (Prohibitive) Fire is used here as an example of forbidden constructive work on Shabbos (the 39 *melachos*). The Jewish courts have a responsibility to execute those who openly violate Shabbos, but cannot carry-out the verdict on Shabbos.

Mitzvos in the Book of Va'yikra:

Va'yikra:

115. Parshas Va'yikra 1:3 "If his offering is a burnt-sacrifice..." (Positive) It is a mitzvah to carry-out the process of offering an *olah* sacrifice following proper procedures (kosher slaughtering, removing the blood....).

116. Parshas Va'yikra 2:1 "And when a person brings a meal offering..." (Positive) This pertains to the mitzvah of offering the *korban mincha* made of flour, etc.

117. Parshas Va'yikra 2:11 "...because no leaven or honey shall you burn as an offering by fire to G-d" (Prohibitive) Anything that makes the offering either sweet or sour is prohibited on the altar.

118. Parshas Va'yikra 2:13 "You shall not leave the salt...out of your meal offering" (Prohibitive) This mitzvah places responsibility on the priests not to leave out the salt from any sacrifice.

Finer Points: Some scholars postulate that since salt is a preservative, it is used on the offerings as a symbol of G-d's "preserving" the Jewish People. It is also a symbol of His eternal covenant with nature.

119. Parshas Va'yikra 2:13 "...with all your offerings you shall offer salt" (Positive) It is a mitzvah to add salt on both meat and flour sacrifices (which is why we put salt on our Shabbos table).

120. Parshas Va'yikra 4:13 "And if all of the congregation of Israel will sin accidentally, and this be hidden from the eyes of the congregation..." (Positive) If the court makes a ruling in error that affects the congregation of Israel (with a sin that bears the punishment of *koreis* (spiritual excommunication), and the majority of the populace sinned, a bull must be brought as a communal offering.

121. Parshas Va'yikra 4:27 "And if an individual shall accidentally sin..." (Positive) This obligates the bringing of a sin-offering (*korban chattas*) if one violates a prohibitive mitzvah in error that bears the punishment of *koreis*.

122. Parshas Va'Yikra 5:1 "...and he is a witness – either he saw or he knew..." (Positive) It is a mitzvah for a person to come forward as a witness to the court if he can offer valid testimony.

123. Parshas Va'yikra 5:6-7 "and he shall bring his guilt-offering to G-d...and if he cannot bring a lamb..." (Positive) It is a mitzvah to bring a *korban olah ve'yored* as a way of achieving atonement.

124. Parshas Va'yikra 5:8 "...and he shall nip its head...but not completely detach it" (Prohibitive) When bringing a bird as a *chattas* offering, (pigeon, dove, etc.) it is not to be killed in a way where the head is completely severed.

125. Parshas Va'yikra 5:11 "...he shall put no oil on it" (Prohibitive) It is not permissible for the priest to put oil on the meal-offering of one who sins unintentionally (*minchas choteh*).

126. Parshas Va'yikra 5:11 "...nor shall he put frankincense on it" (Prohibitive) The priest is also not allowed to put frankincense on the offering of the unintentional sinner. In all other cases of meal-offering, the priest adds frankincense.

127. Parshas Va'yikra 5:15-16 "If a man commits a breach of holiness and sins unintentionally using G-d's holy objects, then he shall bring a guilt-offering...and must pay with an additional one-fifth" (Positive) One who accidentally used objects or food belonging to the Temple must repay its value to the Temple treasury, add a penalty of 20 percent, and bring an *asham me'ilos* offering.

128. Parshas Va'yikra 5:17 "And if a person will sin...and does not know, he is guilty and shall bear his iniquity" (Positive) The mitzvah here is to bring a guilt offering called an *asham talui* (guilt offering of suspension or uncertainty) if the person is in doubt as to whether he violated a commandment that bears the punishment of *koreis*.

129. Parshas Va'yikra 5:23 "...and he shall return the stolen object..." (Positive) Someone who steals an object must return it intact to the owner. He must repay its value to the owner and bring an *asham gezeilah* offering if he broke it or lost it.

130. Parshas Va'yikra 5:25 "And his guilt-offering he shall bring to G-d..." (Positive) This is the mitzvah of bringing an *asham vadai* (guilt-offering of certainty)

Tzav:

131. Parshas Tzav 6:3 "...and he shall take the ash..." (Positive) Every morning, the first service performed in the Temple was the removal of the ashes from the altar (*t'rumas ha'deshen*)

132. Parshas Tzav 6:6 "A continuous fire shall be kept burning on the altar..." (Positive) This mitzvah mandates that a permanent fire be kept burning on the altar.

133. Parshas Tzav 6:6 "...it may not be extinguished" (Prohibitive) The priests are not allowed to put-out the fire on the altar.

134. Parshas Tzav 6:9 "And Aharon and his sons shall eat what is left of it..." (Positive) This relates to the meal offering. The *Kohanim* may eat from what is remaining after a small amount (the *kometz*) is offered on the altar.

135. Parshas Tzav 6:10 "It shall not be baked leavened..." (Prohibitive) The priests may not "overbake" the meal offering in such a way that it becomes leavened (*chametz*).

136. Parshas Tzav 6:13 "This is the offering of Aharon and his sons..." (Positive) This is the mitzvah of the High Priest bringing a meal offering (*minchas chavitin*) on a daily basis.

137. Parshas Tzav 6:16 "Every meal offering of a priest is to be entirely burnt" (Prohibitive) The priests are not allowed to eat from a meal offering that they or another priest brought. They could only eat from those brought by a commoner (see mitzvah 134).

138. Parshas Tzav 6:18 "This is the law of the sin offering..." (Positive) It is a mitzvah for the priests to sacrifice the *chattas* brought by someone atoning for an unintentional transgression that bears the punishment of *koreis*.

139. Parshas Tzav 6:23 "A sin offering...shall not be eaten" (Prohibitive) A *korban chattas* that had its blood sprinkled on the golden altar had to be burnt completely.

140. Parshas Tzav 7:1 "And this is the law of the guilt-offering" (Positive) This is the *korban asham*, the offering of a ram by someone who stole an object or unintentionally used an object owned by the Temple.

141. Parshas Tzav 7:11 "And this is the law of the peace-offering..." (Positive) This is the mitzvah of the priests sacrificing the *korban sh'lamim* brought by the community or an individual.

142. Parshas Tzav 7:15 "...he shall not leave any of it over until morning" (Prohibitive) The meat of the *todah* offering could not be left-over until the next day and had to be burnt.

143. Parshas Tzav 7:17 "But what is left of the flesh of the sacrifice on the third day shall be burned in fire" (Positive) It is a mitzvah to burn meat that passed the allowable time during which it could be eaten.

144. Parshas Tzav 7:18 "...and the soul who eats from it shall bear its iniquity" (Prohibitive) Meat from a sacrifice became unfit (*pigul*) if the *Kohen* designated in his mind a time it would be eaten that is not allowed. It would be a sin to consume it in that scenario.

145. Parshas Tzav 7:19 "And the flesh that touches any unclean thing shall not be eaten..." (Prohibitive) If an offering becomes ritually impure it may not be eaten (this also refers to a ritually impure person eating from sacrifices).

146. Parshas Tzav 7:19 "...in fire it shall be burned" (Positive) Sacrifices like the one in mitzvah 145 (that become impure) must be burned entirely.

147. Parshas Tzav 7:23 "...any fat of oxen, sheep, or goats may not be eaten" (Prohibitive) Fat (*chaylev*), in this case, refers to the fat that surrounds the inner organs of the animal's body such as the stomach kidneys, loins, and entrails.

148. Parshas Tzav 7:26 "And you shall not consume any blood...whether from fowl or animals" (Prohibitive) We are not allowed to eat the blood of birds or animals even if they are slaughtered correctly. The animal is bled and salted, and in the case of organs such as the liver (which retains a lot of blood), we are required to additionally salt the meat and broil it to remove as much blood as possible.

Shmini:

149. Parshas Shmini 10:6 "Do not leave your heads unshorn" (Prohibitive) The priests could not enter the Temple to perform their service with long hair.

Finer Points: Our sages say that if one were to appear like a mourner with long and unkempt hair, it could be interpreted as a display of grief. The Temple was a place of awe and joy.

150. Parshas Shmini 10:5 "...and do not tear your clothes..." (Prohibitive) This could also be seen as a sign of mourning and it is prohibited for priests to enter the Temple with torn clothing.

151. Parshas Shmini 10:7 "Do not leave the entrance of the Tent of Meeting..." (Prohibitive) The priests cannot interrupt their Tabernacle or Temple service.

152. Parshas Shmini 10:9 "Do not drink wine or intoxicating drinks..." (Prohibitive) One is not allowed to enter the Temple (or act as a judge) while intoxicated. Note the story of Nadav and Avihu, two of Aharon's sons who entered the Tabernacle while intoxicated and died (Rashi on Va'Yikra 10:2).

153. Parshas Shmini 11:2 "...these are the living things from which you may eat..." (Positive) It is a mitzvah to choose kosher animals and to look for their signs of kashrus – split hooves and chewing of the cud.

154. Parshas Shmini 11:4 "But of these you shall not eat..." (Prohibitive) One may not eat animals that do not have the two kosher signs.

155. Parshas Shmini 11:9 "These you may eat of all that are in the water...everything that has fins and scales..." (Positive) It is a mitzvah to check to make sure that the fish you are selecting to eat has the two kosher signs.

156. Parshas Shmini 11:11 "...you shall not eat of their flesh..." (Prohibitive) The meat of non-kosher fish is forbidden.

157. Parshas Shmini 11:13 "And these you shall find abominable from among the fowl..." (Prohibitive) Non-kosher species of birds are forbidden. The Torah does not provide kosher signs for birds. Instead, it lists 24 birds that are not kosher. The remainder are technically kosher. Nevertheless, due to the lack of clarity of the translation of the biblical names of many of the bird species, we only eat those birds for which we have a tradition that they are kosher.

158. Parshas Shmini 11:21 "Only this may you eat of the flying and swarming creatures..." (Positive) The Torah lists four insects that are considered kosher and may be eaten (*arbeh, salaam, chargol,* and *chagav*, all from the grasshopper family)

159. Parshas Shmini 11:29 "And this is what is unclean to you from among the teeming things that crawl upon the earth..." (Positive) It is a mitzvah to observe the laws relating to ritual contamination, including touching any of the eight species of *shratzim*; weasels, rodents, frogs, hedgehogs, chameleons, lizards, snails, and moles.

160. Parshas Shmini 11:34 "Of any edible food which water touches shall become contaminated..." (Positive) This relates to the observance of the laws relating to ritual uncleanliness of food. Unlike pots, pans, and clothing, contaminated food cannot become permissible through immersion in a *mikvah*.

161. Parshas Shmini 11:39 "And if an animal that you may eat has died, he that touches the carcass shall become unclean" (Positive) This mitzvah commands us to observe the laws of ritual uncleanliness relating to a *neveilah*, an animal carcass.

162. Parshas Shmini 11:41 "And every teeming creature that creeps along the earth, is detestable – it shall not be eaten" (Prohibitive) We are not allowed to eat rodents or reptiles.

163. Parshas Shmini 11:42 "...among all the teeming things that crawl upon the earth, you may not eat them..." (Prohibitive) Consumption of bugs and worms that breed in plants and fruits is prohibited.

164. Parshas Shmini 11:43 "You shall not make your souls detested with any teeming thing..." (Prohibitive) This law prohibits the consumption of species that swarm in water.

165. Parshas Shmini 11:43 "...and you shall not contaminate yourself with any crawling thing..." (Prohibitive) We are forbidden to eat anything that lives in decaying matter, such as maggots.

Parshas Tazria:

166. Parshas Tazria 12:2-5 "A woman who conceives and gives birth to a male shall be unclean for seven days...but if she bears a female then she shall be unclean for two weeks..." (Positive) A woman who goes through childbirth must observe the laws of ritual impurity.

167. Parshas Tazria 12:4 "...she shall not touch any holy thing" (Prohibitive) One who is ritually impure (such as a woman who gives birth) is forbidden to eat anything *kodesh* – holy.

168. Parshas Tazria 12:6 "And upon the completion of the days of her purity..." (Positive) A woman is commanded to bring two offerings to the Temple following childbirth; a lamb (as an *olah*) and a dove or pigeon (as a *chatas*).

169. Parshas Tazria 13:2 "A man who shall have on his skin a.... he shall be brought to Aharon the *Kohen*..." (Positive) One who discovers on his skin a growth that could be a symptom of *tzaraas* (a skin affliction), he must go to a priest who determines if he is pure or impure.

170. Parshas Tazria 13:33 "...but the *nessek* he shall not shave" (Prohibitive) One who has *tzaraas* may not shave the hair that is within the *nessek* (the afflicted area) if he has the condition in his beard.

171. Parshas Tazria 13:45 "...his garments shall be torn and the hair on his head uncut..." (Positive) One who has *tzaraas* must tear his clothes like a person in mourning and must let his hair grow during his time of affliction.

172. Parshas Tazria 13:47 "And if there shall be an affliction of *tzaraas* in his clothing..." (Positive) If one sees a sign of this disease on his clothing, he must bring it to the priest who will determine whether it is pure or impure. If impure, the clothing is burned.

Parshas Metzora:

173. Parshas Metzora 14:2 "This shall be the law of the Metzora..." (Positive) Once a priest determines that a man has *tzaraas*, when the symptoms subside, it is a mitzvah to follow a specific process of purification as described in this *parsha*.

174. Parshas Metzora 14:9 "And on the seventh day he shall shave off all his hair..." (Positive) This is part of the process of the purification of the person who had *tzaraas*.

175. Parshas Metzora 14:9 "...and he shall immerse his flesh in water..." (Positive) The person recovering from *tzaraas* must immerse in a *mikvah* (ritual bath) as part of his purification. Any person who becomes impure must immerse in a ritual bath before their purification is complete.

176. Parshas Metzora 14:10 "And on the eighth day he shall take two male lambs..." (Positive) This is the final part of the process of purification, bringing two lambs and one ewe.

177. Parshas Metzora 14:44 "Then the priest shall come and look, and behold, the affliction has spread to the house..." (Positive) This is the mitzvah regarding impurity spreading to a house.

178. Parshas Metzora 15:2 "Any man who shall have a discharge from his flesh..." (Positive) This is a mitzvah relating to a *zav*, one who has a discharge from his body and becomes unclean. He is also capable of making others ritually impure through contact.

179. Parshas Metzora 15:13-14 "And when the man with a discharge is cleansed..." (Positive) This is the mitzvah of bringing an offering of turtledoves or pigeons (one as a *chattas* and one as an *olah*) as an element of his purification process.

180. Parshas Metzora 15:16 "A man who has certain discharges must immerse his body in a mikvah..." (Positive) Such a person is contaminated and can contaminate others.

181. Parshas Metzora 15:19 "...When a woman has a discharge of blood..." (Positive) This is the law of the *niddah*, a woman who experiences her monthly cycle and is *tammei* (impure). She can, through contact, make others impure.

182. Parshas Metzora 15:25 "When a woman has a discharge of blood for many days..." (Positive) This is the law of a *zavah*, a female who becomes ritually impure because of certain bodily discharges and can make others impure through contact.

183. Parshas Metzora 15:28-29 "But when she ceases her flow ...and on the eighth day she shall take two turtledoves..." (Positive) A woman healed from being a *zavah* is mandated to bring an offering.

Acharei Mos:

184. Parshas Acharei Mos 16:2 "...that he shall not come at all times into the Sanctuary..." (Prohibitive) The priests may not enter the inner chamber of the Tabernacle or Temple (the *heichal*) unless they are performing their service. Additionally, the High Priest may only enter the Holy-of-Holies (*Kodesh Kedashim*) on Yom Kippur.

185. Parshas Acharei Mos 16:3 "With this shall Aharon enter the holy place" (Positive) This is the mitzvah of the High Priest performing the Yom Kippur service.

186. Parshas Acharei Mos 17:3-4 "Any man...who will slaughter a bull, sheep, or goat in the camp or will slaughter it outside the camp...and has not brought it to the Tent of Meeting..." (Prohibitive) One may not bring sacrifices outside the Tabernacle or Temple.

187. Parshas Acharei Mos 17:13 "And any man...that hunts (traps) an animal or bird that it may be eaten, shall pour out its blood and cover it with earth" (Positive) It is a mitzvah to cover the blood of wild animals or birds with dirt. We do not cover the blood of domesticated animals. There is a Midrash that says that when Cain killed Abel and shed his blood, birds covered Abel's blood by flapping their wings and kicking-up the dust. Therefore, we cover their blood.

188. Parshas Acharei Mos 18:6 "Any man shall not approach a close relative to uncover nakedness..." (Prohibitive) This law begins a section relating to incestuous relationships. Any act of intimacy with these relatives is forbidden.

189. Parshas Acharei Mos 18:7 "The nakedness of your father... you shall not uncover" (Prohibitive) This mitzvah dictates that one is not allowed to commit any act of perversion with their father (as committed by Ham, one of Noach's sons).

190. Parshas Acharei Mos 18:7 "The nakedness of your mother you shall not uncover" (Prohibitive)

191. Parshas Acharei Mos 18:8 "The nakedness of the wife of your father (your stepmother) you shall not uncover" (Prohibitive)

192. Parshas Acharei Mos 18:9 "The nakedness of your sister, the daughter of your father, or the daughter of your mother you shall not uncover" (Prohibitive) This applies to a sister or half-sister.

193. Parshas Acharei Mos 18:10 "The nakedness of your son's daughter... you shall not uncover" (Prohibitive)

194. Parshas Acharei Mos 18:10 "...or your daughter's daughter" (Prohibitive)

195. Parshas Acharei Mos 18:10 Note: It is extrapolated by our sages from the second part of this *passuk* that one's daughter (not from his wife, but from another relationship) is also to be considered one whose nakedness shall not be uncovered. (Prohibitive)

196. Parshas Acharei Mos 18:11 "The nakedness of the daughter of your father's wife...you shall not uncover" (Prohibitive) This refers to one's half-sister from their father's side.

197. Parshas Acharei Mos 18:12 "The nakedness of the sister of your father you shall not uncover" (Prohibitive) This refers to your aunt.

198. Parshas Acharei Mos 18:13 "The nakedness of the sister of your mother you shall not uncover" (Prohibitive) This is your aunt on your mother's side.

199. Parshas Acharei Mos 18:14 "The nakedness of the brother of your father you shall not uncover..." (Prohibitive)

200. Parshas Acharei Mos 18:14 "...do not approach his wife, she is your aunt" (Prohibitive) This prohibits to you the wife of your uncle.

201. Parshas Acharei Mos 18:15 "The nakedness of your daughter-in-law you shall not uncover" (Prohibitive)

202. Parshas Acharei Mos 18:16 "The nakedness of the wife of your brother you shall not uncover" (Prohibitive)

203. Parshas Acharei Mos 18:17 "The nakedness of a woman and her daughter you shall not uncover" (Prohibitive) This is considered a depraved act.

204. Parshas Acharei Mos 18:17 "...you shall not take her son's daughter to uncover her nakedness..." (Prohibitive) This is referring to being with a woman and her son's daughter. This is *zeemah* (depravity).

205. Parshas Acharei Mos 18:17 "...or her daughter's daughter" (Prohibitive) The is referring to being with a woman and her daughter's daughter. Again, this is considered depravity.

206. Parshas Acharei Mos 18:18 "A woman and her sister you shall not take..." (Prohibitive) One could raise the question of how Yaakov was allowed to marry Leah and Rachel who were sisters, but that was before the giving of the Torah.

207. Parshas Acharei Mos 18:19 "A woman in her unclean time (of *niddah*) you shall not approach..." (Prohibitive)

208. Parshas Acharei Mos 18:21 "You shall not present any of your children to pass through (fire) to Molech" (Prohibitive) This prohibits offering children to the pagan god Molech.

Finer Points: Many were persuaded to offer a son as a sacrifice to "appease the gods" because they were convinced that this would result in their other children living long lives.

209. Parshas Acharei Mos 18:22 "You shall not lie with a man as one lies with a woman; it is an abomination" (Prohibitive) This is the injunction against homosexuality. The Torah uses the word *toevah* (an "abominable" act) for this.

210. Parshas Acharei Mos 18:23 "Do not lie with any animal..." (Prohibitive) This refers to bestiality.

211. Parshas Acharei Mos 18:23 "...a woman shall not stand in front of an animal in an act of mating..." (Prohibitive) This is specifically called an act of perversion – *tevel*.

Kedoshim:

212. Parshas Kedoshim 19:3 "Every man, your mother and father you shall revere..." (Positive) This mandates the reverence due to parents.

213. Parshas Kedoshim 19:4 "Do not turn to the idols..." (Prohibitive) This mitzvah prohibits thought or speech that is directed to idol worship.

214. Parshas Kedoshim 19:4 "...and molten gods you shall not make for yourself" (Prohibitive) This law prohibits the actual casting of an idol made of molten metal such as gold, silver, bronze, copper, etc.

215. Parshas Kedoshim 19:6-8 "And that which remains left-over to the third day...those who eat from it shall bear their iniquity" (Prohibitive) Every sacrifice that may be eaten has a designated time period during which it may be consumed. If it is left over (*nosar*) past the appropriate time, it may not be eaten.

216. Parshas Kedoshim 19:9 "...you shall not completely reap the corners of your field" (Prohibitive) One is forbidden to harvest their entire crop. A corner of the field must be set aside (*peah* – corner).

217. Parshas Kedoshim 19:9 "...nor shall pick up the gleanings of your harvest..." (Prohibitive) One is forbidden to pick up stalks of grain that have fallen on the ground during harvest. They must be left for the poor to gather (as did Ruth in the fields of Boaz). This is the mitzvah of *leket*.

218. Parshas Kedoshim 19:10 This *passuk* teaches us six laws, four positive and two prohibitive. It reads as follows: "You shall not harvest the young grapes of your vineyard and you shall not gather the fallen fruit of your vineyard, for the poor and the stranger (righteous convert) you shall leave them." (Positive) The first positive mitzvah here is to leave one edge of your field for the poor to harvest (at least one sixtieth) This is the positive mitzvah of *peah*.

219. Parshas Kedoshim 19:10 (Positive) The positive mitzvah of leaving on then ground that which fell (*leket*).

220. Parshas Kedoshim 19:10 (Prohibitive) This is the law that states that one may not harvest all the fruit of their field.

221. Parshas Kedoshim 19:10 (Positive) It is a mitzvah to leave part of your vineyard for the poor.

222. Parshas Kedoshim 19:10 (Positive) It is a mitzvah to leave for the poor, individual grapes that fall during harvesting (*peret*).

223. Parshas Kedoshim 19:10 (Prohibitive) One may not gather grapes that fall to the ground during the harvest.

224. Parshas Kedoshim 19:11 "You shall not steal..." (Prohibitive) This *passuk* highlights the difference between the law of not stealing as stated in Sh'mos 20:13, mitzvah #36 (in the 10 Commandments) and the one stated here. The first case is speaking of kidnapping and this case refers to stealing money, objects, etc.

225. Parshas Kedoshim 19:11 "You shall not deny falsely" (Prohibitive) Denying that you owe someone money or denying that you are in possession of an object you borrowed or guarded, is a sin.

226. Parshas Kedoshim 19:11 "...nor shall you lie to one another" (Prohibitive) This refers to swearing falsely in court when you deny owing money.

227. Parshas Kedoshim 19:12 "And you shall not swear falsely using My name..." (Prohibitive) When making an oath, one may not invoke G-d's name or any of His attributes if he has no intention of being bound by the oath (or the oath cannot physically be performed).

228. Parshas Kedoshim 19:13 "You shall not cheat your fellow..." (Prohibitive) If you withhold something that belongs to your neighbor you violate this law. Evading payment of a debt would be an example.

229. Parshas Kedoshim 19:13 "...neither shall you rob him..." (Prohibitive) Robbing is classified by our sages as taking something by force, as opposed to stealing (laws numbers 36 and 224 above).

230. Parshas Kedoshim 19:13 "...you shall not hold the wages of hired worker until morning" (Prohibitive) If you hire a worker you must fulfill your terms of payment and may not withhold compensation at the end of the period of employment.

231. Parshas Kedoshim 19:14 "You shall not curse the deaf..." (Prohibitive) Even if someone cannot hear you or understand you (if you are speaking a language they do not understand) you may not curse them.

232. Parshas Kedoshim 19:14 "...and you shall not put a stumbling block before the blind" (Prohibitive) This refers to misleading or taking advantage of someone.

233. Parshas Kedoshim 19:15 "You shall not commit a perversion of justice" (Prohibitive) A judge may not render an unjust verdict.

234. Parshas Kedoshim 19:15 "...you shall not honor the great..." (Prohibitive) A judge may not show favor to a person of great stature (famous, rich, powerful, etc.).

235. Parshas Kedoshim 19:15 "...with righteousness you shall judge your fellow" (Positive) A judge is commanded to be fair to both parties and to give others the benefit of the doubt.

236. Parshas Kedoshim 19:16 "You shall not be a teller of gossip..." (Prohibitive) This is called *rechilus*, commonly described as revealing to someone what someone else said about him, even if true (as opposed to *lashon harah* which is slandering someone, or *motzi shem ra*, defamation).

237. Parshas Kedoshim 19:16 "...you shall not stand aside while the blood of your neighbor is shed" (Prohibitive) If we see a fellow Jew in mortal danger, we must do everything we can to help. Additionally, you must provide testimony if you can save your friend financially.

238. Parshas Kedoshim 19:17 "You shall not hate your neighbor in your heart..." (Prohibitive) Harboring hatred is considered an evil act in itself.

Finer Points: A friend of mine, Renee H. Levy, wrote a book entitled: <u>Baseless Hatred</u>. It deals with this law and the general concept of *Sin'as Chinam*. I highly recommend it as an addition to one's library.

239. Parshas Kedoshim 19:17 "...you shall surely reprove your fellow man..." (Positive) It is a mitzvah to give *mussar* (constructive criticism) to a fellow Jew who is acting improperly. This should be done respectfully, with sensitivity, in private.

240. Parshas Kedoshim 19:17 "...and do not bear a sin because of him" (Prohibitive) We are admonished not to embarrass or humiliate someone.

241. Parshas Kedoshim 19:18 "You shall not take vengeance..." (Prohibitive) Seeking revenge is considered a sin, although this refers to taking action against a fellow Jew. In a case such as the command to remember and take revenge against Amalek, this does not apply.

242. Parshas Kedoshim 19:18 "...nor shall you bear a grudge against the members of your people..." (Prohibitive)

243. Parshas Kedoshim 19:18 "...and you shall love your neighbor as yourself" (Positive) One should love a fellow Jew. He should behave towards others just as he would want others to behave towards him. Rabbi Akiva and Hillel considered this to be the greatest of all behavioral principles and it is often called: "The Golden Rule."

244. Parshas Kedoshim 19:19 "...you shall not mate your cattle with other species..." (Prohibitive) The process of selective cross-breeding is not allowed.

245. Parshas Kedoshim 19:19 "...you shall not plant your field with mixed seeds..." (Prohibitive) One is not allowed to plant different types of seeds (for instance, corn and wheat) together. This is considered a forbidden mixture (*kilayim*).

246. Parshas Kedoshim 19:23 "...for three years they shall be forbidden to you..." (Prohibitive) After you plant a tree, any fruit produced in the first three years is forbidden. This is the law of *orlah*.

247. Parshas Kedoshim 19:24 "But in the fourth year all its fruits shall be sanctified..." (Positive) The fruit of the fourth year (after the planting of the tree) may be eaten, but there is a process that must be followed before the fruit is deemed permissible to eat.

248. Parshas Kedoshim 19:26 "You shall not eat with the blood..." (Prohibitive) This is the law pertaining to eating and drinking in an over-indulgent manner. This law also relates to the *ben sorer u'moreh*, the rebellious and gluttonous child.

249. Parshas Kedoshim 19:26 "...you shall not practice sorcery (divination)..." (Prohibitive) We are not allowed to rely on astrology (or conduct a seance), and are warned not to follow commonly-held superstitions. In *perek* 28 of the Book of Samuel, King Saul went to the witch of Endor and asked her to conjure-up the spirit of the dead prophet Shmuel so he could seek advice. Such divination or sorcery is a sin. The Torah recognizes the existence of black magic and the power of certain types of sorcery as real, but we have a tradition that after the destruction of the First Temple and the absence of the Ark, G-d muted the powers of black magic in order to protect us.

250. Parshas Kedoshim 19:26 "…and you shall not believe in lucky times" (Prohibitive) The superstitious belief in certain lucky days or numbers is not allowed.

251. Parshas Kedoshim 19:27 "You shall not round the corners of your scalp…" (Prohibitive) Shaving the hair completely off of your temple is not allowed.

252. Parshas Kedoshim 19:27 "…nor shall you destroy the edge of your beard" (Prohibitive) This is the prohibition against shaving-off the hair from five specific areas of one's face.

253. Parshas Kedoshim 19:28 "…nor shall you place a tattoo on yourself…" (Prohibitive)

254. Parshas Kedoshim 19:30 "…and My Sanctuary you shall revere…" (Positive) Visits to the House of G-d (Tabernacle, Temple) must be treated in a respectful and reverent manner. Our sages set specific standards for this.

255. Parshas Kedoshim 19:31 "Do not turn to a fortune-teller…" (Prohibitive)

256. Parshas Kedoshim 19:32 "…and to wizards…" (Prohibitive) This *passuk* prohibits relying on wizards (practitioners of sorcery). Relying on someone who claims to be able to foretell the future is not allowed.

257. Parshas Kedoshim 19:32 "In the presence of an old person you shall rise…" (Positive) It is a mitzvah to honor and respect the elderly and the wise and to rise in their presence.

258. Parshas Kedoshim 19:35 "You shall not commit a perversion of justice in measures of length, weight, or quantity" (Prohibitive) This refers to cheating with weights and measures.

259. Parshas Kedoshim 19:36 "You shall have just scales, just weights…" (Positive) It is a mitzvah to utilize accurate tools of measurement so you do not cheat your customers.

260. Parshas Kedoshim 20:9 "Any man who curses his father or mother shall be put to death" (Prohibitive) We are not allowed to curse our parents using G-d's name. This prohibition carries the death penalty.

261. Parshas Kedoshim 20:14 "And if a man takes a woman and her mother…they shall burn him in fire" (Positive) This mandates the *Beis Din* to execute, through *sreifah* (burning) one who violates this crime of immorality. This law also establishes the court mandate to utilize the punishment of *sreifah* when applicable.

262. Parshas Kedoshim 20:23 "Do not follow the traditions of the nations…" (Prohibitive) We are adjured not to follow the customs of other nation. Many things which other nations consider socially acceptable or mandated by tradition can be a danger to us.

Emor:

263. Parshas Emor 21:1 "…each of you shall not defile yourselves by a (dead) person among his people…" (Prohibitive) A priest is not allowed to come into contact with the dead. If one of his 7 close relatives dies, he may attend the burial. They include his wife, father, mother, son, daughter, brother, sister (unmarried). These are known as the *shiv'ah krovim* (see mitzvah #264).

264. Parshas Emor 21:3 "...for her he may contaminate himself" (Positive) It is a mitzvah for a priest to attend to one of his 7 close relatives who dies, even though he will become impure.

265. Parshas Emor 21:6 "...and they shall not desecrate the name of their G-d..." (Prohibitive) A priest who became ritually impure may not serve in the Temple until after sunset one day later, even if he already immersed in a mikvah.

266. Parshas Emor 21:7 "They shall not marry a woman who is a harlot..." (Prohibitive) A *Kohen* is forbidden to marry such a woman.

267. Parshas Emor 21:7 "(They shall not marry a woman) ...who is desecrated..." (Prohibitive) A priest may not marry any woman who was born from a marriage not allowed for a *Kohen*, such as from a marriage to a divorced woman or one who was not born Jewish.

268. Parshas Emor 21:7 "(They shall not marry a woman) ...divorced from her husband..." (Prohibitive) A priest may not marry a divorcee.

269. Parshas Emor 21:8 "You shall sanctify him..." (Positive) It is a mitzvah to honor the priests (the *Kohanim*). An example would be giving them priority to lead the *Birkas Hamazon* at the end of a meal, calling them to the Torah first, etc.

270. Parshas Emor 21:11 "He shall not come close to any dead person..." (Prohibitive) The *Kohen Gadol* – the High Priest, is not allowed to enter a house that has a dead person in it (even if that person is one of his 7 closest relatives as will be seen in the next law).

271. Parshas Emor 21:11 "...for his father and mother he shall not contaminate himself" (Prohibitive) The law is so strict for the High Priest that he may not even carry the dead (nevertheless, if a High Priest were to come across a dead body with nobody around to bury it, he is required to bury the body himself).

272. Parshas Emor 21:13 "He shall marry a woman in her virginity" (Positive) It is a mitzvah for the High Priest to marry a woman who has never been with a man.

273. Parshas Emor 21:14 "A widow...he shall not take" (Prohibitive) The High Priest may not marry a widow (in addition to the other women he is prohibited to marry).

274. Parshas Emor 21:15 "And he shall not desecrate his seed among his people" (Prohibitive) The High Priest is forbidden from relations outside of marriage.

275. Parshas Emor 21:17 "A man from your offspring throughout the generations who has a blemish shall not come near to offer bread to G-d." (Prohibitive) Any priest who has certain physical defects (such as a deformed body), is not allowed to perform the Temple service.

276. Parshas Emor 21:21 "Any man from among the offspring of Aharon the *Kohen* who has a blemish...shall not approach to offer" (Prohibitive) Temporary physical blemishes prevent a priest from serving in the Temple. If the blemish goes away, he may resume his service after following the process of purification.

277. Parshas Emor 21:23 "But he shall not come to the curtain and shall not approach the altar..." (Prohibitive) A priest with a blemish may not even <u>enter</u> the interior areas where the Temple service is performed.

278. Parshas Emor 22:2 "...they should keep themselves away from the holy things..." (Prohibitive) A priest who is defiled may not serve in any capacity in the Temple until he becomes ritually pure.

279. Parshas Emor 22:4 "Any man of the seed of Aharon who is a *metzorah* or *zav* shall not eat from the holy offerings..." (Prohibitive) A priest who becomes ritually impure is not allowed to eat *trumah*.

280. Parshas Emor 22:10 "No stranger shall eat of a holy offering" (Prohibitive) One who is not a priest may not eat *trumah*. In this case, a "stranger" refers to one who is a *Levi*, a *Yisrael*, or a forbidden *Kohen*.

281. Parshas Emor 22:10 "One who resides with a *Kohen* or a laborer shall not eat of holy offerings" (Prohibitive) Temporary or permanent Jewish servants are also not allowed to eat from *Trumah* offerings.

282. Parshas Emor 22:10 This mitzvah, as discussed by multiple commentaries, is not directly attributable to a specific quote from this passuk. The words here, "*toshav*" and "*sachir*" are also used in relation to the *korban pesach* (the Paschal offering) to teach us that one who is uncircumcised may not eat from that *korban*. (Prohibitive) We learn through the similar usage of those words here (using the principle of *gezeirah shavah*) that in this case (*trumah* offerings), one who is uncircumcised may not eat them. This includes a priest who may not have been circumcised due to health concerns.

283. Parshas Emor 22:12 "And if the daughter of a priest shall be married to a stranger, she shall not eat of..." (Prohibitive) If the daughter of a priest enters into a forbidden marriage, she may never again eat *trumah*.

284. Parshas Emor 22:15 "And they shall not desecrate the holy offerings of the people of Israel..." (Prohibitive) This prohibits the eating of produce from which *trumah* or *maaser* was not taken. Such produce is called *tevel*.

285. Parshas Emor 22:20 "All that has upon it a blemish you shall not offer..." (Prohibitive) It is forbidden to offer a defective animal on the altar.

286. Parshas Emor 22:21 "...it shall be pure (unblemished) to be accepted" (Positive) All offerings have to be pure. If a priest detects that an animal has a physical defect or a meal offering contains mold, he must disqualify that offering.

287. Parshas Emor 22:21 "...there shall be no blemish on it" (Prohibitive) It is prohibited to inflict any kind of wound upon an animal that had already been consecrated to the Temple and that would then disqualify it from being brought as an offering.

288. Parshas Emor 22:22 "One that is blind or broken..." (Prohibitive) This refers to the sprinkling of blood on the altar – the blood of a defective animal could not be used for this.

289. Parshas Emor 22:22 "...you shall not sacrifice these..." (Prohibitive) This law specifically forbids the slaughtering of defective animals for Temple offerings.

290. Parshas Emor 22:22 "and you shall not place any of them as a fire offering..." (Prohibitive) This forbids the burning, on the altar, of parts of these prohibited animals.

291. Parshas Emor 22:24 "One whose testicles are squeezed, crushed, torn, or cut you shall not offer and in your land, you shall not do so" (Prohibitive) Castration or sterilization of animals is not allowed (nor is it allowed for humans).

292. Parshas Emor 22:25 "From the hand of a foreigner you shall not offer..." (Prohibitive) We are allowed to bring certain offerings in the Temple from non-Jews, but may not offer defective ones. Reference the story in Gemara Gittin (55b) of Bar Kamsa who wounded an offering brought by the Romans and what resulted from his actions.

293. Parshas Emor 22:26 "...and from the eighth day and onward it shall be acceptable for a fire offering..." (Positive) It is a mitzvah to bring as a korban, only those animals that are at least eight days old.

294. Parshas Emor 22:28 "But an ox, a sheep, or a goat, you may not slaughter it and its young on the same day" (Prohibitive) It is prohibited to slaughter an animal and its offspring on the same day.

295. Parshas Emor 22:32 "You shall not desecrate My holy name…" (Prohibitive) The word used here for "desecrate" is **תחללו** and teaches us the negative concept of **חלול השם** – desecrating or profaning the name of G-d.

296. Parshas Emor 22:32 "…so that I may be sanctified among the children of Israel" (Positive) It is a positive mitzvah to sanctify and honor the name of G-d. This is called: *Al Kiddush Hashem*. Giving up one's life, if necessary, is considered as dying for the sake of G-d. There are three sins for which one must allow himself to be killed (if threatened with death) rather than commit them. They are: *gilui arayos, sh'fichas damim,* and *avodah zarah* – illicit sexual acts, murder, and idol worship.

297. Parshas Emor 23:7 "On the first day there shall be a holy convocation for you…" (Positive) This is the mitzvah of refraining from work on the first day of the holiday of Pesach.

298. Parshas Emor 23:7 "…all manner of work you shall not do." (Prohibitive) We are forbidden from doing any labor on the holiday, except for that which is needed for food preparation.

299. Parshas Emor 23:8 "And you shall bring an offering…seven days" (Positive) This is the mitzvah of offering the *korban mussaf* on each day of Pesach.

300. Parshas Emor 23:8 "…on the seventh day shall be a holy convocation" (Positive) It is a mitzvah to honor the seven day of Pesach by resting and refraining from work.

301. Parshas Emor 23:8 "…on the seventh day…all manner of work you shall not do" (Prohibitive) This is the prohibition of working on the seventh day of Pesach. It is treated like the first day – it is a *yom tov*.

302. Parshas Emor 23:10-11 "And you shall bring an *omer* of your harvested first fruits to the *Kohen* and he shall wave the *omer*…" (Positive) This is the mitzvah of offering a sheaf of barley which was brought on Pesach to the Temple on the sixteenth of Nissan and made into a meal offering.

303. Parshas Emor 23:14 "And you shall not eat bread...until you bring the offerings..." (Prohibitive) One may not eat any grain from the harvesting of a new crop until the end of the sixteenth day of Nissan (the day when the *omer* offering was brought). This is known as the law of *chadash* ("new" grain).

304. Parshas Emor 23:14 "...roasted kernels..." (Prohibitive) This forbids the eating of parched or roasted grain until after the *omer* was brought (this is also part of the laws of *chadash*)

305. Parshas Emor 23:14 "...and fresh grain you shall not eat..." (Prohibitive) This comes to exclude the eating of fresh grain until the *omer* was brought. Again, this is part of the laws of *chadash*.

306. Parshas Emor 23:15 "And you shall count for yourselves from the morrow of the rest day, from the day when you bring the *omer*...seven weeks they shall be complete" (Positive) This is the mitzvah of counting the *omer* by counting forty-nine days; seven weeks beginning on the second day of Pesach, until Shavuos – the day of the revelation on Mount Sinai.

307. Parshas Emor 23:17 "From your dwelling places you shall bring bread that will be waved, two loaves..." (Positive) On Shavuos there is mitzvah to offer two loaves of bread at the Temple from newly harvested wheat.

308. Parshas Emor 23:21 "And you shall proclaim on this self-same day a holy convocation..." (Positive) This is the mitzvah of resting from work on Shavuos.

309. Parshas Emor 23:21 "...all manner of work you shall not do" (Prohibitive) Work is forbidden on Shavuos.

310. Parshas Emor 23:24 "...in the seventh month, on the first of the month, it shall be for you as a day of rest..." (Positive) This is the mitzvah of refraining from work on Rosh Hashanah, the first day of Tishrei. It is called the "seventh" month since Nissan is considered the first month of our <u>historical year</u>, marking our exodus from Egypt, while Tishrei is the first month of our <u>calendar year</u>. The mitzvah of blowing the shofar (even though it is mentioned in this passuk) is associated with mitzvah #405 found in the parsha of Pinchas.

311.   Parshas Emor 23:25 "...all manner of work you shall not do" (Prohibitive) This forbids any labor on Rosh Hashanah (excluding preparation of food).

312.   Parshas Emor 23:25 "...and you shall bring a fire-offering to G-d..." (Positive) This is the mitzvah of bringing a *mussaf* offering on Rosh Hashanah.

313.   Parshas Emor 23:27 "And on the tenth day of the seventh month is the Day of Atonement...you shall afflict your souls..." (Positive) This is the mitzvah of fasting on Yom Kippur.

314.   Parshas Emor 23:27 "...you shall bring a fire-offering to G-d" (Positive) This is the *mussaf* offering of Yom Kippur.

315.   Parshas Emor 23:28 "And you shall not do any work on this self-same day..." (Prohibitive) It is forbidden to do any kind of work on Yom Kippur including food preparation.

316.   Parshas Emor 23:29 "And any soul who will not be afflicted on this day shall be cut off from among her people" (Prohibitive) This forbids eating and drinking on Yom Kippur.

Finer Points: Note the use in this passuk, in Hebrew, of the feminine form when speaking about the soul. It says: **ונכרתה מעמיה** – "and <u>she</u> (the soul) shall be cut off from her people." This is just one example of the many times in Tanach when the soul of man is spoken-of in the feminine.

317.   Parshas Emor 23:32 "It is a day of complete rest for you..." (Positive) This is the mitzvah of resting from work on Yom Kippur.

318. Parshas Emor 23:35 "On the first day shall be a holy convocation" (Positive) This is referring to the first day of Succos, the holiday of "Tabernacles," and the mitzvah to rest from work.

319. Parshas Emor 23:35 "...all manner of work you shall not do" (Prohibitive) Work on the *yom tov* of Succos is prohibited.

320. Parshas Emor 23:36 "For seven days you shall bring a fire offering" (Positive) This is the mitzvah of the *mussaf* offering on all the days of Succos.

321. Parshas Emor 23:36 "...on the eighth day there shall be a holy convocation for you..." (Positive) This is the mitzvah of resting from work on the holiday of Shmini Atzeres (except food preparation).

322. Parshas Emor 23:36 "...on the eighth day...and you shall bring a fire offering to G-d" (Positive) This is the mitzvah of bringing the *mussaf* offering on Shmini Atzeres.

323. Parshas Emor 23:36 "...all manner of work you shall not do" (Prohibitive) This prohibits work on Shmini Atzeres.

324. Parshas Emor 23:40 "You shall take for yourselves on the first day the fruit of the citron tree, the branches of date palms, boughs of myrtle twigs and brook willows..." (Positive) This is the mitzvah of taking the four species on Succos.

325. Parshas Emor 23:42 "You shall dwell in booths for seven days..." (Positive) This is the mitzvah of sitting in a *succah* during the holiday of Succos.

Behar:

326. Parshas Behar 25:4 "But in the seventh year you shall not sow your field" (Prohibitive) This is the prohibition against working your fields during the *shmittah* year.

327. Parshas Behar 25:4 "...and your vineyard you shall not prune" (Prohibitive) During the *shmittah* year one may not work to trim and improve their trees.

328. Parshas Behar 25:5 "That which grows on its own from the harvest you shall not reap..." (Prohibitive) Even those plants that continue to produce during the *shmittah* year cannot be harvested. For example, if you have berry bushes that grow wild on your property, you may not harvest them for commercial use during *shmittah*.

329. Parshas Behar 25:5 "...and the grapes you had set aside as a reserve for yourself you shall not pick" (Prohibitive) You can't take fruit from the trees in the way you would harvest in a normal year. Rather, you must harvest differently. All fields are deemed "ownerless" in that year and anyone can pick enough for their personal consumption, but not for sale to others.

330. Parshas Behar 25:8 "And you shall count for yourselves seven cycles of seven Sabbatical years..." (Positive) This is the mitzvah of counting the cycle of seven *shmittah* years (resulting in the declaration of the *Yovel* – mitzvah #332) which is the 50th year that follows the 7x7 (49 year) cycle.

331. Parshas Behar 25:9 "...on the Day of Atonement you shall sound the *shofar* throughout the land" (Positive) This is the mitzvah of blowing the shofar on Yom Kippur of the 50th (*Yovel*) year. That blast of the shofar was the signal that all Jewish slaves were free from servitude.

332. Parshas Behar 25:10 "And you shall sanctify the fiftieth year and proclaim liberty throughout the land..." (Positive) This is the mitzvah to sanctify the fiftieth (*yovel*) year by not working one's land. The Liberty Bell in Philadelphia is inscribed with part of this *passuk*.

333. Parshas Behar 25:11 "...you shall not sow..." (Prohibitive) It is forbidden to work the land in the *Yovel* year.

334. Parshas Behar 25:11 "...and you shall not reap that which grows on its own..." (Prohibitive) You may not harvest in the *yovel* year that which grows wild (allowances were made for picking for personal consumption, but even then, harvesting had to be done differently).

335. Parshas Behar 25:11 "...nor shall you gather its grapes..." (Prohibitive) The normal way of picking grapes and gathering fruit is not allowed in the *Yovel* year. Again, allowances were made for picking fruit for personal consumption and the laws regulating this are complicated.

336. Parshas Behar 25:14 "And if you make a sale to a fellow or make a purchase from his hand..." (Positive) This is the mitzvah that commands us to seek justice between a buyer and seller and to follow the rules of the Torah in conducting business.

337. Parshas Behar 25:14 "...you shall not deceive one another" (Prohibitive) This is the prohibition against overcharging or misrepresenting the value of an object or a service.

338. Parshas Behar 25:17 "And you shall not deceive a fellow Jew" (Prohibitive) This refers to *ona'as devarim* – deception with words. Causing someone pain by offending them with words is a sin.

339. Parshas Behar 25:23 "The land shall not be sold in perpetuity" (Prohibitive) Land in Israel cannot be sold permanently.

340. Parshas Behar 25:24 "In the entire land of your ancestral heritage you shall grant redemption for the land" (Positive) This is the mitzvah of returning land to its original owner in the *Yovel* year.

341. Parshas Behar 25:29 "And if a man sells a dwelling (house) in a walled city..." (Positive) A walled city in Israel that dates back to the time of Yehoshua has special laws. The family that originally owned a house in such a city could buy it back (redeem it) from the new owners, but only during the first year after such a sale. During a *Yovel* year, this kind of house did not have to be returned to the original owner.

342. Parshas Behar 25:34 "But the fields of the open lands of a city may not be changed..." (Prohibitive) The 48 cities of the Levites (which were also refuge cities (*Arei Miklat*) had buffer zones around them that were declared as "open" land and could not be developed.

343. Parshas Behar 25:37 "Do not give him your money for interest, and do not give your food as increased payment" (Prohibitive) Lending with interest to a fellow Jew is not permitted.

344. Parshas Behar 25:39 "...you shall not force him to work as a slave" (Prohibitive) A Jewish "slave" (for example: one who works as an indentured servant to repay a debt) may not be given work that is so menial that a normal paid laborer would not do it.

345. Parshas Behar 25:42 "...they shall not be sold in the manner of a slave" (Prohibitive) One may not sell a Jewish indentured servant like a slave (in a slave-market, on a stage, or on public display)

346. Parshas Behar 25:43 "You shall not subjugate him through hard labor..." (Prohibitive) One is forbidden to overwork a Jewish indentured servant.

347. Parshas Behar 25:46 "...you shall make them slaves forever..." (Positive) It is a mitzvah to keep a non-Jewish slave as a permanent worker.

348. Parshas Behar 25:53 "...he shall not subjugate him with hard labor before your eyes" (Prohibitive) It is forbidden to stand by as a gentile master abuses his Jewish servant. If that happens, we must step in and take action.

349. Parshas Behar 26:1 "...and you shall not place a flooring stone to bow down upon it" (Prohibitive) It is forbidden to bow-down on a hard surface in prayer. This practice is common among those of other religions who prostrate themselves on tile or marble floors in prayer. This practice was only allowed in the Temple. On Rosh Hashanah and Yom Kippur, when we bow for *Aleinu* or during the *Avodah*, it is common practice to place a fabric covering over the floor, although many do not do this if there is carpet covering the hard surface.

Bechukosai:

350. Parshas Bechukosai 27:2 "...when a man shall articulate a vow to give the value of another person in honor of G-d..." (Positive) It is a mitzvah for a person who vows to donate a person's "value" to the Temple to give according to a fixed value calculation proscribed by the Torah. The value is to be paid in the currency of *shekalim*.

351. Parshas Bechukosai 27:10 "He shall not exchange it nor substitute it..." (Prohibitive) Once an animal was consecrated as a *korban* to the Temple it could not be exchanged for another animal.

352. Parshas Bechukosai 27:10 "...but if he does substitute one animal for another, then it, together with its exchange, shall be holy" (Positive) If mitzvah #351 had been transgressed by the donor consecrating a substitute animal, both animals would be considered holy and could not be used for any mundane purpose.

353. Parshas Bechukosai 27:11-12 "And if any disqualified animal... then he shall stand the animal in front of the *Kohen*...and the *Kohen* shall value it" (Positive) If an animal was consecrated and then became blemished, it was brought in front of a priest for valuation. The donor had to redeem its value (if it was deemed unfit as a sacrifice) and give the money to the Temple treasury. It is a mitzvah to pay the value as established by the *Kohen*.

354. Parshas Bechukosai 27:14 "And if a man consecrates his house to be holy to G-d...as the *Kohen* shall value it so shall it stand" (Positive) This mitzvah establishes the enforcement of valuation of one's house, if one chooses to gift it to the Temple. The owner can redeem the house for the established value plus a fifth (a *chomesh*) if he so desires.

355. Parshas Bechukosai 27:16 "And if a man consecrates a field...the valuation shall be according to its seeding..." (Positive) The value of a field (for donation purposes) is valued based on the volume of crops it produced prior to *yovel*. The Torah specifies here the *shekel* value for each *chomer* (a measurement of volume). The mitzvah is to enforce the system of valuation of a field of crops when redeeming a field from the Temple treasury.

356. Parshas Bechukosai 27:26 "However, a firstborn...among livestock a man shall not consecrate it..." (Prohibitive) A firstborn animal already has a specified holiness. The owner may not substitute another animal as an offering. This mitzvah is also taken as a general rule - one may not take an animal that is consecrated for a specific offering and then exchange it for another and bring the first animal as a different offering.

357. Parshas Bechukosai 27:28 "However, any *cherem* which a person has vowed to give...may not be sold and may not be redeemed" (Positive) If a person consecrates an object (moveable goods) it then becomes forbidden for his personal use. It is called *"cherem."* Since it is already forbidden to him, he cannot redeem it. The mitzvah in this case is to give the consecrated item to the *Kohen*.

358. Parshas Bechukosai 27:28 "...*cherem*...may not be sold..." (Prohibitive) Once an item is *cherem* (has been consecrated and is now forbidden for personal use) it cannot be sold but must be given to a *Kohen*.

359. Parshas Bechukosai 27:28 "...and may not be redeemed" (Prohibitive) The *cherem* spoken-of in the last two laws may not be redeemed by having the owner replace it with another item or exchange money for it.

360. Parshas Bechukosai 27:32 "Any tithe (*maaser*) of cattle or the flock that passes under the staff, the tenth one shall be holy..."

(Positive) Of one's livestock born each year, all are to be counted, with each tenth animal designated as *maaser*. Each tenth animal is marked with red dye and the owner makes a formal vocal declaration that these animals were consecrated.

361.   Parshas Bechukosai 27:33 "...it shall not be redeemed." (Prohibitive) Each tenth animal has to be declared as *maaser*. It is possible that the tenth animal could be externally defective or blemished. Even so, it remained as declared and could not be redeemed or sold.

Mitzvos in the Book of Bamidbar

Nasso:

362.   Parshas Nasso 5:2 "Command the children of Israel that they send out of the camp each *metzora*, each *zav*, and every person contaminated by the dead" (Positive) It is a mitzvah to segregate those who are ritually impure and move them outside the community encampment.

363.   Parshas Nasso 5:3 "...so they should not contaminate their camps..." (Prohibitive) A person who is ritually impure is forbidden from entering the Temple.

364.   Parshas Nasso 5:7 "...they shall confess their sin..." (Positive) It is a mitzvah to verbally confess one's sin (*vidui*) as one element of *teshuva*, repentance. There are four steps to this process, including the confession as commanded in this *passuk*; recognizing the act of sin, regretting it, confessing it, and declaring that they will not commit the sin again.

365.   Parshas Nasso 5:12-15 "Any man whose wife shall go astray...he shall bring his wife to the *Kohen*..." (Positive) If a man suspects that his wife is being unfaithful, it is a mitzvah to bring her

before a priest in the Temple where her innocence or guilt will be tested. This is called the *parsha* of the *sotah* – a woman suspected of an unfaithful act.

366. Parshas Nasso 5:15 "…and he shall bring her offering for her…he shall not pour oil over it…" (Prohibitive) The meal offering brought as part of the procedure of testing the *sotah* could not have oil poured over it (as would normally be done for a *korban mincha*).

367. Parshas Nasso 5:15 "…and he shall not put any frankincense on it…" (Prohibitive) Normally, when one brought a meal offering, a little frankincense was sprinkled over it. This law teaches that in the case of the offering of the *sotah*, none was to be sprinkled.

368. Parshas Nasso 6:3 "…a man or woman who shall separate themselves by taking a Nazarite vow of abstinence…shall separate from wine and strong drink…" (Prohibitive) A *nazir* is not allowed to drink wine or any grape-based drinks. Wine is considered such an intoxicating beverage that the Torah prohibits five different grape products to the *nazir*, including wine, fresh grapes, dried grapes, grape seeds, and grape skins as will be seen in the next four laws.

369. Parshas Nasso 6:3 "…and fresh…grapes, he shall not eat" (Prohibitive) Even plain grapes that have not been fermented are prohibited to a *nazir*.

370. Parshas Nasso 6:3 "…and dried grapes he shall not eat" (Prohibitive) The *nazir* is even prohibited from eating raisins, which are dried grapes and often distinguished by consumers as a different fruit, unrecognizable as a grape.

371. Parshas Nasso 6:4 "…from the seeds he shall not eat…" (Prohibitive) Even the seeds of grapes may not be consumed by a *nazir*.

372. Parshas Nasso 6:4 "…or skin he shall not eat" (Prohibitive) This refers to the consumption of grape skins which also may not be eaten by a *nazir*.

373. Parshas Nasso 6:5 "All the days of his Nazarite vow no razor shall not pass over his head..." (Prohibitive) A *nazir* cannot shave his hair during his period of abstinence.

374. Parshas Nasso 6:5 "...he shall grow wildly the hair on his head" (Positive) It is a mitzvah for the *nazir* to grow his hair long (i.e.: Samson, Shimshon).

375. Parshas Nasso 6:6 "...he shall not come near any human corpse" (Prohibitive) A *nazir* may not defile himself by entering a building that contains a dead person (house, hospital, mortuary, etc.).

376. Parshas Nasso 6:7 "To his father and his mother...he shall not defile himself..." (Prohibitive) A *nazir* is not allowed to attend to any of his close relatives if they die.

377. Parshas Nasso 6:9-13 "And if a man should die near him suddenly...he shall shave his head...shall make a sin offering...an elevation offering...a guilt offering...on the day his abstinence is completed he shall bring himself to the Tent of Meeting" (Positive) A *nazir* who becomes impure during his time of abstinence (as in this case when someone dies right next to him) or one who fulfills his full time that he had vowed to abstain, follows a set formula of coming to the Tabernacle or Temple, offering multiple *korbanos*, and shaving. The observance of these fixed procedures is the actual mitzvah.

378. Parshas Nasso 6:23 "...so shall you bless the children of Israel" (Positive) This is the mitzvah of *Birkas Kohanim*, the daily blessing of Israel by the priests.

379. Parshas Nasso 7:9 "And to the sons of Kehas he did not give since the sacred service was upon them; they carried on the shoulder" (Positive) It is a mitzvah to carry the Ark. While certain families used wagons to carry the parts of the Tabernacle, the family of Kehas was given no wagons since they were to carry the Ark on their shoulders.

They, as *Leviim*, transported the Ark, but the *Kohanim* also carried it at certain times (for example, when Israel went to war).

Beha'aloscha:

380. Parshas Beha'aloscha 9:11 "In the second month, on the fourteenth day, towards evening they shall make it..." (Positive) Those who could not participate in the *Korban Pesach* on the fourteenth of *Nissan* (due to being impure or certain extenuating circumstances) could bring the sacrifice a month later, on the fourteenth of Iyar. This is called *Pesach Sheini*

381. Parshas Beha'alsocha 9:11 "...they shall eat it with matzohs and bitter herbs" (Positive) The observance of *Pesach Sheini* includes eating the *Korban Pesach* with matzoh and marror.

382. Parshas Beha'alsoscha 9:12 "They shall not leave over from it until morning..." (Prohibitive) Just like with the *Korban Pesach* brought in Nissan, the *Pesach Sheini* sacrifice could not be left over.

383. Parshas Beha'aloscha 9:12 "...nor shall they break any bone of it" (Prohibitive) Again, the *Pesach Sheini* sacrifice is treated just like the earlier one, and the breaking of bones is prohibited.

384. Parsha Beha'aloscha 10:9-10 "When you go to wage war in your land...you shall sound blasts of the trumpets...you shall sound the trumpets over your burnt offerings ..." (Positive) It is a mitzvah to blow the silver trumpets (of the Tabernacle and Temple) at certain times.

Shelach:

385. Parshas Shelach 15:20 "As the first of your kneading you shall set aside a loaf as a portion..." (Positive) This is the mitzvah of setting-aside a portion of dough which shall be given to the *Kohen*. This is called *challah*. Today, we separate a ball of dough and burn it.

386. Parshas Shelach 15:38 "They shall make for themselves tzitzis on the corner of their garments..." (Positive) This is the mitzvah of attaching fringes to our 4-cornered garments.

387. Parshas Shelach 15:39 "...and not explore after your heart and after your eyes after which you stray" (Prohibitive) This is the prohibition against following thoughts about heresy or immorality.

Korach:

388. Parshas Korach 18:3 "...but to the holy vessels and the altar they shall not approach" (Prohibitive) The Kohanim are forbidden from doing the work of the Leviim and the Leviim are forbidden from doing the work of the Kohanim.

389. Parshas Korach 18:4 "...and they shall safeguard the Tent of Meeting..." (Positive) It is a mitzvah to establish a system for guarding the Tabernacle and Temple at night and establishing watches.

390. Parshas Korach 18:4 "...and a stranger shall not approach you." (Prohibitive) None of the services assigned to a priest may be performed by a non-*Kohen*.

391. Parshas Korach 18:5 "And you shall keep the watch of the Sanctuary..." (Prohibitive) The Sanhedrin was given the charge to make sure that the Temple not to go unguarded for even one night. Abandoning one's post was a violation of this commandment.

392. Parshas Korach 18:15 "...you shall surely redeem the firstborn of man." (Positive) Every father of a first-born male is commanded the mitzvah to redeem that child from a *Kohen*. Today, we use five silver-eagle dollars as payment for that redemption.

393. Parshas Korach 18:17 "But the firstborn of a cow...you shall not redeem..." (Prohibitive) Firstborn kosher domestic animals such as cows, sheep, and goats, cannot be redeemed and must be given to a *Kohen*.

394. Parshas Korach 18:23 "But the *Levi* shall perform the service of the Tent of Meeting..." (Positive) The Levites have the obligation to perform the mitzvah of serving in the Tabernacle and Temple (such as singing in the choir, playing instruments, standing watch, etc.).

395. Parshas Korach 18:24 "For the tithe of the children of Israel that they raise up to G-d as a gift, I have given to the Levites..." (Positive) It is a mitzvah to give a tithe (one-tenth) of one's produce to the *Levi* (*maaser rishon*).

396. Parshas Korach 18:26 "To the Levites...when you accept...the tithe...you shall raise up from it a gift to G-d, a tithe from a tithe." (Positive) It is a mitzvah for a *Levi* to separate an additional 1/10th from that which was given to him, and present it to a *Kohen* (*trumas maser*).

Chukas:

397. Parshas Chukas 19:2 "...they shall take to you a completely red cow..." (Positive) This is the mitzvah of the *parah adumah*, the red heifer. It was burned and its ashes used to purify someone who had become impure through contact with a dead body. This law is an enigma in that it makes someone pure again and yet makes the one who prepares the ashes impure.

398. Parshas Chukas 19:14 "This is the law when one will die in a tent, anything that enters the tent and anything that is in the tent shall be contaminated for seven days." (Positive) The observance of the laws of impurity of the dead (*tumas mais*) is a mitzvah.

399. Parshas Chukas 19:19 "The pure person shall sprinkle on the contaminated person..." (Positive) It is a mitzvah for the person who became impure (through contact with the dead) to follow the purification process involving the sprinkling of the mixture of the red heifer's ashes and water.

Pinchas:

400. Parshas Pinchas 27:8 "...if a man shall die and he has no son..." (Positive) It is a mitzvah to implement the laws of inheritance.

401. Parshas Pinchas 28:2-3 "...offer to Me... male lambs in the first year..." (Positive) This is the mitzvah of offering two sacrifices of burnt offerings every day. One was offered in the morning and one in the evening. This is the *korban tamid*.

402. Parshas Pinchas 28:9 "And on the day of Shabbos two male lambs..." (Positive) Every Shabbos two extra burnt-offerings were brought (*korban mussaf*).

403. Parshas Pinchas 28:11-15 "On your new moons you shall bring...and one male of the goats..." (Positive) It is a mitzvah to bring the *korban mussaf* on *Rosh Chodesh*.

404. Parshas Pinchas 28:26 "And on the day of the first-fruits when you bring a new meal offering..." (Positive) This is the mitzvah of bringing a *korban mussaf* on the holiday of Shavous.

405. Parshas Pinchas 29:1 "...it shall be a day of shofar-sounding for you" (Positive) This is the mitzvah of listening to the shofar on Rosh Hashanah.

Mattos:

406. Parshas Mattos 30:3 "If a man takes a vow..." (Positive) This law deals with the annulment of vows.

407. Parshas Mattos 30:3 "...he shall not desecrate his word" (Prohibitive) One is not allowed to break their word by not keeping a promise. That is why many Jews, when making a promise, add the words *b'li neder* (בלי נדר) meaning: *without making a promise*

Massei:

408. Parshas Massei 35:2-7 "Command the children of Israel that they give to the Levites from the heritage of their possession cities for dwelling...forty-eight cities, them and their open spaces" (Positive) In Israel, the Levites were allocated 48 cities in which to live that were later designated as *arei miklat* (cities of refuge) as well.

409. Parshas Massei 35:12 "...the murderer will not die until he stands before the assembly for judgement" (Prohibitive) This mitzvah prohibits the killing of a captured murderer until there has been a trial and he has been found guilty.

410. Parshas Massei 35:25 "...and the assembly shall return him to his city of refuge to which he has fled..." (Positive) The Jewish court that tries a killer (and the verdict is that he committed manslaughter, not premeditated murder) must return him to a city of refuge.

411. Parshas Massei 35:30 "...but a single witness shall not testify against any person to cause his death" (Prohibitive) Capital crimes require a minimum of two witnesses and a witness is not allowed to be one of those who renders judgement.

412. Parshas Massei 35:31 "And you shall not accept ransom for the life of a murderer who is worthy of death..." (Prohibitive) It is forbidden to pay off or redeem one's culpability for a capital crime.

413. Parshas Massei 35:32 "And you shall not accept ransom for one who fled to his city of refuge…" (Prohibitive) One who is banished to a city of refuge cannot buy his way to freedom. Only when the High Priest dies are those in sanctuary allowed to return home.

Mitzvos in the Book of Devarim

Devarim:

414. Parshas Devarim 1:17 "You shall not show favoritism in judgement…" (Prohibitive) The court shall appoint only those judges who possess the right qualifications, not those who are popular. They are not allowed to appoint the wrong ones.

415. Parshas Devarim 1:17 "…you shall not tremble before any man" (Prohibitive) A judge cannot allow his fear of retribution from a dangerous litigant to color his judgement.

Va'eschanan:

416. Parshas Va'eschanan 5:18 "And you shall not covet your neighbor's wife…house…field…slave…or anything that belongs to your neighbor" (Prohibitive) Unlike the earlier commandment in Parshas Yisro not to covet that which your neighbor has (to the point you would be willing to use force to get it) this case is speaking of <u>desiring</u> what your neighbor has.

417. Parshas Va'eschanan 6:4 "Hear O Israel, the Lord is our G-d, the Lord is One" (Positive) This is the opening line of the *Shema* and obligates us to believe in the Oneness of G-d, that He created everything, that He is the master of everything, and that there are no other gods but Him. Earlier, in the Ten Commandments (mitzvah #25), we have the mitzvah of believing in G-d's existence.

418. Parshas Va'eschanan 6:5 "And you shall love the Lord your G-d…" (Positive) It is a mitzvah to love G-d with all of our capabilities and all our senses.

419. Parshas Va'eschanan 6:7 "And you shall teach them thoroughly…" (Positive) It is a mitzvah to study Torah and pass it to our children.

420. Parshas Va'eschanan 6:7 "…and you shall speak of them while you sit at home, walk on the way, when you go to sleep, and when you get up." (Positive) This mitzvah dictates that we say the *Shema* twice a day, once in the morning and once at night.

421. Parshas Va'eschanan 6:8 "And you shall bind them as a sign on your arm…" (Positive) This is the mitzvah of *tefillin* worn on the arm.

422. Parshas Va'eschanan 6:8 "…and they shall be as ornaments between your eyes" (Positive) This is the mitzvah of wearing *tefillin* on the head.

423. Parshas Va'eschanan 6:9 "And you shall write them on the doorposts of your house…" (Positive) This is the mitzvah of *mezuzah*.

424. Parshas Va'eschanan 6:16 "You shall not test Hashem your G-d at you tested him at Massah" (Prohibitive) We are forbidden from testing a true prophet.

425. Parshas Va'eschanan 7:2 "…you shall utterly destroy them" (Positive) This is the mitzvah that commands the Jewish People to destroy the seven nations indigenous to the Land of Israel (*Chitti, Girgashi, Emori, Canaani, Perrizi, Chivi, and Yevusi*).

426. Parshas Va'eschanan 7:2 "…and you shall not have mercy on them" (Prohibitive) This refers to the seven nations of the Land of Israel who were idol worshipers.

427. Parshas Va'eschanan 7:3 "You shall not intermarry with them…" (Prohibitive) This is the injunction against marrying a gentile.

Eikev:

428. Parshas Eikev 7:25 "...you shall not covet the silver or gold that is on them lest you be ensnared by it..." (Prohibitive) When the Jewish People conquer enemies, it is expressly forbidden to keep or benefit from any ornamentation that is on their idols.

429. Parshas Eikev 7:26 "And you shall not bring an abomination into your home..." (Prohibitive) Anything that is connected to idolatry is forbidden to us – we cannot derive benefit from it.

430. Parshas Eikev 8:10 "You will eat and be satisfied and bless G-d..." (Positive) This is the mitzvah of reciting a blessing <u>after</u> eating (*birkas hamazon*). The Rabbis later added the requirement to recite blessings <u>before</u> partaking of food and drink, what we call *birchos ha'nehenin* (blessings on things from which we derive benefit).

431. Parshas Eikev 10:19 "And you shall love the stranger for you were strangers in the land of Egypt" (Positive) It is a mitzvah to love those who convert to Judaism.

432. Parshas Eikev 10:20 "You shall fear Hashem, your G-d..." (Positive) It is a mitzvah to fear G-d.

433. Parshas Eikev 10:20 "...Him you shall serve..." (Positive) This is explained as referring to prayer - service to G-d.

434. Parshas Eikev 10:20 "...and to Him you shall cleave..." (Positive) We are commanded to cleave to G-d by associating with those who are wise and teach Torah.

435. Parshas Eikev 10:20 "...and by His name you shall swear" (Positive) When an oath was required in a Jewish court, it was a mitzvah to swear in the name of G-d. Today, we no longer do that since there are too many who will swear falsely and use G-d's name in vain.

Re'eh:

436. Parshas Re'eh 12:2 "You shall utterly destroy all the places where the nations you are driving away worshiped their gods…" (Positive) The conquest of the Land of Israel included the command to completely tear down and destroy places of idol worship.

437. Parshas Re-eh 12:4 "You shall not do this to Hashem…" (Prohibitive) We are not allowed to destroy or erase any name of G-d. This includes those in sacred books and scrolls and also refers to any destruction of part of the Temple. We commonly associate seven sacred names of G-d with this prohibition; **YHVH** (Yud, Heh, Vav, Heh – also known as the Tetragrammaton), **EL**, **ELOAH**, **ELOHIM**, **SHADDAI**, **EHYEH**, and **TZEVAOS**.

438. Parshas Re-eh 12:6 "And there you shall bring your elevation offerings and feast offerings…" (Positive) It is a mitzvah to ascend to the Temple and present any offerings one owes on the three pilgrimage holidays.

439. Parshas Re'eh 12:13 "Beware for yourself that you do not offer your burnt-offerings in any place that you see" (Prohibitive) The only place one can bring a sacrifice is the Temple (and before that, the Tabernacle). Any other location is prohibited.

440. Parshas Re'eh 12:14 "But rather only in the place which Hashem will choose…there shall you bring up your elevation offerings…" (Positive) It is a mitzvah to offer one's sacrifices in the exclusive surroundings of the Tabernacle, and later, the Temple.

441. Parshas Re'eh 12:15 "However, to your soul's desire you may slaughter and eat meat…" (Positive) This is speaking of the mitzvah to redeem and then eat an animal that had an external blemish and was not offered as a sacrifice.

442. Parshas Re'eh 12:17 "You may not eat within your gates the tithe of your grain…" (Prohibitive) *maaser sheini* (the second tithe) may only be eaten in Jerusalem. The prohibition against eating any offering at home is highlighted in laws 442-449.

443. Parshas Re'eh 12:17 "...and your wine..." (Prohibitive) *maaser sheini* of wine may only be consumed in Jerusalem.

444. Parshas Re'eh 12:17 "...and your oil" (Prohibitive)

445. Parshas Re'eh 12:17 "...the firstborn of your cattle..." (Prohibitive)

446. Parshas Re'eh 12:17 "the firstborn of...your flocks..." (Prohibitive)

447. Parshas Re'eh 12:17 "...all of your vow-offerings that you vow..." (Prohibitive)

448. Parshas Re'eh 12:17 "...and your free-will offerings..." (Prohibitive)

449. Parshas Re'eh 12:17 "...and what you offer up with your hands" (Prohibitive) This is known as the "heave" offering or *bikkurim*.

Finer Points: Laws 442 through 449 are all derived from the same *passuk*. The specific offerings listed here may only be eaten in Jerusalem. We also derive from this some finer points of law such as not eating sin-offerings outside the Temple courtyard, not eating burnt offerings, not eating of certain offerings until after the sprinkling of blood, and the fact that only the priests can eat *bikkurim* but cannot do so until the offering has been placed in the Temple courtyard.

450. Parshas Re'eh 12:19 "Beware lest you forsake the Levi..." (Prohibitive) One may not neglect giving the requisite gifts to Levites.

451. Parshas Re'eh 12:21 "If the place...will be far from you, you may slaughter of your herds and your flocks...and you may eat in your cities to your heart's desire" (Positive) One who wishes to eat of a kosher animal must first slaughter it according to the dictates of Torah law.

452. Parshas Re'eh 12:23 "Only be strong not to eat the blood, for the blood is the life and you shall not eat the life with the meat" (Prohibitive) This is the law of *ayver min ha'chai*, eating the limb of a creature while it is still alive (אבר מן החי) and is one of the seven prohibitions originally given to the children of Noach.

453. Parshas Re'eh 12:26 "Only your holy things…you shall take up and come to the place…" (Positive) It is a mitzvah for those who live outside of the borders of Israel to bring their offerings to the Temple. Those from the tribes of Reuven, Gad, and part of Menashe (who lived east of the Jordan River) were required to make a pilgrimage to the Tabernacle (and later, to the Temple) from outside the land of Israel.

454. Parshas Re'eh 13:1 "The entire word that I have commanded you…you shall not add to it…" (Prohibitive) We may not add to the mitzvos of the Torah.

455. Parshas Re'eh 13:1 "…and you shall not subtract from it" (Prohibitive) We may not decrease from the mitzvos in the Torah. For instance, if the law calls for four parchments in the *tefillin* we wear on our head, we cannot put in only three.

456. Parshas Re'eh 13:4 "Do not listen to the words of that prophet…for Hashem, your G-d, is testing you…" (Prohibitive) The Torah tells us that there will be dreamers and prophets who will preach idolatry and perform wonderous acts in the name of their gods. We are commanded to reject them.

457. Parshas Re'eh 13:9 "You shall not accede to him" (Prohibitive) If a fellow Jew tries to entice us to follow him in idol-worship we must reject him. Such a person is called a *maysis*. This law is related to law #87 which speaks of a *maydiach*, one who tries to cause multiple Jews to follow idol worship.

458. Parshas Re'eh 13:9 "…and not listen to him" (Prohibitive) Our sages learn from this that although we are commanded to love our fellow Jew, we must turn against a *maysis* – we may not love him and must, in fact, hate him. See law #457.

459. Parshas Re'eh 13:9 "...your eye shall not take pity on him..." (Prohibitive) We are prohibited to help a *maysis*, even if he is in danger.

460. Parshas Re'eh 13:9 "...you shall not be compassionate to him..." (Prohibitive) We are not allowed to point-out any favorable qualities of a *maysis* and it is praiseworthy to warn others of such a person.

461. Parshas Re'eh 13:9 "...nor conceal him." (Prohibitive) We are not allowed to be silent about a *maysis* and must point-out his guilt.

462. Parshas Re'eh 13:12 "...and they shall not again do such an evil thing in your midst." (Prohibitive) It is forbidden to be a *maysis*.

463. Parshas Re'eh 13:15 "And you shall inquire and investigate and ask well, and behold, if it is true...this abomination was committed in your midst..." (Positive) This is the mitzvah that obligates a Jewish court to investigate and cross-examine witnesses, and to work diligently to arrive at the truth in judgement.

464. Parshas Re'eh 13:17 "...and you shall burn in fire completely the city..." (Positive) This is the mitzvah of עיר הנדחת (*ir ha'nidachas*), the requirement to destroy a city whose inhabitants have gone astray and turned to idol-worship.

465. Parshas Re'eh 13:17 "...it shall be an eternal heap and shall not be rebuilt." (Prohibitive) An *ir ha'nidachas* may not be rebuilt.

466. Parshas Re'eh 13:18 "No part of the banned property shall cleave to your hand." (Prohibitive) The booty of a city destroyed because of idol worship cannot be used. We may not derive any benefit from an *ir ha'nidachas*.

467. Parshas Re'eh 14:1 "...you shall not cut yourselves..." (Prohibitive) We are not allowed to slash ourselves and make cuts in our bodies as some idolaters do in mourning or worship.

468. Parshas Re'eh 14:1 "...and you shall not make a bald spot between your eyes for a dead person." (Prohibitive) We may not tear out the hair of our head as a sign of grief when mourning the dead.

469. Parshas Re'eh 14:3 "You shall not eat any abominable thing." (Prohibitive) One may not eat from an animal consecrated to the Temple and rejected because of a defect that you caused.

470. Parshas Re'eh 14:11 "Every clean bird you may eat." (Positive) It is a mitzvah to determine that a bird one wants to eat is kosher. The Torah lists only those birds that are not kosher.

471. Parshas Re'eh 14:19 "And every flying swarming creature is unclean to you, they shall not be eaten." (Prohibitive) Flying insects are prohibited – we may not eat them.

472. Parshas Re'eh 14:21 "You shall not eat any carcass...you shall not boil a kid in its mother's milk" (Prohibitive) An animal that you could normally eat if slaughtered properly may not be eaten if it died of natural causes or was killed in another way than kosher slaughtering. The prohibition against meat and milk is also referenced here for the third time in the Torah. The three references to meat and milk teach us that you cannot cook, eat, or benefit from this mixture. Nevertheless, most commentators agree that eating and benefiting are both learned from one of the earlier references to this prohibition and that this *passuk* is not the source of the law of not deriving benefit from the mixture of milk and meat.

473. Parshas Re'eh 14:22 "You shall tithe the entire crop of your seeding..." (Positive) This is the mitzvah of *maaser sheini* (the second tithe) in the first, second, fourth and fifth years of the *shmittah* cycle and is to be eaten in Jerusalem.

474. Parshas Re'eh 14:28 "At the end of three years you shall take out all the tithe of your produce..." (Positive) Every third and sixth year of the *shmittah* cycle, it is a mitzvah to separate a tithe for the poor called *maaser ani* instead of *maaser sheini*.

475. Parshas Re'eh 15:2 "Every creditor shall remit his authority...he shall not press for payment from his brother..." (Prohibitive) Once a *shmittah* year has arrived, one cannot demand repayment of a previously-made loan.

476. Parshas Re'eh 15:3 "You may exact payment from a gentile..." (Positive) *shmittah* does not affect loans between a Jew and a gentile.

477. Parshas Re'eh 15:3 "...but over what you have with your brother you shall not remit your authority." (Positive) It is a positive mitzvah to cancel debts in the *shmittah* year.

478. Parshas Re'eh 15:7 "If there shall be a destitute person among you...you shall not harden your heart nor close your hand..." (Prohibitive) One may not turn away from helping the poor.

479. Parshas Re'eh 15:8 "But rather you should open your hand wide to him..." (Positive) This is the positive mitzvah of giving charity.

480. Parshas Re'eh 15:9 "Beware lest you have a thought saying that the shmittah year is at hand and...you will refuse to give to him..." (Prohibitive) This law forbids one from refraining from lending just prior to the *shmittah* year. A system was established that allowed one to register a debt with the Jewish court, the *Beis Din*, through a legal document called a *pruzbul*, which would allow debts to be carried-over past the shine *shmittah* year.

481. Parshas Re'eh 15:13 "...you shall not send him away empty handed.: (Prohibitive) When one sets-free a Jewish servant he may not send him away without gifts.

482. Parshas Re'eh 15:14 "You shall furnish him with much furnishing..." (Positive) When setting a Jewish servant free you must supply him generously with that which will help him establish himself as a functioning member of society.

483. Parshas Re'eh 15:19 "...you shall not work with the firstborn of your bull..." (Prohibitive) Since the firstborn animal is sacred and consecrated to the Temple, one cannot use it as a work-animal. We also learn from this that any animal that is consecrated cannot be used for work.

484. Parshas Re'eh 15:19 "...nor shall you shear the firstborn of your flock." (Prohibitive) Since the firstborn sheep was consecrated to the Temple, its wool could not be used by the original owner, nor could the wool of any consecrated animal.

485. Parshas Re'eh 16:3 "You shall not eat leavened bread with it..." (Prohibitive) On the day before Pesach from mid-day (*chatzos*) one is not allowed to eat leaven (*chametz*).

486. Parshas Re'eh 16:4 "...nor shall there remain any meat which you sacrifice in the afternoon..." (Prohibitive) This prohibits leaving leftovers from the *korban chagigah* (the special festival offering brought, in this case, on the day before Pesach). This sacrifice was permissible to eat for two days, but after that, could not be eaten.

487. Parshas Re'eh 16:5 "You may not slaughter the Pesach offering within any of your cities..." (Prohibitive) The *korban pesach* could only be offered on the altar of the Tabernacle or Temple.

488. Parshas Re'eh 16:14 "And you shall rejoice on your festival..." (Positive) It is a mitzvah to rejoice on the three pilgrimage festivals (Pesach, Shavuos, Succos). This includes wearing special clothing, enjoying sumptuous meals, drinking wine, and bringing special offerings in the Temple.

489. Parshas Re'eh 16:16 "Three times a year all your males should appear before Hashem..." (Positive) This is the mitzvah dictating that adult males make a pilgrimage to the Temple in Jerusalem three times a year.

490. Parshas Re'eh 16:16 "...and no one shall appear before Hashem empty-handed." (Prohibitive) It is forbidden to come to the Temple for a pilgrimage without bringing an offering.

Shoftim:

491. Parshas Shoftim 16:18 "Judges and officers you shall appoint in all your cities..." (Positive) This is the mitzvah of appointing judges and members of a local court (*Beis Din*) as well as the Sanhedrin in Jerusalem, to enforce the observance of laws in the cities in Israel.

492. Parshas Shoftim 19:21 "You shall not plant for yourselves an idolatrous tree...near the Altar of Hashem..." (Prohibitive) We are prohibited from planting any kind of tree near the Altar, due to the fact that idolaters planted trees to beautify the area surrounding their idols. They were also sects that would make trees the center of their worship (*Asheirah*).

493. Parshas Shoftim 16:22 "And you shall not set up a monument..." (Prohibitive) We are not allowed to erect statues, monuments, pillars, etc. that resemble those of idolaters.

494. Parshas Shoftim 17:1 "You shall not slaughter for Hashem, your G-d, any bull or lamb on which there is a blemish..." (Prohibitive) This law prohibits the offering of animals that have a temporary defect or blemish. The animal cannot be offered for sacrifice until it heals.

495. Parshas Shoftim 17:9-10 "You shall come to...Kohanim, the Leviim, the judge...you shall do according to the word they shall tell you..." (Positive) This mitzvah dictates that we follow the judgement of the *Beis Din* and other religious authorities.

496. Parshas Shoftim 17:11 "...you shall not deviate from the word which they will tell you." (Prohibitive) We are commanded not to reject the rulings of the religious authorities. The previous mitzvah (#495) commands us to follow their judgement while #496 establishes a separate mitzvah of not rejecting their judgement or ruling.

497. Parshas Shoftim 17:15 "You shall surely set a king over yourselves..." (Positive) This is one of three mitzvos that the Jewish nation was commanded to observe once the land of Israel was conquered; appoint a king, destroy Amalek, and build the Temple.

498. Parshas Shoftim 17:15 "...you cannot place over yourself a foreigner who is not your brother." (Prohibitive) We are prohibited from appointing a non-Jew as king.

499. Parshas Shoftim 17:16 "...he shall not have too many horses for himself..." (Prohibitive) One of the special commandments directed to a king of Israel is not to have too many horses. A king is additionally commanded not to have too many wives and not to build a personal treasury (as will be seen in laws 501 and 502). King Solomon is said to have violated all three of these commandments and was punished with a period of banishment as king. One opinion is that having too many horses could lead to renewed familiarity with Egypt, which was a major horse-breeding country.

500. Parshas Shoftim 17:16 "...you shall not continue to return on this way again." (Prohibitive) This mitzvah forbids Jews from emigrating from Israel and establishing a home in Egypt. Nevertheless, there appears to be no prohibition against Jews from other lands moving there. This was done by the Rambam (Maimonides) when he left Spain and became a physician in the court of Saladin in Egypt.

501. Parshas Shoftim 17:17 "And he shall not have too many wives..." (Prohibitive) A king of Israel is limited to a maximum of 18 wives.

502. Parshas Shoftim 17:17 "...nor shall he greatly increase gold and silver for himself." (Prohibitive) A king of Israel is not allowed to overtax the people to build his treasury.

503. Parshas Shoftim 17:18 "...he shall write for himself an additional copy of the Torah..." (Positive) A king is required to write a Torah and to keep it with him at all times. It is called "additional" or *mishneh* since the Torah commands all Jews to take part in the writing of a Torah (see mitzvah #613) and the king's Torah is in addition to that.

504. Parshas Shoftim 18:1 "There shall not be for the Kohanim, the Leviim...an inheritance with Israel..." (Prohibitive) The priests and Levites did not receive a portion in the land of Israel, with the exception of the Levite cities which were also cities of refuge. This law prohibits the portioning of land to them.

505. Parshas Shoftim 18:1 "...the entire tribe of Levi...a portion...with Israel..." (Prohibitive) Even spoils of a war of conquest were not to be shared with the tribe of Levi.

506. Parshas Shoftim 18:3 "This shall be due to the *Kohanim* from the people...the shoulder..." (Positive) It is a mitzvah to give to a *Kohen* certain parts of a cow, sheep, or goat that has been slaughtered.

507. Parshas Shoftim 18:4 "The first of your grain, wine, and oil...you shall give him" (Positive) It is a mitzvah to give these gifts to the priest (*trumah*). The Rabbis established this as a minimum of $1/60^{th}$ of one's total production or a maximum of $1/40^{th}$.

508. Parshas Shoftim 18:4 "...and the first of the shearing of your flock you shall give him." (Positive) A portion of the wool sheared from your sheep must be given to the priest.

509. Parshas Shoftim 18:7 "Then he shall minister in the name of Hashem..." (Positive) It is the mitzvah for the *Kohanim* and *Leviim* to work in their designated groups (shifts or watches) in the Temple. There were 24 watches, and every group would serve for one week, at least two times per year.

510. Parshas Shoftim 18:10 "There shall not be found among you...one who practices divination..." (Prohibitive) The act of predicting the future based on divination is forbidden.

511. Parshas Shoftim 18:10 "...a sorcerer..." (Prohibitive) The Torah forbids Jews to practice witchcraft.

512. Parshas Shoftim 18:11 "...or an animal charmer..." (Prohibitive) Jews are forbidden to practice the act of charming.

513. Parshas Shoftim 18:11 "...or one who consults with Ov..." (Prohibitive) Another prohibited type of sorcery or necromancy.

514. Parshas Shoftim 18:11 "...or Yidoni..." (Prohibitive) Again, a type of prohibited sorcery including "consulting the bones."

515. Parshas Shoftim 18:11 "...or one who inquires of the dead." (Prohibitive) This is the act of trying to read the future by holding a séance or performing strange rites in a cemetery.

516. Parshas Shoftim 18:15 "A prophet from your midst...to him you shall listen." (Positive) It is a mitzvah to follow the words of a "true" prophet.

517. Parshas Shoftim 18:20 "But a prophet who shall speak willfully a word in My name, that which I have not commanded him to speak..." (Prohibitive) One is forbidden to be a false prophet and to speak words in G-d's name that do not come from G-d.

518. Parshas Shoftim 18:20 "...or (a false prophet) who shall speak in the name of the gods of others, that prophet shall die." (Prohibitive) Practicing prophecy in the name of strange gods is forbidden.

519. Parshas Shoftim 18:22 "...you should not fear him." (Prohibitive) We are not allowed to let our fear of a false prophet keep us from putting him to death.

520. Parshas Shoftim 19:2 "You shall set aside three cities for yourselves in the midst of your Land..." (Positive) This is the mitzvah of establishing three refuge cities (**ערי מקלט**) inside the borders of Israel.

There were three more on the east side of the Jordan river, one each in the territories of Reuven, Gad, and part of Menashe. Later, another 42 locations (cities where the Levites lived) were added and became sanctuaries.

521. Parshas Shoftim 19:13 "Your eye shall not pity him…" (Prohibitive) A *Beis Din* is not allowed to take pity on a murderer and must honor the court's verdict.

522. Parshas Shoftim 19:14 "You shall not move a boundary of your neighbor…" (Prohibitive) One is forbidden to move property boundary markers in order to make false property claims.

523. Parshas Shoftim 19:15 "A single witness shall not stand up against any man…" (Prohibitive) The *Beis Din* cannot accept the testimony of a single witness if said testimony would result in punishment of the defendant. A minimum of two witnesses is required.

524. Parshas Shoftim 19:19 "And you shall do to him as he conspired to do to his brother…" (Positive) It is a mitzvah for a *Beis Din* to punish those who testifies falsely and are found to be conspiring. They are to give such individuals the same punishment that the defendant would have received. We call this the law of עדים זוממין – *conspiring witnesses*.

525. Parshas Shoftim 20:2 "It shall be that when you come near to war that the *Kohen* shall approach and speak to the people." (Positive) In wartime, a priest was chosen to be a "chosen one of war" (משוח מלחמה) and was given the job of encouraging the soldiers and strengthening their faith before battle.

526. Parshas Shoftim 20:3 "He shall say to them, 'Hear O Israel, you are coming near to battle against your enemies, let your heart not be faint, do not be afraid, do not panic, and do not be broken…'"

(Prohibitive) Jewish soldiers are not allowed to yield and run from an enemy out of fear.

527. Parshas Shoftim 20:11 "And it shall be that if he responds to you in peace…" (Positive) It is a mitzvah to offer the enemy terms of peace before going into battle (in a *milchemes re'shus* – an optional war, as opposed to a *milchemes mitzvah* – an obligatory war). Peace with our enemies (in Israel) is also conditional on their subjugation and their rejection of idolatry.

528. Parshas Shoftim 20:16 "But from the cities of these people…you shall not allow any person to live." (Prohibitive) In addition to mitzvah #425 which commands the Jewish People to destroy the seven nations that occupied Israel, this law dictates that we are not allowed to let any of them remain alive. Note: The Rambam states that this was only the case when they refused to convert or reject idolatry.

529. Parshas Shoftim 20:19 "When you besiege a city for many days to wage war…do not destroy its trees…" (Prohibitive) It is forbidden to cut down fruit trees, even as part of a military siege.

530. Parshas Shoftim 21:1-4 "If a corpse be found…fallen in the field…your elders and judges shall go out and measure…it shall be that the city nearest the corpse, the elders of that city shall take a heifer…they shall break the neck of the heifer with an axe…" (Positive) This is the mitzvah of עגלה ערופה (*eglah arufah*) which places responsibility for someone who was killed (and found, alone in a field) on the elders of the nearest city.

531. Parshas Shoftim 21:4 "…which cannot be worked and cannot be sown…" (Prohibitive) It is forbidden to plant anything in the spot where the *eglah arufah* was killed. This serves as an eternal reminder that someone was murdered on that spot, abandoned and uncared-for.

Ki-Saitzay:

532. Parshas Ki-Saitzay 21:11 "And if you shall see among the captives a woman of beauty..." (Positive) This mitzvah outlines the law concerning a soldier who brings home a captured woman and wants to marry her.

533. Parshas Ki-Saitzay 21:14 "...but you may not sell her for money" (Prohibitive) A woman taken as a captive in war cannot be sold if the soldier had relations with her.

534. Parshas Ki-Saitzay 21:14 "...you shall not enslave her because you have afflicted her." (Prohibitive) A soldier cannot make a woman taken as a captive in war into a slave. If he does not marry her, he must set her free.

535. Parshas Ki-Saitzay 21:22 "If a man shall be committed to death...he shall be put to death and you shall hang him on a tree." (Positive) After the *Beis Din* executes a man, his body is hung from a tree before sunset for all to see.

536. Parshas Ki-Saitzay 21:23 "His body shall not remain all night..." (Prohibitive) The *Beis Din* is not allowed to leave the body of one who was executed to remain hanging in the tree all night. See law #535.

537. Parshas Ki-Saitzay 21:23 "...you shall surely bury him on that day." (Positive) It is a mitzvah to bury a corpse immediately. As this relates to laws 535 and 536, one who was executed and then hung in a tree before sunset must be cut-down just after nightfall and buried immediately.

538. Parshas Ki-Saitzay 22:1 "You shall not see the ox of your brother or his sheep or goat...and hide yourself...you shall surely return them to your brother." (Positive) This mitzvah obligates one to return property lost by their neighbor.

539. Parshas Ki-Saitzay 22:3 "...and you shall do so for any lost article of your brother...you shall not hide yourself." (Prohibitive) If one finds a lost object, he cannot ignore it (due to inconvenience, laziness, etc.) and must make every effort to return it to its rightful owner.

540. Parshas Ki-Saitzay 22:4 "You shall not see the donkey of your brother or his ox fallen on the road..." (Prohibitive) One may not ignore the plight of a pack animal that has fallen and cannot get up (it is our responsibility to help the animal get up from underneath its load as will be seen in law #541.

541. Parshas Ki-Saitzay 22:4 "...you shall surely stand them up with him." (Positive) It is a mitzvah to help the animal stand up and help the owner reload its burden if necessary.

542. Parshas Ki-Saitzay 22:5 "Male clothing should not be worn on a woman..." (Prohibitive) A woman is forbidden from wearing clothing that is commonly identified as being that which is worn by men. Some say this applies to military armament, others say that it is speaking about regular clothing.

543. Parshas Ki-Saitzay 22:5 "...and a man shall not wear the garments of a woman." (Prohibitive) Men are not allowed to wear dresses and other garments that are identified as "women's" clothing.

544. Parshas Ki-Saitzay 22:6 "If a bird's nest happens to be before you...and the mother is roosting on the young birds or eggs...you shall not take the mother with the young." (Prohibitive) We are not allowed to take a mother-bird together with its eggs or hatchlings from a nest.

545. Parshas Ki-Saitzay 22:7 "You shall surely send away the mother and take the young for yourself..." (Positive) It is a mitzvah to shoo-away a mother bird before taking her hatchlings or eggs. We call this the mitzvah of *Shiluach Ha'Kan*. This is one of only two mitzvos in the Torah that have a stated reward. The first is honoring our parents (ref. the Ten Commandments). The second is here, sending away the mother bird. The reward (in both cases) is long life. These two laws are polar opposites in that the mitzvah of honoring our parents extends through all the days of our lives (we must honor our parents even after they have passed-away). The second mitzvah only requires the flick of our hand as we shoo-away the mother bird. Our sages learn from this that we should not try to understand G-d's system of reward – it is beyond us!

546. Parshas Ki-Saitzay 22:8 "...you shall make a fence for your roof..." (Positive) One who has a flat roof on their house is required to build a parapet wall or install a fence to ensure that nobody falls off.

547. Parshas Ki-Saitzay 22:8 "...so that you will not bring blood upon your house..." (Prohibitive) One is forbidden to allow any dangerous impediments on their property or ignore objects that could cause someone to be injured or killed.

548. Parshas Ki-Saitzay 22:9 "You shall not sow your vineyard with a mixture (of seeds) ..." (Prohibitive) This law prohibits the sowing of two types of seeds side-by-side. This is related to law #245, but in this case, is speaking of **כלאי כרם** (forbidden mixtures in a vineyard).

549. Parshas Ki-Saitzay 22:9 "...lest the growth of the seed you plant and the produce of the vineyard become sanctified." (Prohibitive) One may not eat or benefit from the produce of mixed seeds in a vineyard.

550. Parshas Ki-Saitzay 22:10 "You shall not plough with an ox and a donkey together." (Prohibitive) Two animals of different types (and strengths) may not be harnessed or yoked together for work.

551. Parshas Ki-Saitzay 22:11 "You shall not wear *shaatnez*, wool and linen combined." (Prohibitive) If wool and linen are sewed or woven together, the resulting garment is forbidden to us. This is yet another example of the laws of *kilayim – forbidden mixtures*.

552. Parshas Ki-Saitzay 22:13 "If a man takes a wife…" (Positive) It is a mitzvah to perform *kiddushin* (betrothal) as the first step of marriage.

553. Parshas Ki-Saitzay 22:19 "And she shall remain with him as a wife…" (Positive) If one speaks slander about his wife and his claims are proven wrong, he is obligated to remain with her.

554. Parshas Ki-Saitzay 22:19 "…he may not send her away all his days." (Prohibitive) A man who slanders his wife and is proven wrong is not allowed to divorce her.

555. Parshas Ki-Saitzay 22:24 "Then you shall take them both to the gates of the city and you shall stone them…" (Positive) It is a mitzvah for the *Beis Din* to stone those who are found guilty of certain sins. There are four capital punishments – stoning, burning, the sword, and strangulation (*s'kilah, s'rayfah, hereg, chenek*). There are 18 crimes which result in a sentence of stoning.

556. Parshas Ki-Saitzay 22:25-26 "…and the man will seize her and lie with her…only the man who lies with her shall die. But you shall do nothing to the maiden…" (Prohibitive) The court is not allowed to punish someone who was forced, against their will, to sin. In this case, it is a young girl who was attacked in a field and physically violated.

557. Parshas Ki-Saitzay 22: 29 "If a man shall find a virgin maiden who was not betrothed…and the man…" (Positive) If a man forces himself on a maiden who is not engaged, he must offer to marry her. If she agrees, he must marry her.

558. Parshas Ki-Saitzay 22:29 "…he may not send her away all his days." (Prohibitive) The man in mitzvah #557 who marries the maiden, is never allowed to divorce her.

559. Parshas Ki-Saitzay 23:2 "A man with crushed…or a severed organ shall not enter the congregation of Hashem…" (Prohibitive) A man who has been severely disfigured and cannot have children is not allowed to marry a Jewess (but may marry a convert).

560. Parshas Ki-Saitzay 23:3 "A *mamzer* shall not enter the congregation of Hashem..." (Prohibitive) One who is born of a union between a man and woman who are not allowed to marry (such as a case of incest or a married woman bearing another man's child) is considered a *mamzer* and may not marry a Jew (but they may marry a convert or another *mamzer*).

561. Parshas Ki-Saitzay 23:4 "An Amoni and a Moavi shall not enter the congregation of Hashem..." (Prohibitive) A Jewess may not marry a man from the nations of Amon or Moav. This law does not apply to Jewish men marrying women converted from Amon or Moav, since the *passuk* is conjugated in the male form, not the female – it says "*Amoni*" and "*Moavi*," not *Amoniah* or *Moaviah*. Thus, Boaz was allowed to marry Ruth, who was a princess of the nation of Moav.

562. Parshas Ki-Saitzay 23:4-7 "An Amoni and a Moavi...you shall not seek their peace or favor all your days." (Prohibitive) We are not allowed to make overtures of peace to these enemies, Amon and Moav.

563. Parshas Ki-Saitzay 23:8 "You shall not reject an Edomi because he is your brother..." (Prohibitive) Since Eisav was the brother of Yaakov, we are not allowed to reject converts from the nation of Edom which descended from him (but may not marry them until the third generation).

564. Parshas Ki-Saitzay 23:8 "...you shall not reject an Egyptian..." (Prohibitive) It is forbidden to reject an Egyptian convert to Judaism. We may marry them after three generations.

Finer Points: When Moshe asked the leaders of Amon and Moav to assist the Jewish People traveling through their kingdoms (by providing food and water), they rejected Moshe's request. The

Edomites are excluded from harsh treatment because they are relatives, descendants of Eisav. The Egyptians, although they enslaved us, provided food and housing, however meager, to the Jewish People. They are allowed to convert and we can marry them in the third generation.

565. Parshas Ki-Saitzay 23:11 "If there shall be among you any man who is unclean…" (Prohibitive) A person who is ritually unclean is not allowed to enter the midst of the camp (of *Leviim*) and must remain outside the camp until purified.

566. Parshas Ki-Saitzay 23:13 "And you shall have a place outside the camp and to it you shall go." (Positive) A Jewish army is required to have a place, outside the camp, where soldiers can relieve themselves.

567. Parshas Ki-Saitzay 23:14 "You shall have a shovel in addition to your weapons…you shall go back and cover your excrement." (Positive) This mitzvah dictates that soldiers carry an implement that will allow them to dig a hole in which to relieve themselves.

568. Parshas Ki-Saitzaty 23:16 "You shall not turn over to his master a slave who is rescued from his master to you." (Prohibitive) A non-Jewish slave who runs-away from his master outside of the Land of Israel and seeks sanctuary in Israel, may not be returned to his original master.

569. Parshas Ki-Saitzay 23:17 "He shall dwell with you in your midst…you shall not torment him." (Prohibitive) A non-Jewish slave (as in mitzvah #568) may not be oppressed.

570. Parshas Ki-Saitzay 23:18 "There shall not be a harlot among the daughters of Israel…" (Prohibitive)

571. Parshas Ki-Saitzay 23:19 "You shall not bring a harlot's wage or the exchange for a dog into the house of Hashem…" (Prohibitive) An animal given as payment to a harlot and then exchanged for a kosher animal, that kosher animal may not be brought into the Temple. Also, if someone trades a dog for a kosher animal, that kosher animal may not be used in the Temple.

572. Parshas Ki-Saitzay 23:20 "You shall not cause your brother to take interest..." (Prohibitive) In addition to the prohibition against charging interest, this law prohibits a borrower from willfully paying such interest and facilitating the sin of the lender.

573. Parshas Ki-Saitzay 23:21 "You may cause a stranger (gentile) to take interest..." (Positive) It is a mitzvah when lending to non-Jews to charge interest. We are also allowed to borrow from gentiles and pay interest to them. Lending to another Jew without interest is a form of required benevolence to "family." We are not required to show such goodwill and benevolence to non-Jews with whom we do business.

574. Parshas Ki-Saitzay 23:22 "When you make a vow to Hashem...you shall not be late in paying it..." (Prohibitive) Once we accept an obligation upon ourselves to bring a Temple offering, we may not delay performance by passing three consecutive pilgrimage festivals without having fulfilled our obligation.

575. Parshas Ki-Saitzay 23:24 "You shall observe and carry out that which your lips have uttered..." (Positive) We are commanded to fulfill our promises (such as our pledges to charity).

576. Parshas Ki-Saitzay 23:25 "When you come into the vineyard of your neighbor, you may eat grapes..." (Positive) One who comes into a vineyard to work as a hired laborer must be allowed to eat some of the grapes.

577. Parshas Ki-Saitzay 23:25 "...you may eat grapes...to your fill, but you may not put it in a vessel." (Prohibitive) A hired laborer may not collect produce for himself in a container. He is allowed to eat grapes during his time of picking, but cannot take them home.

578. Parshas Ki-Saitzay 23:26 "When you come into the field of standing grain of your neighbor you may pluck ears with your hand but you may not lift up a sickle..." (Prohibitive) A hired worker may eat from the owner's crops but not while working, and may not harvest extra crops to bring home.

579. Parshas Ki-Saitzay 24:3 "...and he wrote her a bill of divorce..." (Positive) It is a mitzvah for one who is getting divorced to follow Torah law and issue a proper divorce document, a *get*.

580. Parshas Ki-Saitzay 24:4 "Her first husband who divorced her shall not again take her to become his wife..." (Prohibitive) It is forbidden to remarry a woman who you had previously divorced and who then married another man who divorced her (or died).

581. Parshas Ki-Saitzay 24:5 "When a man marries a new wife, he shall not go out to war..." (Prohibitive) A newly married man may not leave his wife to go to war during the first year of marriage.

582. Parshas Ki-Saitzay 24:5 "he shall be free for his home for one year..." (Positive) A bridegroom has a mitzvah incumbent on him to celebrate and rejoice with his wife for one year.

583. Parshas Ki-Saitzay 24:6 "One shall not take an upper or lower millstone as a pledge..." (Prohibitive) Since a millstone is critical for food production, it cannot be pledged as security on a loan, nor can any critical utensil be pledged.

584. Parshas Ki-Saitzay 24:8 "Beware the affliction of *tzaraas*..." (Prohibitive) The Torah prohibits cutting-away the symptoms of *tzaraas* and any attempt to hide the affliction.

585. Parsha Ki-Saitzay 24:10 "When you make your neighbor a loan...you shall not enter his home to take security for it." (Prohibitive) Entering a house without permission to take security for a loan is forbidden.

586. Parshas Ki-Saitzay 24:12 "If that person is poor you shall not lie down with his security." (Prohibitive) An item such as a blanket or pillow pledged as security must be returned to a poor person when they need it.

587. Parshas Ki-Saitzay 24:13 "You shall return the security to him when the sun sets..." (Positive) It is a mitzvah for a lender to return a needed object that was taken from a poor person as security.

588. Parshas Ki-Saitzay 24:15 "On that day shall you pay his hire..." (Positive) It is a mitzvah to pay a worker on the same day that their work is performed.

589. Parshas Ki-Saitzay 24:16 "Fathers shall not be put to death because of sons...a man should be put to death for his own sin." (Prohibitive) Testimony in capital cases is not accepted if it is from close relatives.

590. Parshas Ki-Saitzay 24:17 "You shall not pervert the judgement of a proselyte or orphan..." (Prohibitive) A judge or court is admonished not to take advantage of widows and orphans.

591. Parshas Ki-Saitzay 24:17 "...and you shall not take the garment of a widow as a pledge." (Prohibitive) It is forbidden to take security from a widow.

592. Parshas Ki-Saitzay 24:19 "When you reap your harvest...and you forgot a bundle in the field..." (Positive) This is the mitzvah of שכחה – leaving forgotten sheaves in a field so the poor can collect them.

593. Parshas Ki-Saitzay 24:19 "...you shall not turn back to take it..." (Prohibitive) A land-owner is forbidden to return to his field to collect sheaves that he forgot about, then remembered, and now wants to recover.

594. Parshas Ki-Saitzay 25:2 "It will be that if the wicked one is liable for whipping; the judge shall cast him down and strike him."

(Positive) The *Beis Din* itself must carry-out the punishment of giving lashes.

595. Parshas Ki-Saitzay 25:3 "Forty shall he strike him; he shall not add..." (Prohibitive) The court may not whip a person any more than the amount dictated by the Torah. In fact, the maximum number of lashes given by the court was reduced to 39. One is also not allowed to strike a fellow Jew.

596. Parshas Ki-Saitzay 25:4 "You shall not muzzle an ox in its threshing." (Prohibitive) We are forbidden from preventing a work-animal from eating while it is working.

597. Parshas Ki-Saitzay 25:5 "When brothers dwell together and one of them dies, and he has no child, the wife of the deceased shall not marry outside to a strange man..." (Prohibitive) This is the law of the *yevamah*, a woman whose husband did not have children and died. She is forbidden to marry any other man than her husband's brother unless he releases her through a process called *chalitzah*.

598. Parshas Ki-Saitzay 25:5 "...her yavam shall come to her and take her to himself as a wife..." (Positive) The living brother (from mitzvah #597) is responsible to marry his sister-in-law through "levirite marriage" **(יבום)**.

599. Parshas Ki-Saitzay 25:9 "Then his sister-in-law shall...remove his shoe from his foot and spit before him..." (Positive) This is the process of *chalitzah* performed when the brother does not want to marry his widowed and childless sister-in-law.

600. Parshas Ki-Saitzay 25:11,12 "...you shall cut off her hand..." (Positive) This mitzvah deals with the obligation to pay when damaging someone in a way that embarrasses the victim. It is further clarified by some commentaries as obligating us to rescue someone who is being pursued.

601. Parshas Ki-Saitzay 25:12 "…your eye shall show no pity." (Prohibitive) One who pursues someone else to harm them should not be pitied.

602. Parshas Ki-Saitzay 25:14 "You shall not have in your house two sets of measures, a large one and a small one." (Prohibitive) It is a sin for a Jew to own inaccurate weights and measures.

603. Parshas Ki-Saitzay 25:17 "Remember what Amalek did to you on the way when you were leaving Egypt." (Positive) It is a mitzvah for every Jew to remember the evil done to our people by Amalek.

604. Parshas Ki-Saitzay 25:19 "…you shall wipe out the memory of Amalek from under the heaven…" (Positive) It is a mitzvah to kill Amalek (as the prophet Shmuel did to Agag, the king of Amalek, after King Saul allowed him to remain alive) and to completely blot out that nation.

605. Parshas Ki-Saitzay 25:19 "…you shall never forget." (Prohibitive) We are forbidden to forget what Amalek did to us. This statement is associated by many with the Holocaust. We warn our children: "Never forget!"

Ki-Savo:

606. Parshas Ki-Savo 26:5 "And you shall call out and say before Hashem…'An Aramean tried to destroy my forefather…'" (Positive) When the *bikkurim* first-fruit offerings were brought in the Temple, it was a mitzvah to recite *pessukim* 5-10 of this *parsha* beginning with: ארמי אבד אבי in *passuk* 5) and ending with the words 'אשר נתתה לי ה (in *passuk* 10).

607. Parshas Ki-Savo 26:13 "Then you shall say before Hashem… 'I have removed the holy things from the house and I have also given it to the Levi, the stranger, the orphan, the widow…'" (Positive) It is a mitzvah to make this declaration at the Temple at the end of the holiday of Pesach (in the 4th and 7th years of the *shmittah* cycle) stating that all portions of *trumah* and *maaser* have been properly given.

608. Parshas Ki-Savo 26:14 "I have not eaten from it in my deep mourning…" (Prohibitive) One is forbidden from eating parts of the 2nd tithe (*maaser sheini*) when in a state of *aninus* (between death and burial) for a family member.

609. Parshas Ki-Savo 26:14 "…neither have I consumed it in a state of contamination…" (Prohibitive) The 2nd tithe (*maaser sheini*) could not be eaten while a person was in a state of ritual impurity or if the tithe itself became impure.

610. Parshas Ki-Savo 26:14 "…and I did not give of it for the needs of the dead…" (Prohibitive) If one exchanged the 2nd tithe for money, they could only use that money to purchase food. It is forbidden to spend that money on anything else, even burying the dead.

611. Parshas Ki-Savo 28:9 "…you shall observe…and you shall walk in His ways." (Positive) It is a mitzvah to follow in the righteous path of G-d by making every effort to emulate G-d's traits of kindness, forgiveness, honesty, etc.

Va'Yaylech:

612. Parshas Va'Yaylech 31:2 "Gather together the people, the men, the women, and the small children…" (Positive) This is the mitzvah of *Hakhel* (הקהל) when, on the second day of Succos in the year following *shmittah* (the sabbatical year), the entire nation assembled at the Temple to hear the king read from the Torah.

613. Parshas Va'Yaylech 31:19 "And now, write this song for yourselves…" (Positive) The final mitzvah in the Torah is to write a *Sefer Torah*. Each Jew should participate in this mitzvah by hiring someone to write a Torah on their behalf or by being part of a group that arranges for the writing of a Torah. Today, the building of a Torah library is considered by some to be a fulfillment of this commandment.

Every Jew should have books of Torah at home and take part in teaching Torah to their children and grandchildren, as it says in the same *passuk* as the command to write a Torah: ולמדה את בני ישראל שימה בפיהם - *and you shall teach the children of Israel, place it in their mouths.*

Learning Torah and teaching it to the next generation in the key to passing along our traditions.

A PERSONAL LIBRARY AND A LIFETIME OF STUDY

It is important to point out that just because someone learns all day, that does not mean they know <u>how</u> to learn. It is common for some teachers to refer to their yeshiva students as "good learners," but how do you really quantify one's ability to absorb their studies or pass them along to others?

I was visiting a prominent rebbe of a Jerusalem yeshiva who was active in recruiting for his kollel. He told me the story of a young man who came to him, wanting to join. In his interview, the rebbe asked him what Gemara he had learned in the previous year. The prospective kollel member answered that he had learned Gemara Nazir.

The rebbe said: "I will ask you one question that will tell me whether you really know the Gemara. Can a woman become a nazir and can she take the same vows of abstinence as a man?"

The gears in the young man's brain began to turn. He searched his memory for a clue and started to sweat when he could not find an answer. Finally, he admitted to the Rebbe that he did not know.

The rebbe responded: "The answer is written directly in the Torah. It says in Bamidbar, *perek* 6, *passuk* 2: "...איש או אשה כי יפלא לנדר נדר נזיר..." (*...a man or a woman who shall separate themselves by taking a Nazarite vow of abstinence...*). The answer is not in the Gemara, it is in the Torah, the original source!"

Needless to say, the young man was not recruited into the kollel.

The world of Jewish learning often focuses on one's proficiency in Talmud and their ability to decode complex tractates. Priority is given to memorizing multiple series of discussions and arguments while referencing a host of commentaries. While this is important and is a valuable tool in acquiring knowledge and sharpening the mind, one must not neglect the study of Tanach.

The Torah is so filled with mystery and our laws are so intricate and complex that only through dedicated study and investigation can one hope to come to a deeper and more meaningful understanding of them.

I have consulted with numerous educators and have come up with a list of sources that should be the basic foundation of one's library. This does not mean that one should buy them, stack them neatly on shelves, and leave them there to look impressive. These are meant to be studied and used as reference tools. One has to make time to learn them regularly and to progress from the first *passuk* of *B'reishis* to – there is no end.

To be a lifelong student of Torah means to never stop studying, learning, investigating, and asking questions. My father lived a long and happy life and never stopped learning. He had a weekly Gemara shiur for over 40 years and learned the weekly *parsha* every Friday night. He never went to shul without being prepared with *divrei Torah* to discuss with others, and admitted, to the day he passed, that the ways of G-d and the world remained a mystery to him.

The first set of books we all need in our homes is a Chumash – the five books of the Torah, with commentaries. I recommend this in two forms: First, we need a Mikros Gedolos with the commentaries of Rashi, Ramban, Or Ha'chayim, K'lei Yakar, Sifsei Chachamim, and S'forno. Additionally, an Artscroll set of Chumash and Rashi with English translation is an invaluable tool.

A full set of Neviim and Kesuvim is also a must. Whether it is from Judaica Press or Artscroll, make sure that it has Rashi and Radak's commentaries and an English translation of the primary text.

Too many "serious" yeshiva students do not take the time to learn Chumash and Rashi, let alone Nach, and dismiss them as something that seminary girls study. There have been numerous times when I have approached a rabbi with a question on Yirmiyahu or Amos, only to have them admit to me: "I never really learned it."

I made the commitment last year to learn at least 2 chapters of Nach every night. I have been studying the Judaica Press edition with Rashi and Radak and recently finished its final book; *Sefer Divrei Hayamim - Chronicles*. It has been a true eye-opener and I regret not having done it earlier in life.

Next, we all need a set of Talmud (Mishna and Gemara), whether it be a Vilna Shas or the Artscroll Schottenstein edition of the Talmud, which has 73 volumes. The advantage of the more traditional Vilna Shas is that it contains the commentaries of the Rif, the Ran, and others that are not in the Artscroll. Nevertheless, the Artscroll translation with its bottom-of-the-page commentary is an excellent study tool.

For studying Halacha – Jewish law, there are a few primary sources that must be considered, including the Rambam's *Mishna Torah* as well as the *Mishna B'rurah*, and a one-volume *Kitzur Shulchan Aruch*.

If possible, a number of resource books should be purchased. This would include Pirkei Avos (Ethics of our Fathers), and a Codex Judaica or Jewish Timeline Encyclopedia (each is in one volume). Ishei Hatanach Encyclopedia of Biblical Personalities is a great resource (also in one volume), as is *Hamaftayach*, by Daniel Retter – a key to any subject in the Talmud in a single volume. Just look up a subject alphabetically, and it will give you the source page. It is available in either English or Hebrew but there is no combination set.

The Book of Legends (*Sefer Ha'Aggadah*) by Bialik and Ravnitsky translates into English and indexes the stories from the Talmud and Midrash.

Another invaluable tool, a concordance, is one that will help you look up any word and find its source in Tanach.

For studying Jewish history, I recommend four books. The first three are by Rabbi Berel Wein, Faith & Fate, Herald of Destiny, and Triumph of Survival. The fourth is a phenomenal book on the Holocaust by Publications International, Ltd., The Holocaust Chronicle.

Finally, I want to recommend a mostly overlooked resource. It incorporates Torah, Neviim, Kesuvim, many of the stories of the Talmud as well as the Midrash. It is *Me 'Am Lo'ez*.

While this has been a staple in Sephardic homes, synagogues, and schools for almost three centuries, Ashkenazic yeshivas have historically dismissed or ignored it. Nevertheless, many rabbis and teachers count it to be among the best commentaries ever written on Tanach. The original was composed in Ladino by Rabbi Yaakov Khuli (Culi) in 1730.

Today, we can study this magnificent work as translated by Rabbi Aryeh Kaplan. It is a complete anthology, with twenty volumes covering the first five books of the Torah. The full set, including Nach, is 45 books. Ownership of this set is a must for anyone building a Jewish library and making the commitment to learn Tanach!

Establishing a library and studying from its books on a regular schedule will help anyone become a lifelong student of Torah. This will also help one to fulfill the 613th mitzvah in the Torah.

We must continue our tradition of deep study and pass this knowledge as well as our books to our children and grandchildren

BIG QUESTIONS

In some circles it would be considered heretical to ask these questions. I believe it is important to expose students to this information and to offer a path to an answer, when possible. I have worked with students for many years and these questions come directly from them.

Posing difficult questions often stimulates one to open a dialogue with family, teachers, and friends in an effort to come-up with an acceptable answer. But remember, nobody but G-d has the definitive answers. That is why the Talmud often ends contentious discussions with the word "תיקו" which is a mnemonic device used to remind us that at some point in the future at a time of G-d's determination, Tishbi – Eliyahu Ha'Navi, (who is given a respectful title and named after the city from which he came, Tishbe in Gilead) will answer all of our questions. The four Hebrew letters of תיקו, **tuf – yud – kuf – vav** begin the words *Tishbi Yetaretz Kushios V'abayos*. In Aramaic, this suggests to us: "leave the discussion where it is."

These questions are important and the answers I have provided are those that work for me. I encourage the reader to consult the works of many scholars who have provided additional answers and deep perspective on these questions, including Rabbi Jonathan Saks, Rabbi Akiva Tatz, Rabbi Aryeh Kaplan, Rabbi Mattis Weinberg, Rabbi Dovid Gottlieb, and Rabbi Ken Spiro (from Aish Hatorah).

If we have scientific proof the earth is billions of years old, why is our Jewish calendar only in the year 5781?

Our count of the years begins with man's creation on day six. What happened in the previous five days? If the sun, the moon, and the stars (and the cosmic system that established the 24-hour day) were not created until the fourth day, how long were each of the "days" leading up to that? The Torah also says in the first chapter, at the end of the creation of light and dark; ויהי ערב ויהי בקר יום אחד – "And there was evening and there was morning, <u>one</u> day." It never calls it the "first" day. What happened before that?

In that light, the Zohar hints at the creation and destruction of "other worlds" as part of the process of the creation of <u>this</u> world. The Gemara in Avodah Zarah discusses the idea of creation and destruction of previous worlds.

There is also the philosophical concept of our universe being contained (metaphorically) within a piece of pottery which was shattered in an explosion at the outset of creation (perhaps this is what some scientists refer-to as the "big bang"). Our job, according to this theory of "*tikkun olam*" (repairing the world) is to repair the world piece-by-piece through doing mitzvos.

Unfortunately, *tikkun olam* has been appropriated by many Jews as a "religion" in-and-of itself. There are those who only see our responsibility as Jews as one which involves promoting peace among man and physical repair of the world – ecological pursuits, responses to global warming, joining "peaceful" protests, etc. Have you heard the story of the Jewish first-time visitor to Israel who asked his tour guide how to say *tikkun olam* in Hebrew?

It is possible to view the first days of creation as eons, which to G-d are viewed as "days." It is not difficult to reconcile our calendar with the scientific or archaeological record. Creatures such as dinosaurs and prehistoric "man" for which we have ample evidence, did roam the earth, but they existed before G-d's creation of the first rational man, Adam. In fact, the Torah tells us in the creation narrative that on day five

G-d created the giant sea creatures and all "creeping living souls." Who or what were they?

But what about cave paintings of prehistoric man fighting creatures like wooly mammoths? Why does man have a tail bone? What about the evolutionary process of man's development? How does one reconcile evolutionary theory with the Torah?

The process of evolution as espoused by Charles Darwin is actually described in the Torah. Follow the sequence of creation in the first Parsha in the Torah and you will see "evolution" before your eyes. It is important, though, to see this through a lens that allows for the first days to viewed as eras or millennia. Nevertheless, Jewish theology teaches that creation was not random (see the Ramban's commentary on the first passuk in the Torah). Therefore, we disagree with Darwin on the origin of creation. We believe in The Divine Conductor.

The World's Creation in the Torah

Day 1: Heaven(s) and earth, light and dark

Day 2: The sky

Day 3: The seas, dry land and vegetation

Day 4: The sun, moon and celestial bodies (stars, planets, etc.)

Day 5: Birds, sea creatures, creeping living beings, winged fowl

Day 6: Mammals (land animals), then rational man and woman (as opposed to man-like creatures)

Day 7: The creation of Shabbos – the 7th day ("of rest")

We believe that creation was not a random event but one of intelligent design. Judaism teaches us that the grand symphony conductor, G-d, initiated and controlled this entire process.

We do not have to view creation with a fundamentalist's rigid and literal interpretation. Did G-d create the animals with a wave or a word and they instantly appeared? Is it possible that G-d set the process of creation of the animal kingdom into motion? We know that monkeys preceded man on the 6th day, but no monkey can become a man unless G-d specifically declares it.

Yes, we have a tail bone. What does that mean? The Midrash says that there were other man-like creatures that came before Adam, but G-d breathed the spirit of life into Adam making him unique, with a *neshama* – a soul.

Do I really have free will?

G-d did not create us to be puppets. We were created with free will. One of the basic beliefs of Judaism is that we are endowed by G-d with two sides, one of *Yaytzer Ha'tov* and one of *Yaytzer Ha'ra*. We can always choose between doing good or bad. The Torah tells us in B'reishis that *"the Yaytzer of man is evil from his youth."* It is balanced by the existence of the *Yaytzer Ha'Tov* – the "good" side of man, but is, nevertheless, a very powerful force that often leads man to sin.

This stands in stark contrast to the Christian belief that man is flawed from birth and is endowed with "original sin." We, as Jews, do not agree with that. Instead, we ascribe to a belief that G-d created us with the potential to do good or bad in even measure and we have the free choice to do either. We make these choices every day. Can we choose to eat a cheeseburger at McDonalds? Yes. It is against the laws of the Torah, but

G-d is not going to stop us. Can we turn on the television or make a bonfire on Shabbos? Again, it is against the laws of the Torah, but G-d gave us free will and we can choose either way!

Why do bad things happen to good people and why do people sometimes suffer?

Just because a person decides to sin does not mean that G-d agrees with them. This is a key to reconciling bad things happening to good people and good things happening to bad people. G-d lets the world operate and the chips fall where they may! We have absolutely no idea why G-d does what He does. All we can do is observe and absorb His judgement while trying to be the best we can be!

Today, the world has imposed on many of us a revised definition of justice, with "social justice," "environment justice," and "economic justice" serving as tools to micro-manage a society where people want to "virtue signal" so they can feel better about themselves.

When we ask: "Why is G-d doing this?" we are questioning why something seemingly unjust has happened. As Jews, we view suffering differently than many adherents to Christianity or Islam who seem to welcome suffering as an important element of their observance. While we may not understand the need for suffering, we definitely do not welcome it and often struggle with the "why." We are willing to acknowledge that G-d actively runs the world, but sometimes question His actions. We can recognize His dominion and the fact that there is an ultimate wisdom behind His actions, but it is, nevertheless, difficult to reconcile the apparent injustices in the world.

When things are going well, when we are profiting financially, having a smooth and healthy life – we don't ask: "Why is G-d doing this to me?"

When things don't go well, we start to question our fate and ask whether G-d's actions are fair. Perhaps we should consider other options for why seemingly bad things happen to us. Did we do something wrong? Is this a good time to reflect on our past behavior?

There is a Jewish concept that *yesurim* (afflictions) are G-d's way of waking us up. We all experience times that demand that we look inward and make an effort to improve. Do we want afflictions? No, but sometimes, when we look at events in hindsight, we can appreciate the value of past experiences, many of them painful.

Is the world fair? Is everyone rich, attractive, and healthy? I don't believe that is the case. In Hebrew there is no word for "fair." Today, in Israel, there is an exclamation, "***Zeh lo fair!***" – "**This is not fair!**" There is no concept of fairness in Judaism. Everything is relative.

Similarly, in Hebrew, there are no words for "I have." Instead, we say: "יש לי" which means "**There is to me.**" All we have is that which is to us – that which we have been given. We recognize that everything we "have" is what has been given to us by G-d. Our lives have purpose and meaning and we do not believe that everything that happens to us is merely random or sheer luck. We all want to believe that we are moving in the right direction in life.

In many colleges, a typical question asked in Philosophy 101 is: If G-d is all-powerful, can He create a rock that is so heavy that even He cannot lift it? You can go around in circles all day on this question, but I will provide you with a possible answer I heard from one of my teachers.

G-d already has created such a rock and it is called: "Free Will." By giving humans the ability to make choices in life, G-d has essentially hamstrung Himself and cannot get involved on a regular basis in micro-managing our choices or those of people who often affect us. Otherwise, we would be nothing but puppets.

Our enemies murder us. People lie, cheat, and steal. Do they have free choice? Could they choose to be good? Of course, but G-d is not going to make every choice for man. If you choose to stuff a pork sandwich into your mouth is G-d going to stop you? What happens when you make the conscious decision to hurt someone else either physically or verbally? Does G-d stop you?

G-d set this world in motion and told us to "work it" and "watch over it." Life goes along as affected and influenced by the free choices of man. But G-d also has a plan and a direction for the world. There are times when the choices made by man can affect the direction or fate of the world so profoundly that G-d <u>must</u> get involved. Sometimes, free will must be suspended for a short time so G-d can nudge the world back onto its "path," and that is usually when overt or hidden miracles are performed. Our history is full of such moments and miracles and they continue to this day.

This is where the discussion gets more complicated. There is a precarious balance in our world between free will and G-d's will. We do not understand the concept of a Divine Plan. What direction are we going in and why? We have no idea. We were placed on this earth to work it and guard it.

Every Friday night in Kiddush we repeat words from the Torah that describe our purpose on this earth when we say: "...אשר ברא אלקים לעשות." – "...that G-d created to do." To do what? We were created and given this world and then commanded **to do** – to work, to innovate, to create, and to build, while in the process, doing mitzvos and taking care of one another.

Many of us, in our desire to gain power or riches make terrible choices. We literally choose the "dark side." We are free to choose to do good or bad and are responsible for our own choices. We must each choose our own path and fight our *Yaytzer Ha'ra* – our dark and evil side. Nobody said the world is fair. It is what it is, a deep mystery. All we can do is try our hardest and make every effort to choose the side of good and life. As the Torah says: "ובחרת בחיים" (*And you shall choose life*).

I am a member of the technology generation and I have grown accustomed to getting answers at the touch of a keyboard. Why should I follow laws I can't find reasons for? Aren't I entitled to an answer?

Every generation that came before us saw themselves as the most civilized in history with the most modern conveniences. Today, we are amazed by the lives of our predecessors who lived without flush toilets, clean running water, televisions, cellphones, and computers. We have grown accustomed to turning to technology for the answers to our questions. We have no need to go to the library and do research there.

For the observant Jew, there is an additional challenge. A large percentage of the Torah's commandments are *chukim* – laws that have no stated reason. We are expected to follow them without questioning their reasoning or rationale.

Imagine your parents telling you to take out the garbage right now. Your response may be: "Why?"

If they respond: "Because I told you so!" would that be enough of a reason for you to do it?

The parent-child relationship mirrors G-d's relationship with us. Essentially, G-d expects us to follow the laws He commanded us. Why were we given *chukim*? Why not tell us the reason? I suppose the simple reason would be: Because He said so! When we do His will because He said so, it demonstrates our trust that G-d wants what is best for us.

That raises a famous Jewish legal question relating to mitzvos. Is it better to perform a mitzvah because we are commanded to or because we genuinely want to? The majority of our sages agree that it is a higher level of observance to follow the laws because we are commanded to. This recognizes our human condition of normally resisting doing things "on command." Maybe this is an outgrowth of western culture, but we have a tendency to fight those things that appear to deprive us of the right to choose how to behave.

Since the dawn of the technology revolution, we have grown increasingly lazy. We have learned or been conditioned to expect quick answers to our questions and have revolted against the expectations of what some call an ancient culture or antiquated laws.

One of our greatest blessings as Jews has been our Talmudic tradition of putting greater emphasis on the questions than the answers. We ask, we pry, we search and investigate. Sometimes we find an answer and sometimes we don't. We follow hundreds of laws without knowing the reasons for them. We keep kosher; not because it is healthier to do so but simply because we are Jews and follow the word of a higher authority – G-d.

I may have a great question, but G-d does not owe me an answer. To expect one is to follow an arrogant path that seeks to place man on a level with G-d. We need to change our expectations. Technology has its place and is a wonderful tool, but it cannot answer our deep questions. It can't tell us why G-d does things and it surely has no moral compass.

We all need to re-train and re-educate ourselves to place more emphasis on finding the good questions. At the same time, we must be able to move forward in life without all the answers.

I titled this book <u>The Choosing People</u> because our ancestors chose to follow the path of G-d and the Torah thousands of years ago. If we deny our laws, break with tradition, marry outside our faith, or give-up on our past, our link to our ancestors breaks and we cease to be relevant. I don't believe we have the right to break that connection.

We are G-d's "choosing people" and chose to accept His laws at Sinai before even hearing them. To end it all now because of our intellectual arrogance would be a terrible crime committed against G-d, our families, our communities, our nation, and our future.

How do you justify the Holocaust? How could a loving G-d allow such a thing to happen?

I acknowledge that it is a difficult challenge to believe in a G-d that could allow millions of people to suffer, be slaughtered, and humiliated. One way to maintain our faith is to believe that the Holocaust shows how critical Judaism is to the world's existence and how far our enemies will go to try to eliminate us!

The Holocaust indicates to us the weakness of man, not the weakness of a G-d who gave man free will. I prefer to believe that as G-d witnessed the killing of His nation, whether it was during the slavery in Egypt, the Inquisition in Spain, or in the Holocaust, He was figuratively "crying" with His hands tied. He was "powerless" to stop our enemies, who also had free will, from choosing to do evil.

But why allow things to go that far? Why did He not stop it with a miracle before millions died?

I believe that one day, after I die, I will have the opportunity to see the inner-workings of G-d's plan and to ask questions. My first question will be: "Why do children sometimes suffer?" My second question will be: "Why didn't you step in earlier to stop the Holocaust?"

G-d operates on a frequency that man cannot tune into. An AM radio cannot tune-in to an FM signal. We exist in this world for a finite time and then our soul moves on, after death, to another level.

We must learn to live with these questions until we reach a point where G-d will provide us with His answers. It is a difficult challenge and provides us with an opportunity to test our dedication and faith. It is too easy to blame G-d and use that as an excuse to reject Judaism.

Modern Israel was a direct outgrowth of World War II. Our enemies try to deny the Holocaust as a way of removing any justification for the declaration of Israel as a Jewish country. We must never forget the terrible crimes committed against our People and we must use those memories as a way to build, from the ashes of the Holocaust, a free and godly nation in Israel.

Avraham, the first Jew, was born in the year 1948 from creation. Israel was "born" in 1948 of the modern age. Over six million Jews died in the Holocaust and Israel now has over six million Jewish citizens.

Circumstance?

I think not!

TAKING PRIDE IN BEING A JEW

It is sometimes difficult, in the face of antisemitism and uncertainty, to take pride in being a Jew. Many of us are afraid, when confronted, to admit that we are Jewish.

Looking at some famous Jews of modern times can help us take pride in their accomplishments and make us more comfortable in our place in the world.

A friend in Alaska sent me the following listing of historical figures of known Jewish lineage.

1. The Roosevelt family were Dutch Jews who arrived in New York in 1682. The first American Roosevelt was Claes Rosenvelt. The mother of Franklin Roosevelt (Sara Delano) was a descendant of Sephardic Jews.
2. Dwight Eisenhower's father was a Swedish Jew (and appears in the West Point Yearbook, 1915).
3. Fiorella LaGuardia (past mayor of New York City) spoke Hebrew and Yiddish. His mother's last name was Jacobson.
4. Winston's Churchill's mother was Jenny Jarome, a Jewess from Brooklyn, although her father claimed to be from Anglo-Saxon Protestant descent.
5. Cary Grant, Peter Sellers, David Bowie, Robert DeNiro, Shari Belafonte, Harrison Ford, Gwyneth Paltrow, William Shatner, and Geraldo Rivera all had Jewish mothers. Marilyn Monroe, Elizabeth Taylor, and Sammy Davis Jr. converted to Judaism.
6. Jewish musicians include Paula Abdul, Neil Diamond, Lenny Kravitz, Bob Dylan, Adam Levine, Michael Bolton, Pink, Billy Joel, Simon & Garfunkel and many more. Jewish comedians have had a very strong influence in radio, television, and movies.

7. The first full-length movie with sound (The Jazz Singer) was produced by Jews, Samuel Goldwyn and Louis Mayer, the founders of MGM Studios.
8. Jewish doctors, surgeons, scientists, physicists, and engineers have received more Nobel Prizes per capita than any other ethnic group. Jews are "over-represented" in this group by a factor of forty.
9. Levi Strauss, inventor of jeans and Levis, was Jewish.
10. Four Jews were among the original signers of the Call for National Action which created the NAACP.
11. European Jews founded all of the original Hollywood movie Studios.
12. Over 70% of all Pulitzer Prize winners have been Jews.
13. Albert Einstein, Niels Bohr, Sigmund Freud, and Carl Sagan – all Jewish.
14. Irving Berlin, a Jew, wrote the most popular holiday song in modern history – White Christmas.
15. Jonas Salk, a Jew, created the polio vaccine.
16. One of the most famous baseball pitchers of all time, Sandy Koufax, a Jew, refused to pitch in the first game of the World Series in 1965 for the Los Angeles Dodgers – it was Yom Kippur.
17. Designers Calvin Klein, Ralph Lauren, and Kenneth Cole – all Jewish.
18. Many members of the US Supreme Court have been Jewish including Louis Brandeis, Benjamin Cardozo, Abe Fortas, Ruth Bader Ginsburg, Stephen Breyer, and Elena Kagan.

Although any list I could generate of Jewish sports stars would be relatively short, I could list literally thousands of famous Jews from modern times who have been ground-breaking contributors to society.

Whether it be in the areas of business, science, medicine, or entertainment, Jews have contributed more to our world than any other ethnic group. For that we are often reviled, and many are jealous of our accomplishments.

Nevertheless, we should take pride in the collective and individual successes of our people and our tireless pursuit of education, excellence, innovation, and achievement.

ADDITIONAL TERMS – A SHORT GLOSSARY

A.

Aggadah: Rabbinic interpretation (midrash) of the Bible including elaborative stories.

Aliyah: Immigration to Israel. Literally, "going up" or "ascending." In ancient days it referred to pilgrimage to Jerusalem. In modern times it refers to waves of immigration to the Holy Land. It is also used as a term for being called-up to the Torah in synagogue.

Aninus: The time of mourning between death and burial that carries specific restrictions.

Arbah Minim: Lulav, Esrog, Hadassim, and Aravos – brought on Succos.

Ashkenazim: Jews of German or Polish ancestry.

Atbash: (א-ת ב-ש) A method of encrypting the Hebrew alphabet by taking letters and opposing them with their reverse associated letters. For instance, the first letter Aleph, has as its opposite, the letter Taf, the last letter of the Hebrew alphabet. The Beis has Shin as its opposite, Gimmel has Reish, etc. Hebrew commentaries sometimes draw lessons from utilizing this system of looking at the alphabet. The Hebrew word for charity is צדקה and the opposites of these letters using the Atbash method are הקדצ which is the same word spelled backwards. This teaches us a lesson that giving charity reverses back to us and we are repaid for our good deeds. Another example is from the book of Jeremiah where we are told of the king of ששך (Sheshach) and the Atbash of that word is בבל (Bavel – Babylon) hinting that Sheshach is Babylon.

Aveirah: Sin

Avelus: Mourning the dead

Auto-da-fe: A Portuguese term for "act of faith" and the exposure and punishment (torture and death) of converted Jews during the Spanish Inquisition.

B.

BCE: Before the **C**hristian (or **C**ommon) **E**ra – Before year #1 of the common or Christian (Gregorian) calendar.

Beis Din: Jewish court. Literally, "House of Judgement."

Beis Hamikdash: The Temple in Jerusalem.

Beis Knesses: Literally, "House of Assembly" – synagogue.

Bilu: The movement of Eastern European Jews of the first wave of immigration to Israel in 1882. A mnemonic device for the Hebrew words that translate as: *House of Yaakov, come, let us go!*

Bimah: Pedestal or platform for Torah-reading in the synagogue or pulpit from which services are led.

C.

Chalutzim: Jewish pioneers (in Israel).

Chassidim: From the Hebrew for "pious" or "kind." Originally, Jewish followers of the Bal Shem Tov. Today, a generic term for sects of ultra-orthodox Jews.

Cherem: Banishment or excommunication from a Jewish community.

Chevra Kadisha: Jewish "holy" society that organizes the preparation of the dead for burial.

Chilul Ha'shem: That which desecrates or profanes G-d's name, or an action by an individual or group that projects Judaism in a bad light.

Chol Ha'moed: The intermediate days of Pesach or Succos during which work is permitted.

Conversos: Jews who faked conversion to Christianity (and practiced Judaism in secret) in Spain and Portugal during the Spanish Inquisition.

D.

Decalogue: The Ten Commandments (from the Greek words for "ten" and "word").

Diaspora: From the Greek word for "dispersion," Jewish community life outside of Israel following expulsion.

E.

Ethics of the Fathers: Pirkei Avos – a section of the Mishna devoted to moral and ethical teachings, adages, and Rabbinic words of wisdom from the Mishnaic period.

Exilarch: The title of head of the Babylonian Jewish community during the first millennium of the modern calendar. Called, in Aramaic, the *reish galusa* (head of exile).

F.

Final Solution: The Nazi plan for genocide against the Jews during World War II (1939-1945) and the stated goal of exterminating all Jews.

G.

Gaon: The head of a rabbinical academy and communal leader in Babylon during the period from years 500 to 1000.

Gemara: Aramaic for "learning." The discussions and commentary on the Mishna, incorporated together with the Mishna into the Talmud.

Gehennom: From the Bible – from the words *Gei Hinnom* (the Valley of Hinnom) in Jerusalem (the valley outside the Jaffa gate running north to south) where ancient idol-worshipers would sacrifice children to their god, Molech. It has been interpreted by Christians as "Hell."

Get: The Hebrew word for a contract of divorce (also, *sefer k'risus*).

Gematria: A method of interpreting Biblical words based on their numerical values. This is from the Greek word "gamma" (the third letter of their alphabet) and "tria" (meaning "three") its associated numeric value based on its position in the alphabet.

Genizah: A storehouse of Jewish sacred writings that were not buried or properly disposed-of. Many ancient synagogues had hidden rooms where old contracts, parchments, and books were discarded. The most famous were the Genizah of Cairo, Egypt and the Geniza of Aleppo, Syria.

Ghetto: The Italian word for "foundry." In Venice, in the early 1500's, the Doge of Venice segregated the Jews from the general populace by housing them in an old cannon-casting factory, a foundry. During World War II, the word "ghetto" became synonymous with a walled-off portion of a city where Jews were concentrated.

H.

Haredi: A term used for describing ultra-orthodox Jews. Derived from Isaiah 66:2 – one who "trembles" at the word of G-d.

Halacha: Jewish law. Literally, "the path" or "walking the path."

Hashem: Literally, "The Name." When we are not davening or reading Torah or Nach in synagogue, it is customary not to pronounce the written name of G-d, the Tetragrammaton of Yud, Heh, Vav, and Heh. The word *Hashem* is substituted.

Haskalah: "Enlightenment" which brought modern thinking and practice to European Jews in the late 1700's and continued for over 100 years.

Hatikvah: Literally, "The Hope." Israel's national anthem. It was written by Naftali Imber (a Galician Jew) in the 1880's.

I.

Inquisition: An investigation. The Catholic Church investigated Jews during the period the Spanish Inquisition (from 1478 to 1834) to see whether they were faithful followers of Christianity. Its violent reach stretched from Western Europe to South America.

J.

Judea: The Southern Kingdom of Israel following the death of King Solomon. The Romans originally called Israel "Judea," named after the tribe of Yehuda (Judah). Following the Assyrian conquest of the northern tribes, the only tribes remaining in Israel were Yehuda and Binyamin as well as some *Kohanim* and *Leviim*.

K.

Kabbalah: Jewish mysticism.

Kaddish: The Aramaic prayer recited for eleven months following the death of a close relative or on the anniversary of their death.

Kahal - Kehilla: Congregation or organized community.

Kashrus - Kosher: Jewish dietary laws. Literally, "fit" or "proper."

Kavanah: Deep concentration. It is a state-of-mind that leads one to effectively reach out in prayer or do a good deed.

Kesuvah: Jewish marriage contract.

Kibbutz: A communal settlement in Israel. Originally, a collective farming community in which all income was held in common and all profits were reinvested internally. Today, many kibbutzim manufacture sophisticated commercial or industrial products but are still governed by a communal or socialist system.

Kibbutz Galuyos: Ingathering (return) of exiles to Israel.

Kiddush Hashem: Sanctification of G-d's name. A term often used for Jewish martyrdom or for an act that brings glory to G-d's name.

Kiddushin: The act of sanctifying a marriage and establishing a legal relationship.

Kittel: A white robe (reminiscent of burial shrouds) that is a symbol of purity worn at High Holiday services and by some grooms at weddings.

Kol Nidrei: Literally, "All My Promises." The first prayer of Yom Kippur. A nullification of vows and promises of the past year.

Koreis: Literally, "cut off." A category of heavenly punishment wherein a sinner is cut-off from the future of the Jewish People. It connotes spiritual banishment.

K'riyah: The act of tearing one's clothing as a sign of mourning.

L.

Ladino: A Judeo-Spanish language developed and spoken by Jews in pre-Inquisition Spain. Its use continues to this day, mainly in poems, songs, and prayers in Sephardic synagogues descended from Turkish, Greek, Spanish, Portuguese, Italian, and North African communities.

Lechem Ha'panim: The twelve loaves of bread baked each week in the Temple and placed on the *Shulchan* – the Showbread Table.

Luchos: Tablets (the two stone tablets of the Ten Commandments).

M.

Magen David: Literally, "Star of David." It is constructed of two equilateral triangles, one facing up and one facing down. Some says it was first used as a symbol of the army of King David on the shields of soldiers, calling upon G-d to be the "shield" of Israel. It has become synonymous with Jewish identity and was used by the Nazis, who ordered all Jews to sew a yellow Star of David onto their clothing. The overlapping triangles are also symbolic of the synthesis of man and woman.

Manna: The food G-d provided to the Jews in the desert.

Marrano: A derogatory term ("pig" or "swine") used primarily by Italian Jews to describe Spanish and Portuguese Conversos who moved to Italy during the Inquisition.

Maseches: A single tractate of the Mishna (and Talmud).

Mashgiach: One who certifies food as Kosher. This term is also used for a rabbi in a religious institution who oversees the moral direction of his students or congregants.

Middos: Character traits or qualities.

Midrash: A collection of stories that elaborate on the Bible and that are often used to teach lessons in morality. These stories are not to be taken literally.

Mikvah: Ritual bath utilized in the process of purification.

Minhag: Custom or customary religious practice.

Misnagdim: "Opponents." Jews who are not Chassidic. This term emerged from a dispute between the Vilna Gaon and the Bal Shem Tov (who was a proponent of Chassidus) in 1772.

Mizrachi: "Eastern" or "Oriental." Refers to Jews from exotic lands who returned to Israel from places like India, China, or Yemen. It is also the name of a religious Zionist political party.

Moshav: A cooperative agricultural settlement in Israel. As opposed to a kibbutz, profits are distributed to individual families based on their production. Nevertheless, the land and equipment are owned by the co-op.

Mussaf: "Additional." Initially referred to additional sacrifices that were brought in the Temple on Shabbos, Rosh Chodesh, and holidays. After the days of the Temple, it became an additional prayer service.

N.

Nasi: "The prince." The head of a tribe of Israel. Later, in Roman times, it referred to the head of the Jewish court, the Sanhedrin.

Nazir: One who separates himself (or herself) from the community and takes a vow not to cut their hair, consume grape products, or become impure.

Neilah: The closing prayer service of Yom Kippur.

Ner Tamid: "Eternal light." A light that is kept burning in our synagogues as a remembrance of the Menorah in the Temple which was perpetually lit.

Nichum Aveilim: The act of comforting mourners.

Niddah: A woman in a state of physical impurity brought on by her monthly cycle.

Nissuin: "Elevation." In a marriage, the second part of the wedding is called *nissuin* and following that, the couple may live together legally.

O.

Olam Ha'bah: The World-To-Come.

P.

Pale (of Jewish Settlement): An area in western Russia where Jews were forced to live during the period of the czars from 1791 to 1917.

Pentateuch: The five books of the Torah (from the Greek words "penta" for 5 and "teukhos," meaning book or scroll).

Peroches: Originally the curtain that separated the Holy-of-Holies in the Tabernacle and Temple from the *Kodesh*, the area that held the Menorah, etc. Today, it refers to the curtain covering the ark in our synagogues.

Pharisees: A group of Jews who formed a social movement and (following the destruction of the 2nd Temple) became the forebearers of Rabbinic Judaism.

Pidyon Ha'ben: The act of redeeming a firstborn son from a *Kohen*.

Pogrom: A Russian term for a violent and unprovoked attack against a Jewish neighborhood, town, or community.

S.

Sabra: A fruit that grows in desert climates that is prickly on the outside and sweet inside. Commonly used to identify those born in Israel.

Sephardim: Jews of Spanish/Portuguese descent.

Shechita: Kosher slaughtering.

Shoah: The Hebrew word for the Holocaust. Literally: "whirlwind of destruction." "Holocaust" comes from the Greek words that describe the *olah* sacrifice which was completely burnt. The word "holos" means "burnt" and "kaustos" means "sacrificial offering."

Shiva: The period of seven days (based on the Hebrew word for 7, *sheva*) of mourning following burial.

Shmittah: Sabbatical year, declared once every seven years. A time to let fields remain fallow, release indentured servants, and forgive certain loans.

T.

Tabernacle: The portable *mishkan* in the desert – In Israel it was moved to Gilgal, Shilo, and Givah, and later replaced by Solomon's Temple in Jerusalem.

Taharas Ha'mishpacha: The Jewish laws of family purity.

Takanah: A law or edict enacted by rabbis for the protection of the people, but not as having been directly commanded in the Torah.

Teshuva: Repentance.

Tikkun Olam: The mystical concept of repairing the world. This is based on the teachings of the Zohar (book of Jewish mysticism) that in the process of creating our world, G-d metaphorically broke-apart the primal elements like shards of pottery. Every time we do a mitzvah, we put one of those shards back into place, helping to "put the world back together."

Tzedakah: Charity. Literally; "act of righteousness."

Y.

Yahrtzeit: A Yiddish term for an anniversary of the death of a close relative. In Hebrew; *azkarah* or *hillula*. In Ladino; *meldado*.

Yiddish: A Judeo-German language spoken primarily in Eastern Europe beginning in the Middle Ages. This language was brought to many countries by Jewish immigrants from Eastern Europe and is still in use today.

Yizkor: A prayer service for remembrance of the dead, recited on Yom Kippur and during the three pilgrimage festivals; Pesach, Shavuos, and Succos.

Yovel: The 50th year following seven **Shmittah** cycles (49 years). The "Jubilee" year.

FINAL MUSINGS

I had a fascinating conversation with Rabbi Solomon Maimon, a patriarch of the Seattle Jewish community. We were discussing community dynamics and volunteerism and he told me the following:

There are four types of people who are members of synagogues, and this is a general rule that applies in most communities.

1. Basic members who do not attend services on a regular basis. Perhaps they come to shul on the High Holidays. Basic donors who pay their dues but do not do much more.
2. Members who volunteer and can be counted-on to help with activities, dinners, kiddushim and fundraising.
3. Donors. Those who are the financial sustainers of the congregation and give generously.
4. The *"klei kodesh."* These are the rabbis, teachers, and those learned in Torah who sustain the community and our traditions.

Rabbi Maimon continued.

"The largest number in most congregations is category 1, the basic membership. Next, come your active members and volunteers, then your big donors and your teachers. It is common for those in categories 2, 3, and 4 to be in two categories at the same time. You will have volunteers who are also big donors or volunteers who are also *klei kodesh*.

Rarely, if ever, do we find those who fit into categories 2, 3, and 4 at the same time as active volunteers, large donors, and teachers of Torah. If you can find a person like that, they are often reviled because of envy or jealousy. The fact that they are perceived as 'having it all' or 'doing it all' is inexcusable to those who cannot see themselves making the same sacrifices.

Rabbi Maimon opened my eyes that day with his perspective and clarity, even as he approached his 100th year. We live on this earth for a short period of time. We have the opportunity to maximize our potential and to learn, to work, and to give. Our families, shul, and community, should be the center of our lives.

Unfortunately, we let either laziness or ego get in the way. It is possible to have it all and to do it all. It takes time and effort as well as sacrifice. Our 2nd Temple was destroyed because of baseless hatred and unwillingness or stubbornness that prevented us from seeing the good in others. Before we can deal with the problems of the world around us, we must first conquer the conflicts between us. Only then will we be worthy of seeing the days of Mashiach.

In 1983 Dennis Prager and Joseph Telushkin published a book entitled: <u>Why the Jews?</u>

The introductory chapter of its second printing in 2004 was: "Is it 1938 again for the Jews?" In it, the authors documented multiple cases of antisemitism in Europe and the United States including physical assaults and the defacing of synagogues and cemeteries.

Now, here we are, in the year 2021, with antisemitism exploding around the world. In times of trouble (such as the Covid-19 pandemic) Jews are sought-after as victims and attacked as scapegoats.

Our 2nd Temple in Jerusalem was destroyed by the Romans almost 2000 years ago. We have survived in exile and are thriving in Israel. More Jews live in Israel than in the United States. The world continues its attacks on the Jewish People through its accusations directed against Israel of apartheid and genocide.

We cannot buy favor from the gentile world. Jews who donate to build symphony halls and give to the arts or public education instead of Jewish causes, think that they will earn acceptance and respect from neighbors and civic leaders. What they don't realize is that when we do not observe and respect the tenets of our own religion, we are despised. No one respects a Jew who does not respect himself.

Too many Jews are caught-up in a culture that advocates for religious and societal change, which some want to label as: "The New Normal." Keep in mind that today's problems are yesterday's solutions. We don't have all the answers, but still, must reject societal pressures that advocate for the abolishment of long-held beliefs and practices.

It is time for us to come home. We need to start by studying what Judaism is all about and return to observance of the Torah. We need to respect each other and be active in our communities. We must work and sacrifice as we expand the horizons of our Torah study and practice.

The Maharal of Prague said that G-d blessed Avraham and gave him the power to bless others (*parshas Lech Lechah*, 12:2,3). The word for "blessing" comes from three root letters, *beis*, *reish*, and *chaf*. These three letters have numerical values (gematria) of 2, 200, and 20 (222 total). The message in these letters is that blessing connotes doubling, increasing, and multiplying. We are blessed when we exert extra effort and increase our strength by literally doubling-down in our service to our G-d, our community, our study, and our charity. That is the secret to our blessing and is the secret to how we can "have it all!"

G-d's gift to us is the Torah, **THE** Book of law, morality, and history, that transcends time and place. Study it. Learn from the wisdom of our ancestors and over 3800 years of Jewish history. There is no time better than right now to start learning Tanach!

AFTERWORD
By: Rabbanit Shani Taragin

What does it mean to be a "Choosing People?"

Throughout the Torah, the root word *"bechar"* (*chose*) appears 39 times. It is predominantly in reference to G-d's choice of us as a Chosen Nation, or as a Chosen Place for his *Shechinah* (*Divine Presence*) to rest.

When man does choose in the Books of Bereishis or Sh'mos, it is in reference to Lot choosing the iniquitous location of the city of S'dom (Bereishis 13:11) or Moshe or Yehoshua selecting men for war or judicial appointments. The only reference in the Torah to an entire people choosing is found in the Book of Devarim, where the etymology of choice, *"bechar,"* appears 31 times!

Amidst numerous pesukim teaching us of G-d's choice of people and place, the Torah teaches us:

העדתי בכם היום את השמים ואת הארץ החיים והמות נתתי לפניך הברכה והקללה **ובחרת בחיים** למען תחיה אתה וזרעך

"I call heaven and earth to witness against you this day, that I have set before you life and death, the blessing and the curse; therefore, **choose life***, that you may live, you and your seed"* (Devarim 30:19)

The Torah implores us to choose life, thereby transforming us from a Chosen People (Devarim 4:37, 7:6) to a Choosing People who choose to value and maximize every day as mitzvah observing Jews.

Rashi understands that choosing life should be understood as choosing continued existence in this world through performance of mitzvos, as opposed to perishing if one does not. The choice we have is one of cause-and-effect: doing good leads to life, whereas doing evil leads to death –

perishing. *"Therefore, choose life"* – choose for yourself the good recompense, the blessing. But this interpretation is difficult. Is it necessary to command a person to choose what is good for him and what he should pursue? Surely all living things choose life and flee from death! What is novel in this case?

Rashi answers based on the Sifrei Re'eh 53 as follows: *"Therefore, choose life."* G-d is saying: "I show you this in order that you may choose the portion of life." It is comparable to a man who says to his son: "Choose a good portion of my estate," and then sets him in the best portion, saying to him, "Choose this!" As we are taught in Tehillim 16:5, *"You place my hand on the good lot, saying: 'Choose this.'"*

According to the Targum Yonasan, however, "life" is "the way of life," the way of the Torah and the commandments. Therefore, the words in Devarim 30:19 *"Therefore, choose life"* are rendered: *"Therefore, choose the way of life, which is Torah."* In verse 20, the words *"for that is your life, and the length of your days"* are rendered as: *"for the Torah in which you occupy yourselves is your life in this world."*

Indeed, the word *chayim* (*life*) is, in Tanach, sometimes used in the sense of the content of one's life – the proper way of life (i.e., Mishlei 3:18 or Mishlei 4:13). G-d is not impartial to Israel's choice, but rather, He strongly desires that we should choose life so that we may **live**! Man has choice – it is in our hands, but it is also of clear interest to G-d, who bestowed upon us free choice, to reveal how He wants us to exercise this power of choice.

"Therefore, choose life" is not only because such life involves cleaving to G-d and performing His commandments, but also because such life bestows upon us, the choosers, "life" in its literal sense. *"That you may live"* is not only a promise of reward, but an expression of G-d's desire

that man whom He created should live, since G-d is *"the King who desires life"* (Yechezkel 18:23).

We are instructed to choose "life" in two ways; as a means and as an end!

This does not interfere with our free choice but is merely an expression of G-d's love and care for each member of the Jewish People.

Moshe bids us farewell at the end of his life with the mitzvah of *Hakhel*, reminding us to assemble once every seven years to re-experience the covenantal event at Mt. Sinai. He encourages Yehoshua and the entire Nation to perpetuate the observance for all future generations.

Yehoshua ends <u>his</u> final message to the people (Book of Joshua, 24:22) in a similar manner:

ויאמר יהושע אל העם עדים אתם בכם כי אתם בכרתם לכם את ה' לעבד אותו. ויאמרו עדים.

"And Joshua said to the people: 'You are witnesses against yourselves that you have chosen the Lord to serve him.' And they said: '(we are) Witnesses.'" They made a choice, at that moment, to accept G-d's will!

This covenant of symbiotic selection stems from G-d's love and patriarchal promises (Devarim 7:7-8), and yet, with that comes a tremendous responsibility: *"You only have I singled out of all the families of the earth. Therefore, will I visit upon you all your iniquities."* (Amos 3:2)

G-d charged the Jewish People with a specific mission to follow a covenant of social and Divine commandments that is designed to create a society of sanctity and responsibility.

Rabbi Norman Lamm z"l, wrote:

"The chosenness of Israel relates exclusively to its spiritual vocation embodied by the Torah. The doctrine, indeed, was announced at Sinai.

Whenever it is mentioned in our liturgy – such as the blessing immediately preceding the Shema…it is always related to Torah or Mitzvot. This spiritual vocation consists of two complementary functions, described as *"Goy Kadosh,"* that of a holy nation, and *"Mamlechet Kohanim,"* that of a kingdom of priests. The first term denotes development communal separateness or differences in order to achieve a collective self-transcendence…the second term implies the obligation of this brotherhood of the spiritual elite toward the rest of mankind; priesthood is defined by the prophets as fundamentally a teaching vocation." (Lamm, Norman. <u>Seventy Faces: Articles of Faith, Volume I</u>)

Sanctity and responsibility are not passive terms of being chosen, but rather are active terms of choosing-ness! We make choices every day – to follow the commandments or not, to continue the traditions and teachings of our ancestors or to assimilate into modern society.

As Rabbi Lord Jonathan Sacks z"l, wrote:

"To be a Jew is to be a link in the chain of the generations. But there are times when the chain begins to break, when the continuity of Judaism and the Jewish people can no longer be taken for granted…At such moments, questions are unavoidable. Who are we? Of what story are we a part? Why were our ancestors so determined that it should continue? Does what spoke to them speak to us? …We cannot order our children to be Jews. We cannot deprive them of their choice, nor can we turn them into our clones. All we can do is show them what we believe and let them see the beauty of how we live …I can tell them where we came from, and where our ancestors were traveling to, and why it was important to them that their children should carry on the journey. This is our story, unfinished yet. And there is a chapter only they can write." (<u>A Letter in the Scroll</u>, Rabbi Jonathan Sacks)

When Moshe renewed the Sinaitic covenant in Devarim to a generation that did not actually witness the Divine revelation at Mt. Sinai, he turned to the new generation of Choosing People and addressed (as Rashi explains) even those not yet born (Rashi, Devarim 29:14). He explained the basis of Jewish identity: *"You are standing here in order to enter into a covenant with the Lord your G-d, a covenant the Lord is making with you this day as His people, that He may be your G-d as He promised you and as He swore to your fathers, Abraham, Isaac, and Jacob. I am making this covenant with its oath, not only with you who are standing here with us today in the presence of the Lord your G-d but also with those who are not here with us today."* (Devarim 29: 11-14)

But how can Moshe ask the Jewish People to bind their as-yet unborn descendants to uphold the covenant, to impose obligations on them in their absence and without their consent? Especially when one considers that Judaism is a religion of freedom "of the priority of faith over fate" (Sacks) and of a **Choosing** and not just a **Chosen** People!

Just as G-d called upon Avraham to undertake a journey, and again to Moshe, and then to the enslaved Jewish People, so too G-d calls upon us. We are free to decline. We may choose not to continue the chain built-upon by those before us. We may not choose to follow our grandparents and parents. But doing so means that we are also denying who we are; heirs to our history as well as our personal and national identity.

That is why we must study the story of our People. The journey of our past creates a feeling of responsibility and a trajectory for the future. That is the essence of this magnificent educational tool written with labor and love by my uncle, Reb Avraham Russak, an educator par excellence.

I vividly recall annual Pesach visits to Seattle, Washington where my grandfather, Yosef "Joe" Russak z"l, would host all of his children and grandchildren. My grandmother, Savtah Adina z"l, would prepare for the holiday for weeks in advance and would make delicacies for her beloved family. My time spent at the Seder and the experiences of both the food and divrei Torah, created everlasting memories. That is exactly what the Seder is meant to do!

We would not only hear "his-story" of the Haggadah, but our stories of Jewish faith and commitment as Reb Avraham (i.e., Uncle Larry), dressed in a Kittel and a Tallis would fly into the Seder room to distribute Afikomen gifts from "Eliyahu Ha'Navi," heralding messianic times.

My grandfather would regularly repeat the wise aphorisms of Chazal, especially those contained in the Mishna of Tractate Avos.

His favorite was:

עקביא בן מהללאל אומר, הסתקל בשלשה דברים ואי אתה בא לידי עברה. דע מאין באת, ולאן אתה הולך, ולפני מי אתה עתיד לתן דין וחשבון.

"Akavyah the son of Mehal'el said: 'Mark well three things and you will not come into the power of sin: Know from where you come, and where you are going, and before whom you are destined to give an accounting and a reckoning.'" (Ethics of our Fathers 3:1)

"Remember where you come from," Saba Joe would teach us! He taught us our personal family and national history. With love and pride he would speak of personal sacrifices made to observe a life of Torah and Mitzvos even while serving in the US Army.

Yet, with even greater enthusiasm, he would challenge our knowledge of Tanach and Jewish history, trivia, and Biblical personalities. He would teach Rashi and the beautiful stories of the Midrash.

As his son, Avraham Russak has continued these traditions of pedagogic love and determination as he enthusiastically and creatively teaches these messages to his children and grandchildren around his Shabbos table. He also teaches them to the children who attend the Junior Minyan at his shul that he has been leading for over 40 years.

I have personally merited participating in his Shabbos parsha quizzes and have watched as he entertains his family and guests with engaging and thought-provoking questions that lead to Torah discussions.

Now, he has laboriously invested in reminding us all of "where we come from" through this phenomenal educational resource of Jewish history – our people and our choices, our remarkable accomplishments and contributions to civilizations, and the Jewish community we have built throughout so many years of exiles and tribulations.

May this educational masterpiece, *b'ezrat Hashem*, enrich the hearts and minds of every student of Torah. It should remind us all where we have come from, to where we are going, and to whom we are ultimately accountable.

Through surveying our history and the scope of Tanach and the Talmud, we shall be reminded of our responsibility and G-d's directive and gift: *"Uvachartah B'Chayim" – And you shall choose life*!

We are the Choosing People, girded with knowledge, confidence, and responsibility, ultimately to reap tremendous benefits from choosing a Torah lifestyle.

May we merit "life" and a legacy of meaning.

ACKNOWLEDGEMENTS

I would like to thank those who helped me with the production of this book.

The book design and the front and back covers were done by Sefira Lightstone of Sefira Creative. She recently made Aliyah and can be reached at Sefiracreative@gmail.com.

The cover art is from an original oil painting from my personal collection entitled: "Man with Torah" by the Israeli artist Huvy. Her gallery is on King David Street in Jerusalem across from the Citadel Hotel. I would like to thank her and her family for granting me permission to use this copyright-protected image and I highly recommend visiting her gallery where you can appreciate her visual images of stories from Tanach.

I must first thank those who taught me how to formulate the right questions; Rabbi Morris Besdin, Rabbi Benjamin Blech, Rabbi Shlomo Riskin, Rabbi Manfred Fulda, and Rabbi Pesach Oratz. Together, they shaped the JSS Program of Yeshiva University and inspired thousands of young men and women to continue studying, searching, and investigating the words of Tanach and the Talmud.

Rabbi Daniel Lintz of the Torah Academy of the Pacific Northwest assisted me in editing and enhancing much of the material, especially the section on the 613 Mitzvos.

Rabbi Yaakov Tannenbaum of Bikur Cholim Machzikay Hadath Congregation in Seattle assisted me whenever I had halachic questions or needed help interpreting complex tracts.

Rabbi Yonah Margolese of Torah Day School of Seattle helped with the Big Questions chapter and was instrumental in giving me feedback and suggestions.

Rabbi Eytan Feiner of the White Shul in Lawrence, New York, and his sister, Rabbanit Shani Taragin of MTVA Seminary in Jerusalem wrote the Introduction and the Afterword and also helped with editing, suggestions, and corrections.

It took a lot of time and effort to write this book and I want to additionally thank my wife, Shelly, for encouraging me to keep studying, writing, and editing.

During the Covid-19 crisis it would have been very easy to give in to laziness and boredom and to become discouraged. For months I did not go to services at shul and it took a lot of effort to keep our family together.

Beginning right after Purim last year, we davened at home, brought together children and grandchildren, sang much of the tefilla out loud, and had a kiddush afterwards. We ate Shabbos and holiday meals together, took road trips together, and formed a family "bubble." I put together so many puzzles I lost count and learned Tanach every day, finishing my first cycle of learning all of Tanach last summer.

We made every effort to keep each other healthy, especially in the company of Shelly's mother who is over the age of 96. It all worked well until December of 2020 when one member of the family contracted the Covid-19 virus and it spread to most of our children and grandchildren. We give thanks to G-d that everyone recovered. Now, most of us have received the vaccinations due to the dogged determination of my wife, who has spent countless hours online trying to sign-us-up, working the system.

When our shul re-opened in a tent I would sometimes wake on Shabbos and tell my wife I didn't want to go to davening. She insisted I go and reminded me that she "signed-me-up" to be there. Reading Torah in shul while wearing a mask was exhausting. Nevertheless, we did not give in to the curse of Covid and hopefully, we will all be through this soon!

Shelly was the one who worked the hardest to keep the family on track and never let up! I want to thank her for all of her tireless efforts and for her constant reminders to finish this book, saying: "You promised Shani you were going to do this!"

Shani – thank you for your edits and for your Afterword. I hope this book will be a tool that students will use for many years to come.

Manufactured by Amazon.ca
Bolton, ON